The Life and Times of Dudy Noble

Other books by Steve Robertson

Flim Flam
Stark Villains
Alpha Dawgs
DAWG PILE
Blooms of Oleander
When the Bottom Falls

The Life and Times of Dudy Noble

By Steve Robertson

Copyright © 2024 Steve Robertson

All rights reserved. No part of this publication may be reproduced, stored in a retrieval system, or transmitted or used in any form by any means, electronic, mechanical, photocopying, or otherwise without prior written permission of the copyright holder.

Library of Congress Control Number: 2024937623

ISBN: 978-1-7352892-4-3

Manufactured in the United States of America
Crane Publishing Group, LLC
Publisher and Editor: Paul T. Brown
Managing Editor: Vicki T. Gardner
Design & Production Director: Dennis Heckler
Website design and manager: Keith Boudreaux
Publishing Assistant: Janet B. Watkins

Distributed to the book trade by:

Crane Publishing Group, LLC
133 Harbor View Drive
Madison, Mississippi 39110
601-946-8745
www.dudynoblebook.com

First Edition

Preface

In the following pages, you, my beloved reader, will learn more about Dudy Noble than has been written in recorded times. I have done my best to bring this story and this remarkable man to life in hopes of detailing his legacy.

It's essential to understand how this process began. I never know where my inspiration may come from, and the genesis of this book came from a football firing.

Mississippi State fired Coach Zach Arnett in 2023 with two games to go in the regular season. Coach Greg Knox was the interim head coach in the games against Southern Miss and Ole Miss.

Firing a coach before the season ends isn't a very Mississippi State thing. It's a rarity in Bulldog sports. In the days after Arnett's dismissal, I wondered if such an occurrence had happened.

My research led me to Major Ralph Sasse, who you will read about in the chapters ahead. Sasse didn't complete the 1937 season, and an interim coach served in his place for the campaign's duration.

I dug into the archives and found a picture of that 1937 football staff. There was Dudy Noble in the yearbook photo. He coached one of the best freshman football teams in SEC history that year.

I thought to myself, *That's pretty neat. Why have I never heard about this?* The more I searched, the more I realized there was little information about Dudy Noble or his career. I said out loud, "Someone should have written a book about him."

A bell went off in my head, and I decided that it was my book to write. It's a work that likely should have been published 50 years ago, but here we are.

I have combed through box scores, newspaper accounts, and yearbooks and heard some family stories passed down through the years to bring us to this point.

The Dude is my seventh book, perhaps the one I'm most proud of.

They are all my babies, but this one means a little more to me due to its historical nature.

I have come to know the Noble nieces and nephews and consider many of them my friends. This work would never have gotten off the ground without them.

I hope that I have made them proud. I have worked tirelessly on this book for them, you, and Mississippi State University.

We all know about Dudy Noble Field, but most have no clue why Dudy deserved the honor of having the venue named after him. In this book, you will learn about his time at Mississippi State as a player, coach, and administrator.

I'm proud of many things in my life, but near the top is this book. I consider *The Dude* one of the greatest gifts I could ever give the Mississippi State family.

Steve Robertson

Introduction

Mississippi State University is an institution built upon significant qualities. The value system of those who claim allegiance to Dear Ole State is built on accountability, family, hard work, humble beginnings, and love for one another.

State athletics brings together a cross-section of people who likely disagree on many other issues. On game day, people from all backgrounds gather as one to celebrate solidarity. There is an irresistible pull to campus and a need to feel a part of something bigger than oneself.

Fans eagerly count down the days until they can gather for a common cause. They can set aside their differences and unite under a maroon and white banner. While the time spent making new friends and reconnecting with old ones is precious, winning is the most essential item on the agenda. The story of Clark Randolph Noble embodies the spirit of Mississippi State. Noble, the firstborn of a farming family, was drawn to Mississippi A&M, as it was known at the time, as a student who wanted to become a better farmer.

Along the way, Noble developed a love for sports. Having never played organized sports, Noble learned the nuances of competition during intramural events as an A&M student beginning in 1910.

Noble's love and skill grew so that he could compete with the varsity in games that mattered. The Hinds County farm boy could get his name in the paper for doing something significant to others.

Noble's career as an athlete hasn't been adequately documented until now. His time as a college coach has served mainly as a footnote with a handful of schools. One wonders if his name didn't adorn Mississippi State's historic baseball venue if fans of today would even know who he was.

They know the name, and now it is time for fans of all ages to learn about his story. Noble is the most decorated student-athlete in the history of Mississippi State athletics. His exploits are legendary.

Noble enrolled for college courses in Starkville at just 16 years of age. Apart from a few years coaching elsewhere, Mississippi State athletics was his life. As he matured as a player, coach, and administrator, State matured right along with him.

The Noble era encompasses some of the most significant events in world history. He helped the school navigate the World Wars, the Great Depression, and the early stages of the Civil Rights movement in the South.

He also coached, hired, and trained some of the most prominent names that laid the foundation for what Mississippi State fans enjoy today.

The Dude: The Life and Times of Dudy Noble documents the history of Mississippi State. There were peaks and valleys. There were wins and losses. There were friends and enemies. There were even some friends who wound up being enemies upon closer inspection.

It's all chronicled in the pages that follow. Members of the Mississippi State family will read in detail the path that has brought the University to this point and Dudy Noble's role in leading it there.

Contents

Dedication

Introduction

Preface

1. A Learned Man 1
2. Randolph Goes to College 6
3. Becoming the Dude 12
4. Aggie Athletics Grow 18
5. Chadwick's Revenge 25
6. For The Folks Back Home 35
7. A Journey into "Hell" 45
8. Back Home to Stay 53
9. The Grassroots of a Coaching Legacy 61
10. Building a Baseball Brand 71
11. Going From Hunter to Hunted 82
12. The Chadwick Era Comes to a Tragic End 92
13. The New Boss 101

14. A Major Change 110

15. A Shock to the System 119

16. Back in the Saddle 131

17. A Hire for the Ages 137

18. Champions 148

19. Uncommon Men 159

20. Unrest in the House of Maroon 174

21. Honoring the Legend 187

22. Be Careful What You Wish For 194

23. Atta Babe! 206

24. The End of the Road 219

25. A Lasting Legacy 229

Pictures and Letters 239

Epilogue

Acknowledgements

Chapter 1

A Learned Man

Born with a name worthy of the presidency, William Alexander Noble breathed his first breath of life on November 26, 1865, in Learned, Mississippi.

Will was part of the first generation of Nobles to be born in the Magnolia State. His parents, Patrick Henry and Bettie Noble, migrated to Mississippi from their native state of South Carolina before the Civil War.

The Noble family has ties to the confederacy as Patrick's first cousin, Edward Noble, was the second man to sign the articles of succession for the state of South Carolina.

The Palmetto State was the first to secede from the Union before the Civil War. The outcome of the 1860 presidential election didn't sit well with many Southerners. Abraham Lincoln defeated the southern candidate of choice, John C. Breckenridge of Kentucky, rather decisively.

Breckenridge and running mate, Joseph Lane of Indiana, largely swept the South but garnered just 72 votes from the Electoral College. Lincoln received 180 electoral votes and collected more than a million more ballots in the popular vote to win the presidential election.

It's documented that the southern states left the Union in opposition to Lincoln and his platform. While Mississippi Governor John J. Pettus pushed the state legislature for a secession convention just a week after Lincoln was elected, the Magnolia State didn't leave the Union until January 9, 1861.

During the 1860 census, Mississippi had a free population of just 354,674. There was little in the way of industry in the state. People used their hands and were hard-knuckled folks.

Timber was a considerable commodity then, and most who worked outside their farms found work in "timbering." Textile mills popped up around the state as farmers harvested the cash crop of cotton and, in turn, manufactured other goods.

With very little "book learning" taking place, most Mississippi families simply farmed their land. This included the Nobles who settled in the tiny hamlet of Learned in Hinds County.

Today's residents wax nostalgic about days gone by as if Learned was some booming metropolis. The population hit its zenith in 1900 when the census takers counted 138 heads.

Those yarns of yesteryear may have a small ring of truth to them, but Learned remained a charming small Mississippi community tucked away from the hustle and bustle of big city life.

While the town didn't have much development, the fertile ground provided locals with more than enough farming opportunities. The Noble family planted both personal and professional roots.

One anecdote passed down through the generations involved the founding families of the Lebanon Presbyterian Church. The church was located just outside of Learned. The McNairs and the Nobles are credited with raising the church and filling the first pews.

Back in the days of horse-drawn carriages and wagons, a dispute arose involving the patriarchs of both families.

One particular Sunday morning, Patrick Noble arrived with his family in tow only to discover that old man McNair had taken his usual parking spot and tied up his horse on the regular Sunday tree typically used by Noble.

A fistfight ensued right there on the church grounds. It may seem trivial in hindsight, but the few vestiges afforded to small-town Mississippians were something to be taken seriously. At times, too seriously.

As William, better known as Will, matured, he started to assist on the family farm and learned to make his way in the world.

When he came of age, Will married Vivia Seabelle Smith and took the next steps into adulthood on December 18, 1889.

Like his father before him, Will made his way into the world as a farmer. He also became an integral part of the community. In addition to farming the land, Will served on the school board for the Learned Consolidated School, worked as the constable, and even served as an election official.

If there was work to do to move the town forward, Will was involved. His passion and community spirit were evident, serving as a shining example to his future children. Simply put, Will Noble was a pillar of his community.

As post-Civil War reconstruction took place, there were some ruffled feathers around the South concerning state's rights and the like, and Will tried to do his best for his family and neighbors.

Stories handed down through the generations suggest Will was a strict man with solid values. He believed in hard work and self-reliance. If there was ever a man's man, it was Will Noble.

On May 6, 1893, Will and his wife Vivia welcomed their first child. A son named Clark Randolph Noble made the young couple a party of three.

In January of 1895, Ellen Elizabeth Noble was born. The family called her Bettie. Alice Rebecca Noble joined the family in May of 1897. Somehow, she earned the nickname of Ditter.

Sadly, in 1899, after three children and 10 years of marriage to Will, Vivia died. She was laid to rest in the Lebanon Church cemetery.

With a farm to run and a family to feed, Will did what many young widowers did in those days: he married his first wife's sister.

Will and Merab Jessie Smith tied the knot and returned to what most would consider an everyday Southern life. Better known as Meb, Merab had three children with Will. William Lacy Noble was born in 1901. Pickens Alfred Noble made his Earthly debut in 1905. Mildred Jessie Noble's birth in 1906 marked the sixth descendant of Will Noble. It was also the final child Will sired with Meb.

Amid the family expansion, Will's oldest son and the actual subject of our story, Randolph, completed high school at Learned and enrolled at Mississippi A&M, now called Mississippi State University, to learn more about farming.

The Noble farm was one of prosperity, but it was also one of experimentation. While cotton and other crops were the mainstay in Mississippi, Will Noble agreed to allocate some of his acreage for corn as part of the rehabilitation of the state's agricultural industry following the Civil War.

As part of this initiative, former Mississippi Commissioner of Agriculture Henry Edwards Blakeslee supported youth corn clubs. Blakeslee even encouraged those who managed the state fair to allocate some space for corn exhibits and recognition of corn club winners around the state.

In 1911, Randolph was the blue-ribbon winner of the Hinds County Corn Club growing contest, producing 80.41 bushels of corn. That relatively new cash crop in Mississippi fetched about .50 per bushel.

At his core, Randolph was a farm boy. It's all he knew. The goal of going to college was to learn how to farm more efficiently and someday take over the family farm or create one of his own.

Shortly after Randolph's enrollment at A&M, tragedy struck the family again. The typhoid fever epidemic hit the nation hard. Mississippi wasn't immune from its spread.

The biggest illness outbreak occurred over a decade before, but that was of little defense when it swept through the Magnolia State. Meb and some of the Noble children became infected. The disease took Meb in 1916, which left Will with five children at home and still a farm to run.

Will didn't forsake the Biblical command to "go forth and multiply" for long. Wife number three, Ida Pecquet Phillips, soon took the Noble name and took responsibility for raising the children.

Will and Ida had three additional children before she, too, passed away. William Junior was born in 1920. James Phillips Noble joined the fun in 1921, and Cary Louie Noble became the caboose of the family in 1923. A year later, Ida was laid to rest.

In all, there were nine children born to the three wives of Will Noble, but Will wasn't quite done.

With small children to raise and a farming business to attend to, Will had a series of housekeepers who helped with all home and child-rearing duties. He eventually married one of them, Celia Augusta Ballard, in the fall of 1928.

While Augusta never had any children, she raised the Noble youngsters as if she had carried them in her womb. To this day, all within the family who knew her have held her in high regard.

Chapter 2

Randolph Goes to College

When Mississippi A&M welcomed the 1910 freshman class to campus, the enrollment swelled to over 1,100 students. One of those brand-new Aggies was Clark Randolph Noble. His family called him Randolph.

As the fall semester began, Randolph was just 16 years of age. Growing up on the farm likely had him wise beyond his years. Going off to college is difficult for any teenager, but Randolph was younger than most of his peers.

Transitioning from a small rural school to an institute of higher learning presented some real challenges. College professors were undoubtedly less forgiving than the town folks of Learned.

The sole purpose of going to college was for Randolph to learn more about farming. With a land grant school like A&M available to him, the eldest of Will Noble's children planned to learn all he could to help the family farm back in Learned.

Randolph's freshman curriculum included Agronomy, Anatomy and Physics, Botany, Geology, History, and Math. While some of those early agricultural classes may have seemed like old hat, college-level mathematics was a bit of a chore.

With progressive farming methods being taught in Starkville, Randolph had access to new information that his father and grandfather before him had likely not even considered.

Farming was the primary industry in Mississippi, and it was also the Noble family business. Randolph had little aspirations beyond building upon the foundation laid by his forefathers when it came to living off the land.

Soon after Randolph set foot on campus, he met a man who would change the course of his college days and the trajectory of his life.

Coach Billy Chadwick was hired as the Aggie director of athletics in 1906. A native of Ohio, Chadwick moved from Albion College to Mississippi A&M.

In time, Chadwick coached every varsity sport and ran the physical education department. He handled these duties simultaneously and was wildly popular with the student body. Affectionately called "Chad," Chadwick was among the most well-liked and well-known people on campus.

While not every male student was talented enough to represent A&M on the fields and courts of play, Chadwick wanted them to participate in physical fitness. In addition to varsity sports, A&M had an assortment of club teams that allowed students to compete in their favorite sports. P.E. was also required for those who attended classes, even if they were part of the Aggie Cadet Corps.

Randolph had never played organized sports a day in his life. No Little Leagues or Pee-Wee football programs were available for young athletes to hone their skills. Youth sports were non-existent for the most part, especially in small-town Mississippi.

Many Aggie athletes who won their Varsity M sweaters were cut from the same cloth as Randolph. They were farm boys who built their speed and strength working the fields or herding cattle. They were unrefined, but they were country-strong.

It didn't take long for Randolph to catch the eye of Coach Chadwick. While his knowledge of sports was lacking, Randolph was fleet of foot. He listened. He worked hard. He was coachable. After two years of learning sports on the club level, Randolph was ready for something more meaningful.

Chadwick encouraged Randolph to come out for fall football tryouts. He took his first athletic steps on the practice field, becoming named the fastest man in the South.

When the final cuts for football were made for the Aggies football team of 1912, Randolph wasn't relegated to the freshman team or a club team made up of castoffs. Randolph made the Aggie varsity squad without ever having played a real game of football in his life.

Being on the football team had its privileges. Perhaps the most important was the training table. The gridders gathered for meals together, and the portions were more substantial than those available to the regular students.

During pre-season camp, one breakfast feast was notable in the life and times of Randolph Noble.

As the players filed in and found their seats, Randolph sat at the end of the table with a burly upperclassman seated to his left. The player's name is unknown, but he had a reputation for being a guy no one wanted to mess with.

Randolph waited expectantly for the southern breakfast delicacies to reach him. He corralled a biscuit and some bacon that morning, but his eyes were on the scrambled egg platter.

Eventually, the poultry products made their way to Randolph's table. Just before he could rake off a fork full for himself, his breakfast table neighbor took the entire platter of eggs for himself.

With a smug look of satisfaction, the brooding veteran player handed Randolph an empty platter. To say that the measure of hazing around the breakfast table didn't sit well with Randolph would be to understate the obvious.

Recognizing what had taken place and the intended disrespect that went with it, Randolph sprang to his feet and challenged the player to a fight.

"If you ever do anything like that again, I'll kick your ass," Randolph said.

Though just a freshman, Randolph was ready to duke it out. While he had a measure of respect for all people, Randolph wouldn't be disrespected, especially in front of his peers.

With fire in his eyes and bass in his voice, Randolph let his teammate know that he wasn't someone who was going to sit back and be treated poorly.

Randolph's fire stung. Just before the sparks began to fly, the egg platter bandit took Randolph's plate and scrapped all the eggs onto it, hoping to keep the peace.

The matter was settled without fisticuffs, but Randolph was no longer Randolph on the football field. No, he was now Eggs Noble or simply "Eggs." A man willing to fight over a plate of eggs might have the temperament for football.

While Randolph played with no prior experience above the club level in 1912, he did play. The Aggies posted a winning season, but it wasn't the season it likely should have been.

A&M opened the season with a 3-0 record. The Aggies shut out Mississippi College, Tennessee Medical College, and Alabama by a combined score of 58-0.

The wins over the Choctaws and Crimson Tide had the squad tied for first place in the Southern Intercollegiate Athletic Association (SIAA) standings.

Randolph got his first taste of real football playing as a reserve right tackle in the season opener against MC. In the win over Tennessee Medical, Randolph started at right end. Randolph watched from the sidelines in the 7-0 victory over Alabama.

The Aggie winning streak was snapped at Rickwood Field in Birmingham. Auburn scored a first-quarter touchdown and made it stand up to win 7-0. While he wasn't in the starting lineup, Randolph was back in action as a reserve at right end.

In what was deemed a "Battle for Blood" by the Memphis *Commercial Appeal*, A&M defeated LSU by the score of 7-0. The game was mired in a bit of controversy.

The lone score resulted from a tremendous defensive play and a miscue from the Tiger special teams. LSU had the ball at their 20-yard line and attempted an end-around play. The Aggies were ready. The LSU ball carrier ran back toward his own goal line and was stopped at the one-yard line.

After the massive loss of yards, the Tigers elected to punt. In those days, the uprights for the field goal were at the goal line rather than at the back of the end zone.

A&M brought an all-out blitz and forced a quick kick. The punt attempt caromed off one of the uprights and fell back into the LSU end zone. The Aggies recovered and were credited with a touchdown. A&M and the officials were booed off the field down in Baton Rouge.

Now 4-1, Coach Billy Chadwick's team seemed poised to make some noise down the stretch. With Randolph now taking some snaps at fullback, A&M held a 24-7 lead over Tulane at the half.

The Aggies fell apart and surrendered 21 points unanswered. The coup de gras came when Tulane scooped up a live ball and returned it for a touchdown when a high snap on a punt attempt rolled free. The final score was 27-24 Tulane.

The final game of the campaign ended with a 41-7 blowout loss at Texas A&M. Randolph didn't play in the game, but he played enough that season to earn his varsity letter. It would be the first of many, but perhaps this one meant more.

A farm boy from rural Hinds County, Mississippi, with no prior experience, made the team at A&M and earned some varsity starts.

Randolph handled himself well and proved to be a very talented athlete. He was precisely the type of player Coach Chadwick was looking for. When basketball tryouts rolled around, Randolph once again made the cut.

Sadly, during the Christmas break, Randolph had an accident. Details are scarce about the incident, but the result was that Chadwick's rising star severely burned his hand.

Due to the injury's severity, Randolph couldn't dribble and shoot the basketball. The impairment also sidelined him during baseball season. Catching and throwing with a bum hand was torture, so Randolph served as a manager of sorts.

Chadwick liked having Randolph around, and the time spent with the team allowed him to learn more about sports. Randolph was learning the nuances of athletics by observing as more than just a casual observer. He wanted to understand and get an education from seeing it all up close.

When baseball season opened, Randolph was right there, taking it all in. His most important job as a baseball manager was heading to the locker room in the eighth inning to fire up the furnace. Randolph's key responsibility on game day was ensuring the Aggie baseball players could take hot showers once their time on the baseball diamond was over.

It was a job that Randolph took seriously. While he wasn't part of the 1913 lineup, Randolph was vital to the A&M baseball program. The seeds sown during this year took root.

The Aggies were good that year. Not as good as they were two years earlier when they won the 1911 SIAA title, but it was still big-time college baseball.

Baseball has always mattered in Starkville. For Randolph, being around a program with high expectations motivated him to work even harder to belong.

As the winter gave way to spring, Randolph participated in track events. Even though his hand wasn't wholly healed, Randolph could run wide open without any issues. A&M benefited from his participation.

When the 1912-13 academic year ended, Randolph "Eggs" Noble had a pair of varsity letters. The only thing that prevented him from having four as a freshman was that injury that forced him out of action.

Sports were different back then, but players didn't make the varsity by default. Randolph earned everything he got. He was a natural-born athlete blessed with God-given talent and a rural upbringing by a family that valued hard work.

One suspects that the Noble family back home in Learned, Mississippi, celebrated Randolph's exploits, but some may suggest that any son of Will Noble was expected to do great things.

As Randolph made the trip home for the summer, he had already accomplished more than most athletes in their careers, but it was only the beginning for him. The ascension of this star was still in its genesis.

Chapter 3

Becoming the Dude

As the fall semester beckoned in 1913, change blew in like the autumn wind. Coach Billy Chadwick was ready to lead his fifth Aggie football team into battle. The 1913 campaign proved to be the last A&M played on Hardy Field.

The sport of football was growing around the country and on campus. The demand for better facilities was evident. Several college gridiron events were hosted on lined fields with no stands. As a result, spectators piled up on the sidelines. In some cases, fans would wander onto the field for some trash talk.

No matter how well-intended those well-wishers may have been, they needed somewhere to sit. They also needed to be back from the festivities.

With the blessing and financial backing of A&M's fourth President, George Robert Hightower of Grenada, Mississippi, Chadwick began planning a cleaner and more organized fan experience.

The "New Athletic Field" was already being designed when the Aggies took the field to open the 1913 season against Howard, now known as Samford.

Howard and the Aggies were somewhat regular opponents. There had been six previous meetings between the two programs. A&M held a 5-1 record in the series and outscored the Baptists 230-6 in those six contests. Howard's lone win came in a 6-0 affair in 1909.

The 1913 meeting went the way of the Aggies by a score of 66-0. That gaudy score is not an indictment on the quality of the Howard team. They went on to post a 5-3-1 record for Coach Balpha Lonnie Noojin.

On that opening Saturday, though, it was all A&M. Newspaper accounts of the day noted several injuries to the Howard roster as the

Aggies manhandled the Baptists.

Howard's most promising drive reached the A&M three-yard line. To avoid the shutout, Howard attempted a drop kick that the Aggies blocked and recovered.

A&M didn't escape the game unscathed, though. Ole "Eggs" Noble started the game as the left halfback but suffered a severe shoulder injury. Many wondered if the ailment would sideline our budding hero for the rest of the season.

The physicality of the Aggie team continued in week two. A&M came from behind to take a 14-13 lead in what was deemed a real war of attrition. In the fourth quarter, with darkness drawing nigh, Mississippi College cried for mercy.

A&M had sidelined so many MC players that Coach Dana Bible decreed that his team no longer had enough players to field an 11-man formation. Despite the protests of the officials, Bible refused to continue the game. While considered a forfeit then, the game is recorded in the books as a 14-13 Aggie win.

In week three, the pain train continued down the tracks, literally and figuratively. Nearly the entire A&M student body, complete with the marching band, enjoyed a locomotive ride from Starkville to Columbus, Mississippi, to see the Aggies shutout Central University 31-0.

Chadwick likely could have run for Governor and put up a decisive tally at the voting precincts, but the air in the Aggie balloon ran out the following weekend.

Once again, Auburn played the villain and dashed A&M's dreams for the fifth straight time. The Tigers overwhelmed the Aggies and won, going away 34-0. The final score loomed large in the conference standings.

A&M didn't surrender a single point the rest of the season. Chadwick's crew won at the Texas Fairgrounds in Dallas over Texas A&M, 6-0. Only one penalty was called the entire game.

Noble returned to good health and service a week later in a 34-0 shelling of Tulane in Starkville. Noble carried the football, served as a punt returner, and even intercepted a pass.

On November 15th, A&M and LSU played to a draw. Neither team could muster much offense. Both teams attempted multiple drop kicks, but neither could convert and put points on the board. The game ended with no score.

Alabama was the foe on Thanksgiving Day for the season finale. Unfortunately for the Crimson Tide, they were without their star player, William Van De Graaff, who would later become Alabama's first All-American football player.

Van De Graaff was needed on that day as the Aggie offense had their way with things early and scored the game's only touchdown in the first quarter. The A&M defense made that slim margin hold up. Former *Tuscaloosa News* reporter Thomas Owen praised the Aggie defense, saying, "Their tackling was of the highest order."

When the season was over, State recorded a 4-1-1 record and finished second in the SIAA standings to an undefeated Auburn team. On the season, the Tigers rushed for over 5,800 yards in their eight games.

As the holiday break began at the end of the fall semester at Mississippi A&M, Noble had a bit of a quandary. He quickly became a big man on campus, but unlike some of his peers, Noble didn't have much luck with the ladies.

The female enrollment at Mississippi A&M was relatively minuscule at the time, as most of the students from the fairer sex seeking higher education elected to take classes in Columbus at the girls' college.

The Industrial Institute and College for the Education of White Girls, now known as "The W," was commonly referred to as II&C. The full name was quite a mouthful, so the abbreviated nomenclature was easier to say.

The II&C, the first women's college in the United States, was a target-rich environment for Aggie cadets and students looking for a date. The competition was fierce as young men did their best to woo a career-minded young lady to join them on a date.

Courting was a considerable part of the college experience. While he would soon become a hero on the baseball diamond, Noble was striking out with the ladies. The matter reached a head during a trip home to the family farm in Learned for Christmas.

A chance meeting with a family friend proved life-changing in more ways than one. One of Will Noble's friends and fellow farmers asked young Randolph how college was going.

After exchanging the usual pleasantries and platitudes, Randolph had a bit of a confession. While many of his teammates had healthy social lives, young master Noble was challenged to get a girl to say, "Yes!"

The voice of experience from an earlier generation explained to Noble that he needed some "courting" clothes. Randolph had his school clothes, athletic attire, and some knock-about outfits, but he didn't have the wardrobe to take a young lady on a proper date.

The clothes make the man is an old adage. It likely applies better in first impressions with dating prospects than in any other arena. A wrinkled suit might pass at work or church, but it's a real turnoff when trying to impress a woman.

After sharing this sage advice, the Noble family friend put a few dollars in Randolph's hand and encouraged him to ask his father, Will, for more.

Once Randolph fought back the embarrassment that goes with the naiveté of youth, he explained the calamity to his father. Will's eldest son wanted a girlfriend and needed his dad's help to get one.

After one of the foremost father-son talks that all fathers and sons have at some point, Randolph had the funds to buy himself some proper clothes to entertain young ladies.

Once back in Starkville, Randolph was ready to spend his "girl money" on some gentlemen's wear. He could have gone to M. Rossoffs in Starkville or Simon Loeb & Brother's Department store in Columbus. No matter which cash register received those precious funds, Randolph was walking out looking spiffy, or so he thought.

While Noble had funds, he had little fashion sense. To be fair, how could he? Randolph was raised on a farm where most of his social interaction was at church, school, or when he rode to town with his daddy. Dating was foreign to him. His Sunday best was fine for services at the rural Lebanon Church, but courting was something he had to figure out for himself.

After Randolph paid for his purchases, he wore his new suit to the dorm to show it off to his friends and teammates. The three-piece ensemble was made from a loud green fabric. One could surmise that it may have come from the clearance rack. No matter the price point, Randolph had some sure enough threads to court the women folk properly. He also had a dressy hat to accompany it, but the brim of the topper wasn't to his liking, so Noble pushed up the front.

As Randolph returned to campus, he steeled his nerves for the big reveal. He could hear some of his friends' voices from beyond the closed door, so he sprang in with a grand entrance decked out in his newly purchased clothes.

Nearly in unison, the first words out of their mouths were, "Dude!" While the connotations of today don't convey the compliment perhaps the way Noble's friends intended, Randolph was a hit.

It didn't take too long for Dude to become Dudy. It simply stuck. In time, the nickname Eggs was retired, and the only people who used the name Randolph were the folks back in Learned.

Noble made the cut to join the varsity basketball team not long after the spring semester began. He likely would have played for Coach E.C. Hayes as a freshman, but the injured hand prevented it. Now, back to good health, Noble was set to learn how to shoot hoops on the fly. Somehow, a farm boy with no experience on the court was part of a SIAA men's basketball squad intent on defending back-to-back conference titles.

The 1913 Aggie cagers went 13-2 and posted a 10-2 mark in league play to earn a three-peat. Besides a pair of losses to Alabama, A&M ripped through the schedule, regularly blowing out opponents. The

Aggies capped the season by beating Ole Miss in four straight games, including an 84-18 beatdown in Starkville.

When the college baseball season began, Noble found himself in the starting line-up, batting second and playing left field. Noble was running the 100-yard dash in nearly 10 seconds flat at the time. As a result of that top-end speed, Noble became a prolific base stealer and a guy who could stretch a single into a double when an outfielder got a little lazy getting the ball back into the infield.

A&M turned in a 15-11-2 season and ended SIAA play with an 8-6-1 mark. Perhaps the season's highlight was a three-game sweep of LSU in Baton Rouge.

In the series' first game, Dudy Noble went 2-for-4 and added a sacrifice in a 10-2 shelling of the Tigers to hand them their first home loss of the year.

For the second straight spring, Noble once again lettered in track. While he wasn't a podium participant just yet, those days were coming.

As the semester ended, the sportsman, now named Dudy Noble, had collected four varsity letters in a single year. With a pair of letters in football and track now to his credit, Noble added varsity M's in basketball and baseball for a two-year total of six.

Just two years into his college career, Noble was making the most of his opportunities. Despite never having played in a real game before enrolling at A&M, Dudy had already built a reputation for being an all-around athlete.

The Noble name grew in popularity and prestige, but the best was still to come.

Chapter 4

Aggie Athletics Grow

As the 1914 college football season approached, the demands on Coach Billy Chadwick were countless. With Mississippi A&M growing in enrollment and the business of sports becoming a more significant part of the college experience, Chadwick had to empower others around him.

Coaching everything, teaching P.E., and running the athletic department was too much for one man to handle. Chadwick surrendered the reigns of the basketball program to Coach Earl C. Hayes before the 1911 season. When Chadwick was prepared to do the same in football, he again turned to Hayes, who served as his most trusted assistant.

Hayes knew the Aggie players well, and his promotion to head coach was well-received by the squad. That isn't to suggest that Chadwick was no longer involved; he couldn't handle the demands of a growing athletic department and the commitment to coaching football at a high level.

A veteran and talented crop of Aggie players returned for the '14 campaign, hoping to get the Hayes era off on the right foot.

The season opened with a 53-0 shelling of Marion. Dudy Noble drew the start at left end on a rain-soaked day. With the weather and the score worsening by the moment, the two teams elected not to play the fourth quarter. A&M was declared the victor once the third-quarter whistle blew.

Cumberland served as the Aggies' second victim of the year. After one-quarter of play, A&M raced out to a 31-0 lead. At the halftime intermission, the Aggie advantage was 44-0.

Hayes finally called off the dogs with A&M ahead 64-0, but the Aggies weren't done scoring. Noble took over at quarterback in the fourth quarter and found the end zone twice to cap the scoring at 77-0.

A&M traveled to Lexington, Kentucky, for the first road game of the season. This contest began like the previous two, with the Aggies roaring to an early lead. After A&M went ahead 13-0, Kentucky head coach Alpha Brumage complained to the lead official, Dan Blake, that the Aggie players were competing with "greased trousers." Those words were brushed aside until Brumage finally got his way at halftime. The Aggies had to change their pants during the intermission.

Perhaps Brumage was correct in his claims that the Aggies had an unfair advantage, or his team played better in the second half.

Kentucky came from behind to win 19-13. A&M was shut out in the second half, and the Wildcats earned a league win. The victory was so significant to Kentucky that they held a victory parade through campus with university president Henry Stites Barker serving as the unofficial grand marshal.

The following week, the Aggies went to Birmingham to face their familiar rivals from Auburn. This meeting went similarly to the previous five. The Aggies couldn't find the end zone. A&M fell 19-0.

Shutouts against the Tigers were common for those early Aggie teams. In the first six meetings, A&M managed just five points.

Halloween saw the Aggies playing at Sanford Field in Athens, Georgia. Georgia (UGA) hadn't suffered a home defeat since moving their football games from Herty Field to Samford Field in 1911.

Like A&M, UGA had lost their two previous games, so someone was bound to have something to smile about at day's end.

It was an unseasonably warm day on the Georgia campus, leading to sweat-covered fumbles. Simply put, it was a sloppy day of football for players who had grown accustomed to autumn temperatures.

The game was a stalemate for three quarters. Aggie standout Harry "Buzzard" McArthur scored on an end-around play from 25 yards to open the fourth quarter. It would prove to be the only touchdown on the day. A&M missed the extra-point attempt.

With the game still in the balance, Dudy Noble gave the Aggies all the breathing room they needed when he connected on a 23-yard drop kick that sailed through the uprights to make it 9-0 A&M.

The Aggie defense made the two-score margin hold up as A&M became the first visiting football team ever to win at Sanford Field.

The shutout over Georgia appears to have buoyed the Aggie spirits. Their strong play continued, with some lopsided scores.

Noble started at right end in a 73-0 cakewalk over Mercer. Noble was one of three Aggies to score four touchdowns in the game. One of Dudy's trips to paydirt came via the forward pass, which was still a relatively novel part of college football then.

The strong play for A&M continued against Tulane in a game played at the Jackson Fairgrounds. Some tomfoolery mired the contest. The Maroon and White bested the Olive and Blue 62-0, but the score was only part of the story.

In the second quarter, Tulane standout T.T. Gately had to leave the game with a severe injury to his face. Whisked away in an automobile to a nearby hospital, Gately was diagnosed with a severely broken cheekbone. Emergency surgery had to be performed.

Gately wasn't the only Tulane football representative with medical issues. Head coach Edwin Sweetland was relieved by assistant E.W. Gillis as he recovered from a severe ankle injury when he was struck with a foul ball before the season. The pain lingered throughout the year.

Gillis complained throughout the game of rough play, slugging, and greased trousers. If there was something to cry about, Gillis did it.

While the media accounts of the time painted the Tulane players as choir boys and the Aggies as bullies, the game did get a little chippy, and the officials had to intervene. One scrum led to the ejection of A&M guard Jimmy Spurlock.

The finale of the eight-game regular season came against Alabama. A&M won 9-0 in a war of attrition in a game shortened by darkness. The two squads continued to play as long as they could until the officials called the game, as they couldn't tell the difference between the teams on the field.

A&M ended the season with a 6-2 overall record. Auburn and Tennessee were named co-champions of the SIAA as both went undefeated on the year.

As football ended, the preparations for basketball season took place. Heading into the 1914-15 season, the Aggies had won three straight SIAA regular season titles.

Things started well enough as A&M steamrolled to a 6-0 start. The Aggies took a pair from Mississippi College, Auburn, and Alabama. A potential four-peat as league champions seemed like a probability rather than a possibility.

The final eight games of the season were all played on the road. The Aggies went 2-6 down the stretch to finish the campaign 8-6.

Dudy Noble served as the starting point guard on the team and was voted captain of the squad by his teammates. It was a rebuilding year, and A&M was due one after three SIAA titles. The '14 and '15 squad was dubbed state champions by the media scribes after going 6-0 against Mississippi college foes. Such modest and noble goals were still worth celebrating even way back when.

In his first four seasons as the Aggie baseball coach, Chadwick recorded winning years. The 1914 season was his most difficult challenge in the A&M dugout.

The Aggies returned just four regular positional starters, including Noble, who was placed in leftfield. Just as he had been in basketball, Noble was voted captain of the 1914 baseball team. In the previous three seasons, Albert Critz served as captain.

Critz anchored the infield at first base during his time in Starkville. When graduation forced him to move on, Chadwick moved former right fielder George Frentz to first.

The season started well enough as the Aggies rattled off four straight wins to open the slate. Mississippi College nipped A&M by the score of 2-1 to break the streak.

Things were hit or miss the rest of the way as A&M went 11-9-2 overall and finished 5-6-1 in SIAA play.

Later in life, Noble shared that one of his favorite moments from his playing career was a "grand slammer" he belted against Georgia Tech. The box score from the 9-1 win over the Yellowjackets from the 1914 season credits Noble with a solo shot. His use of grand slammer was simply a euphemism to describe the majesty of the shot as it left the park.

Frentz, Noble, and second baseman H.C. McKinney were the stars of the 1914 squad. The team went 2-0 against Alabama, 1-3 against Ole Miss, and finished the schedule 0-2-1 against Vanderbilt.

That season, Ole Miss was coached, in part, by future Major League Baseball Hall of Famer Casey Stengel. While recovering from injury, Stengel wanted to be close to the game but out of the spotlight. Stengel's former high school coach, Bill Driver, hired him to help coach the Rebel baseball program while he rehabbed.

While Driver was the head coach, Stengel is listed in the record books as the skipper despite his work as an assistant coach. Driver handled the press conferences and filled out the line-up card despite some revisionist history in modern media accounts.

When the regular season ended, there was no College World Series. The SIAA didn't even host a conference tournament to determine the league's winner. The regular season standings determined who claimed the championship.

Many members of the SIAA supported a post-season, but it took some time for things to come together. Only track and field held a championship event in the league's infancy.

Another point of contention among the members was freshman eligibility. Smaller schools supported the inclusion of freshmen on varsity rosters, while some of the larger institutions were staunchly against it.

Mississippi A&M was one of those supporters of four-year eligibility. Had the future rules been in place, Noble himself would have been impacted. In the first two years at A&M, Noble played on class teams, which are on par with today's intramural programs.

Before his varsity play that started in 1912, Noble fine-tuned his skills playing against his classmates before playing in games that made the newspaper.

In the spring of 1914, Noble turned 21. While that age was like his junior-level classmates, the future legend had already been on campus for nearly four calendar years. Noble wasn't your typical athlete, nor was he your typical junior college student.

While the SIAA leadership squabbled over eligibility matters, Noble kept competing. He kept winning.

Heading into the 1914 track season, Noble was reported to be the only college sprinter in the country to have finished the 100-yard dash in ten seconds in three different meets during the previous year.

During the '14 running season, Noble won the event on what was considered a slow track at Alabama with a time of 10.25.

At the SIAA championships held in Meridian, Mississippi, Noble rose to the moment and proved himself to be one of the fastest college athletes in the South and the nation.

In the 100, Noble tied his own SIAA record with a 10-flat time. In the 220, Noble tied the SIAA gold standard time of 22.15.

When the running events were completed, Mississippi A&M was first in the standings. LSU was able to clinch the overall conference title with some solid work in the throwing events.

As the day darkened, the Tigers won the meet with 34 points. The Aggies posted a second-place finish with 30 points. Tulane tallied 24 points for third overall.

For reasons unknown, Noble didn't participate in the 1912 or 1913 championship meets despite having qualifying times. In 1914, Noble proved himself on the big stage. Not only did he have another varsity letter, but he also held a pair of SIAA championship medals and records.

Noble wasn't the only rising track star to wear the Varsity M. Friend and teammate Don Magruder Scott of Woodville, Mississippi, was also breaking hearts and records. While Noble was a sprinter, Scott was a middle-distance runner specializing in the 440-yard dash.

With three years of varsity experience, Noble held 10 varsity letters in four sports and multiple SIAA championships. Noble wasn't just good for around here. Noble was undeniably good. He was excellent and capable of competing and winning on stages much grander than those in his home state of Mississippi.

Chapter 5

Chadwick's Revenge

Astute readers may have noticed that no details regarding football games between A&M and Ole Miss have been shared thus far. There is a good reason for that. The Aggies and Rebels didn't meet on the gridiron in the 1912, 1913, or 1914 seasons.

What is unknown to most who follow both programs and the annual Battle for the Golden Egg are the reasons behind the three-year interruption in the rivalry.

Details regarding what amounted to a massive scandal during that period haven't been properly published for over a century. The tale is very sordid, involving corruption, blatant rule-breaking, an attempted cover-up, and eventually sanctions for Ole Miss football.

The more things change, the more they stay the same. Malfeasance, regarding the pigskin, is a long-held tradition for the folks in Oxford. Corner-cutting efforts to find an unfair advantage is a practice that dates back decades and generations for the red and blue.

The trouble began before the 1912 football season. Just days before the Rebels were set to take on Memphis High School in the season opener, the SIAA deemed half a dozen Rebel players ineligible.

At the center of the allegations that involved charges of professionalism were Rube Baker, Billy Cahall, Fred Carter, "Mr. Botts" Causey, Monk Randolph, and Byron "By" Walton. That half a dozen were star players and labeled as "ringers" (alleged football players only, rather than student-athletes who attended class).

The first sign of any issues regarding the eligibility of the players in question came from within the Ole Miss faculty itself. Dr. Robert C. Rhodes, an assistant professor within the medical school, brought the initial allegations forward at a spring faculty meeting in May of 1912.

Rhodes reportedly had proof that the players weren't amateurs and shouldn't be allowed to play college football.

To their credit, the educators in Oxford elected to pass the information off to the board of trustees who oversaw Mississippi's institutes of higher education. Despite a June 5th hearing being scheduled, no one appeared to argue the charges against the players. All six were reinstated, but our story has truly just begun.

Shortly after the "exoneration," the SIAA began an inquiry. Dr. William Dudley, the founder of the league and first president, sent word to Ole Miss head coach Nathan Stauffer that the two needed to discuss the players in question.

In addition to his coaching duties, Stauffer worked as a physician. With a medical degree in hand from Jefferson Medical College in Pennsylvania, Stauffer planned to use some time during the summer to study abroad in Europe and take a bit of a vacation.

Dudley informed Stauffer that he should delay his trip until the matter could be resolved. Following the reinstatement hearing from the board of trustees, Stauffer sailed to Europe anyway. Upon his return to the United States, Stauffer learned that he and the six players at the center of the probe had all been suspended by the SIAA.

The Ole Miss Alumni Association and the student body joined to protest the decision. They demanded justice and suggested that Dudley and the whistleblower, Rhodes, colluded with one another as Vanderbilt alums to derail the Rebel football program.

Vandy had gone undefeated in 1910 and 1911 and won at least a share of the SIAA football title in both seasons.

Resolutions were passed, and Rebel folks signed petitions to demand another hearing and reinstate the players. Interestingly enough, the Ole Miss Alumni Association admitted that alums had provided outside financial assistance to football players in the years prior.

The Ole Miss faculty voted to reinstate the charges against the players and Coach Stauffer. The ballots were nearly evenly divided. The final tally was 15-14 to bar the players from athletic competition. The findings were forwarded to the SIAA, along with the request to ban all involved parties.

In the wake of the decision, many Ole Miss alums pushed to have the game against Mississippi A&M canceled even before the season had begun. As noted in the *Jackson Daily News*, one supporter shared that he would take 20 to 1 odds that Ole Miss wouldn't even score against the Aggies with a roster primarily of scrubs.

The Rebels got out to a 3-0 start to the season. Ole Miss shut out Memphis High 34-0, claimed a forfeit from Castle Heights, and then edged out LSU 10-7 in Baton Rouge. Maybe things weren't so bad after all.

Ole Miss traveled to Nashville the following week to take on Vanderbilt on Dudley Field. Considering the backdrop of the suspensions and the harsh feelings about Commodore alums, the game was a big one for both squads.

Vandy crushed Ole Miss 24-0. The result stirred up more feelings of resentment over the suspensions.

Ole Miss beat Mississippi College in Oxford to improve their record to 4-1. A competitive 10-9 loss to Alabama came the next week. Texas walloped Ole Miss 53-14 the week before Thanksgiving.

With the season winding down, a decision still had to be made about the rivalry game against Mississippi A&M. The annual football feud was scheduled for November 28th, but there was a lot of doubt about the game taking place.

When the game was finally canceled officially, Ole Miss and its media partners in Jackson blamed A&M head coach Billy Chadwick for the game being called off. The rumor then was that the Aggies didn't want to play against Ole Miss's quarterback, Ralph Fletcher.

Fletcher was being branded a sports mercenary, essentially a free agent, brought in by first-year Rebel head coach Leo DeTray. Before arriving in Oxford, DeTray, a former University of Chicago player, served his second stint as an assistant at his alma mater in 1911.

With the hubbub surrounding the SIAA coach and player suspensions, DeTray and Ole Miss needed a quarterback desperately. They found one in Fletcher.

Fans had no clue that Fletcher's enrollment at Ole Miss had already been a matter of conversation and controversy behind the scenes. The Rebel narrative in the papers pointed the finger at Chadwick. The propaganda was very self-serving and devoid of facts.

In an exposé worthy of a Pulitzer Prize, the *Hattiesburg Daily News* got to the bottom of the matter. It made the details of the entire fiasco available for public consumption.

Just as Ole Miss was preparing to play LSU on October 19, 1912, the University faculty deemed Fletcher ineligible. They forwarded their findings to the SIAA. League president Dudley instructed his staff to review the facts and independently decide Fletcher's eligibility.

The matter took some time to resolve. In the interest of fairness, Dudley permitted Fletcher to play in the loss against Vanderbilt, mainly due to Ole Miss chancellor Andrew Kincannon's repeated assertions that Fletcher hadn't played at any previous institutions.

Another matter involved in the probe was the allegation that Fletcher had coached football at Ada High School in Ohio. Fletcher stated to the SIAA that he hadn't been employed as a paid football coach, which was prohibited for college athletes then.

Ole Miss professor Christoper Longest penned a letter to the SIAA on November 6, 1912, revealing that he had received confirmation that Fletcher had been a student at the University of Chicago in 1910 and 1911. The case was clear. DeTray recruited Fletcher to Ole Miss, and many conspired to cover up his prior college playing and high school coaching experience.

Dudley wrote to Kincannon two days later, expressing his disappointment over the ruse and Ole Miss's attempts to circumvent eligibility rules. Transfers were required to sit a season, but the Rebels felt that rule didn't apply to them.

"Mr. Fletcher is unquestionably ineligible on account of the one-year rule," Dudley penned. "I do not understand how you or any member of the faculty committee on athletics can see it any other way."

Despite the ruling from the league, Ole Miss continued to play Fletcher in ball games. After the loss to Alabama, Kincannon and the Ole Miss leadership drew the ire of Dudley.

"I learned that Fletcher played in your game with Alabama Saturday, although he had been ruled out by the vice-president, and his case was before me on appeal," Dudley's November 11th correspondence read. "I wrote you last Friday that I sustained Dr. Walker's ruling. You should presume that the action of the vice president would hold until reversed by the president or the executive committee.

"I desire an explanation from you at once, or it will become my duty to blacklist Mississippi. I desire to inform you that Fletcher cannot play on the Mississippi team again under any circumstances.

"A blacklist means that you cannot play any team in the SIAA in the future and that all games you now have are canceled regardless of contracts."

Despite the stern warning from Dudley and the SIAA leadership, Ole Miss still planned to play Fletcher on the football team.

On November 19th, the Ole Miss athletic department sent a telegram to A&M athletic director Billy Chadwick. The *Hattiesburg Daily News* got a copy of the back-and-forth correspondence, which flew in the face of the nonsense that the Jackson media had been fed out of Oxford.

"Will you play our annual Thanksgiving game with Fletcher in the game? If you refuse to do this, you will be the cause of us having no game. Wire answer tomorrow noon," the message read.

President Dudley and the SIAA had informed Ole Miss officials that Fletcher wasn't permitted to suit up again as a Rebel football player. Ole Miss was bound and determined to play him anyway, and if A&M wouldn't let him play, then it would be the Aggies' fault that the rivalry game was canceled.

Undeterred by the attempted manipulation from Ole Miss, Chadwick informed Rebel officials that the game was set to proceed as scheduled.

"Telegram received," Chadwick wired in response. "We are expecting you to play the Thanksgiving game. Have nothing to do with deciding personnel on your team."

With the ploy foiled, Ole Miss leaders fired another telegram to the SIAA.

"Unless you remove the ban on Fletcher and accept the affidavit produced, there will be no game on Thanksgiving. Wire answer this evening."

The league stood firm, and the game was canceled. On November 23rd, Ole Miss informed Chadwick that the game was indeed off.

In place of the rivalry game, Ole Miss scheduled a game against the Tennessee Medical College of Memphis, in which they won 47-6. With that win, Ole Miss celebrated a winning season at 5-3 and didn't have to suffer through a loss to A&M without Fletcher on the field. The whole matter was preposterous.

Ole Miss's faculty committee deemed Fletcher ineligible before the season began. A kangaroo court session was scheduled to reverse that ruling prior to the SIAA taking steps to intervene.

Despite the SIAA's stance, Ole Miss elected to flaunt the rules. The Rebels thumbed their noses at Dudley and the league, and they paid for it handsomely. Dudley kicked Ole Miss out of the SIAA. The blacklist impacted baseball, football, and track.

During the 1913 season, Ole Miss played as an independent. The *Jackson Daily News* opined that Ole Miss could get along just fine without being a member of the SIAA, and the league may fold without their inclusion.

A year later, Rebel leaders filed for reinstatement. A handful of games were permitted against SIAA teams during the 1914 season, but Mississippi A&M wasn't one of them.

Considering the campaign of misinformation designed to cast aspersions at Coach Billy Chadwick, it made sense for the two to have a cooling-off period. While the bitter rivals had a three-year hiatus on the gridiron, the fires of bitterness still burned in Chadwick.

When the 1915 schedule was released, it was officially known that the A&M and Ole Miss series would resume. Fans were beside themselves with anticipation. The annual grudge match was considered the most important sporting event on the calendar each year for Mississippi folk. In 1915, though, the game wouldn't be held on Thanksgiving.

Dudy Noble played all over the field throughout his college football career. In the early days, Noble served time at tackle or end. Eventually, Chadwick moved him to fullback and, in time, halfback. In his final season with Hayes as the head man, Noble won the starting quarterback job.

A&M opened the 1915 season with a 12-0 win over Mississippi College at the state fairgrounds in Jackson.

The Pioneers of Transylvania College made their way to Starkville in week two. Dracula didn't make an appearance. This Transylvania was tucked away in Lexington, Kentucky, rather than central Europe. At the time, the Pioneers were part of the SIAA.

The game ended in a scoreless tie and was the only time the Aggies failed to earn a win in the series. The record reads 3-0-1 in favor of A&M. In the '15 tie, A&M missed one field goal and had another blocked.

Week three brought Kentucky to the Athletic Field on the Mississippi A&M campus. Noble ran the offense with greater proficiency, and the Aggies scored a 12-0 win.

Keeping with the tradition of the time, Auburn blasted A&M 26-0. Noble and the offense couldn't get anything going. Even when the Aggies had opportunities to score, they turned the ball over. The Tigers simply had their number, and Noble never celebrated a football win over Auburn during his playing career.

LSU kept A&M off the board the following week in a 10-0 win. In a hard-fought game, the lone touchdown was a scoop and score by the Tiger defense. Fumbling was a big part of football in the early 1900s, and that was the case on this day.

With a 2-2-1 record, A&M prepared to take on Ole Miss in Tupelo. The 1915 meeting between the two schools was the first time the contest had ever been held in Tupelo. The previous seven meetings were all held in Jackson.

Ole Miss entered the game with a 2-3 mark. The biggest blemish was a 91-0 shellacking at the hands of Vanderbilt in Memphis. Considering the bad blood between the Rebels and the SIAA office headed by Dudley, the lopsided affair was likely more personal.

After all the hubris that originated in Oxford and was hurled toward Starkville and Chadwick, the Aggies also had an axe to grind. While it had been years since Rebel officials tried to use Chadwick as a scapegoat to back out of the 1912 game, A&M folks had not forgotten.

Legend has it that Chadwick told the coaching staff and the team that he wanted to score every point the team could. Noble and the rest of the Aggies took that directive to heart.

Otto Schwill scored the first Aggie touchdown and Noble the second as A&M charged out to a 14-0 lead.

Schwill added his second rushing touchdown in the second quarter. Noble connected on his first pass of the day, and it went for a long touchdown. The Aggies were comfortably ahead 33-0 when the whistle blew to signal halftime.

At some point in the third quarter, Ole Miss earned a first down. It was their lone offensive highlight of the day and the only first down the Aggie defense allowed in the game.

While the Rebels were seeing their offense sputter, the Aggies kept humming. Schwill added his third and final touchdown run of the day just before Noble threw a 30-yard touchdown pass to put A&M up 46-0.

The Aggies were far from done. Chadwick wanted the score run up, and run up it was. A&M tacked on 19 more points in the final period of play to push the score to 65-0. On A&M's last offensive possession, Noble attempted one more Hail Mary pass. It fell incomplete, but the Aggie superstar wouldn't waste an opportunity to avenge the man who believed in him in the early stages of his college career.

To add insult to humiliating injury, there was nearly a brawl during the halftime of the varsity game when the Aggie bulldog and the Rebel goat got a little too close together. The goat retreated amongst the Ole Miss coaches and players as Bully pursued. Hundreds of Aggie cadets rushed the field as one of the Rebel footballers stood to confront the Aggie dog handler for not subduing his mascot.

Ole Miss head coach Fred Robins is credited with avoiding a near riot on the playing surface. Eventually, cooler heads prevailed, but it was simply that kind of day for the in-state rivals. The Aggies won every fight on the field and were ready for another one that didn't involve a scoreboard.

Later in the season, in the freshman football game, A&M trounced the Rebels again by the score of 29-0. Chadwick's charges dominated Ole Miss every chance they got.

With the Rebels thoroughly defeated and the Aggies emboldened by the most lopsided score in the history of the series, A&M pressed forward.

Noble and crew traveled to Knoxville the following week and posted another shutout, 14-0. A blocked drop kick attempt by the Volunteers was scooped up and returned for a score to give the Aggies an early 7-0 lead.

Special teams were the difference that day. The coup de gras came when A&M blocked a punt and returned it 70 yards for a score to cap the scoring at 14-0.

The season ended with a 7-0 win over Texas A&M. High winds wreaked havoc on nearly every attempted pass. The oval regularly sailed away from its intended targets. Only one pass attempt between the two teams resulted in a completion.

The Starkville contingent went "old school" and resorted to a ground-and-pound game. The lone score came on a Schwill run to glory. Noble led the team on one final drive that nearly ended in the end zone as the final seconds ticked away.

When the final horn sounded, scores of Texas A&M Cadets

stormed Kyle Field and carried Noble, Schwill, and other Aggie players off the field on their shoulders. It was a fitting show of respect between warriors, and Dudy Noble certainly qualified for such distinction.

As the 1915 college football season ended, there were no bowl games. The Rose Bowl didn't begin its run as an annual postseason game until the following year.

There was no SIAA title game. There wasn't even a Golden Egg. That annual rivalry token between the two Mississippi rivals was still over a decade away from being introduced.

At the core of it all was the love of the game and the unending desire for bragging rights. Mississippi A&M earned those and then some with the 65-0 drubbing of Ole Miss. The Rebels had it coming.

While the only evidence we have of that glorious November Saturday is the scant written accounts and the record books, Chadwick's desire to rub Ole Miss's face in the mud has stood the test of time. The result of that game has endured.

Over 100 years later, 65 points is the highest tally that either team has ever scored in the rivalry game. The 65-point margin of victory is the largest in the history of the Magnolia State's biggest grudge match.

That 1915 meeting ended with the most substantial ass-whoopin' that Mississippi A&M or Mississippi State ever doled out to Ole Miss. Billy Chadwick gave the Rebels their comeuppance for attempting to sully his name and reputation for the 1912 game being canceled.

Dudy Noble took out three years of unbridled fury and frustration on the Rebels in his only meeting against them on the football field. In Mississippi A&M's finest hour against Ole Miss, Noble called the cadence and led the Aggies to a historic win that remains the gold standard in the battle for instate football supremacy.

Chapter 6

For the Folks Back Home

The International Olympic Committee awarded Berlin the host site on July 4, 1912. The German Stadium, erected to house the festivities, was dedicated on June 8, 1913.

Grand plans were being made to have the finest Olympic event, but the region soon became unsettled. Just over 13 months after the Olympic venue opened, Austrian Archduke Franz Ferdinand and his wife, Sophie, were assassinated. The killings set off a chain reaction that led to World War I.

While day-to-day life in America was largely unaffected, Europe had a major crisis. Many in the United States went on with their lives. That included church, school, and ball games.

In the early stages of the conflict, many believed peace would be achieved well before the 1916 games began. As the war drug on, decisions had to be made. The International Olympic Committee canceled the Berlin Olympics. As a result, there were no Olympic trials in the United States.

The United States Olympic officials selected the earlier American Olympic teams based on regional events. Things were changing as the 1916 team was being assembled. There was talk about a national event rather than several regional trials.

Two runners in the discussion for invitations to those meets were Mississippi A&M's own Dudy Noble and Don Scott.

For the second straight year, Noble dominated the ranks of the SIAA and won the 100-yard and 220-yard dash at the Amateur Athletic Union (AAU) sanctioned Southern Intercollegiate meet in 1916.

The Memphis *Commercial Appeal* reported that Noble was "the best sprinter developed by a southern college in the history of athletic competition in this section of the country."

In back-to-back years, Noble was timed as the only college 100-yard sprinter to record times of 10-flat in the event nationally.

Noble was dubbed the "fastest man in the south" by Mississippi A&M's student newspaper, *The Reflector*, and yearbook, *The Reveille*. In those early days of student scribing, the unofficial title may have been the product of hometown homiletics. As a proven track star on the big stage, Noble made that early praise appear to be prophetic.

Scott was more of a middle and long-distance runner. As the captain of A&M's championship track team in 1916, Scott set the record in the quarter mile in 49:1.5 seconds. He ran the half-mile in 1:55:3.5, which was a blistering pace even on a reported slower track. Scott had some faster personal records but weren't considered official as they were run at AAU non-sanctioned events.

Noble and Scott were invited to the AAU National Championships in San Francisco, California. With no Olympics to run in, both ran for national glory and in honor of their home state of Mississippi at an event called the Panama Exposition Meet.

The trip out west was an expensive one. Noble and Scott were both from modest blue-collar families. The great people of Learned and Woodville, Noble and Scott's hometowns, raised the money necessary to fund the expenses for both runners. Their quests suddenly became one of civic pride as well as personal accomplishment.

Scott and Noble were running for A&M. They were running for Mississippi. The two were also running as pathmakers for the young dreamers of Mississippi who had never known a life beyond the state lines. The two were proof positive that there was a bigger world out there, and they were determined to find it.

With Noble's sprinting acumen well documented, many expected him to win the national championship in the 100 and the 220-yard dash. Noble was quick off the line in the 100, but his top-end speed served him better in the 220. The longer dash was considered his best event. He rarely sprinted across the finish line since his competitors trailed far behind.

Noble found the competition stiff on the national level and came up short of a place on the podium in both events. Noble didn't win his qualifying heat for the final in the 100 or 220. Perhaps it was a bad day, but the first-place finisher crossed the line in the 100 with a 9:4.5 time. Even with a good day, Noble would have needed the fastest race of his life to earn the gold medal.

Scott fared a little better with a fourth-place finish in the 880. He missed the podium in the 440, but the winner, Frank Sloman, tied the world record at the time with a 47-second flat time to the finish.

In the fall of 1916, Scott won the AAU National Championship in the half-mile at 1:54. Not only did Scott win the gold medal, but he also ran the fastest time ever in the event in the history of the AAU. When the dust settled, Scott became the first national title winner in Mississippi A&M history.

When the Olympic Games resumed in 1920, Scott was part of the US contingent that competed at Antwerpen, Belgium.

Scott qualified for one event, the 800 meters. In round one, Scott turned in a time of 1:56.9, which was second best in his grouping. In the semifinals, Scott finished first at 1:57.2.

After making it through the qualifying heats, Scott had the chance to compete for a gold medal. On the first lap of the final, Scott led the field. He faded down the stretch and finished fifth. Not bad for an ole boy from South Mississippi, but a little short of the Magnolia State hope.

Shortly after his first Olympic appearance, *The Reflector* suggested that A&M officials change the "The New Athletic Field" name to honor Scott, the school's first-ever Olympian. "The name of a thing, in order to be appropriate, must bear some direct relation to whatever thing that bears the name," the student writer wrote.

"New Athletic Field does directly relate to our athletic field in the sense that it is news, but why not call the baby The New Baby, or the store The New Store?

"In selecting a name for our athletic field, we ought to stop and say,

'Ink has written A&M athletic history' and select the name of some great athlete whose feats have added the most laurels to A&M's athletic glory.

"If we review the records of the great football men, there is no man whose feats are outstanding enough to warrant the naming of the field in his honor. The same may be truthfully said about our baseball men.

"There is but one A&M athlete who has gone out from this institution and demonstrated his superiority over any athlete he has come in contact with. Don Scott, A&M's great half-miler, has met and defeated the best athletes of this country. He now holds the SIAA record for the half-mile and his records still stand unbroken for the same distance in the Western Conference and the National AAU.

Why not name our new athletic field Scott Field in appreciation of Don's untiring efforts to bring athletic fame to his Alma Mater?"

It didn't take a lot of persuading. To this day, the Mississippi State football program still calls Scott Field home. While the stadium surrounding that sacred patch of grass has been dubbed Davis-Wade Stadium, the name Scott Field has endured for over 120 years.

In 1924, Scott again made the US Olympic team that competed in Paris. He participated in the modern-day pentathlon this go-around and finished 26th out of 38 competitors.

Scott finished eighth in the field in the running portion of the competition. His worst event was shooting, where he finished 34th. It's ironic considering his upbringing in South Mississippi, where hunting is a way of life.

While Scott went on to Olympic glory in the years following his enrollment at Mississippi A&M, Noble went to work.

Despite some accounts to the contrary, when Noble left A&M following the spring semester in 1916, he did so without his college degree. The original plan was to head back to Hinds County and work on the farm.

An exciting opportunity arose that changed Noble's professional career. Mississippi College needed a coach.

Dana Xenophon Bible was a name on the rise in the college football coaching profession. After three seasons at MC, more prominent budget schools contacted Bible about running their programs. The *Hattiesburg Daily News* shared on August 17, 1916, that Bible had been in talks with Texas A&M and had resigned from his post at the Clinton, Mississippi college to pursue an opportunity there.

The brief said that Mississippi College president, John William Provine, had already come to terms with Noble as Bible's successor.

There is an interesting aside related to Bible and A&M. His departure was expected to take him to Aggie land in 1916, but he spent that season working as an assistant coach at LSU. Bible was the Tigers' head coach for that year's final three games.

Coach E.T. McDonnell ran the LSU program for the previous two seasons but left abruptly after a 7-0 loss to Sewanee. Assistant Irving Prayer supervised the team for two games, but Bible blew the big whistle for the final games.

LSU went 7-1-2 during the season, and Bible departed for A&M the following year, where he stayed for 10 seasons. Bible had successful stints at Texas A&M, Nebraska, and Texas. He was eventually an inaugural selection in the College Football Hall of Fame.

Noble inherited a strong roster in '16 led by star quarterback Edwin "Goat" Hale.

Legend has it that on a touchdown run in a high school game between Central High School and Brookhaven, Hale broke through the line for a touchdown. His run to glory ended when he collided with a wooden building behind the end zone with his head. The old shack got the worst end of the encounter as Hale splintered some of the wooden planks.

The head butt to the building led to Hale being nicknamed Goat. It stuck.

Hale wasn't the only person in Noble's life who experienced a name change. With a paying job and aspirations to start a family, Coach Noble asked Elizabeth Montgomery to marry him.

Elizabeth attended the II&C in Columbus, now known as The W, at the same time Noble attended A&M. Their courtship took off as college graduates.

Following her time in college, Elizabeth took a job teaching in Edwards, Mississippi, and lived in the teachers' dormitory. Noble asked for her hand, and she agreed. Soon after, Elizabeth Montgomery became the first lady of Mississippi College football.

Whether it was the need to support a wife or satisfy his competitive fire, Noble went to work, proving himself as a college coach.

While the Collegians were expected to be outsized and outclassed by many of their SIAA opponents, Noble refused to buy into that line of thinking. After his team's first fall scrimmage, Noble shared with sports writers that he was encouraged by what he saw.

The season opener brought Marion to Provine Field on the Mississippi College Campus in Clinton. If there were any first-game jitters, the Collegians didn't show them.

A wet and rainy day did little to dampen the day's events. MC won 32-0. Hale had a pair of touchdown runs, including a 65-yarder that broke the game open.

The second game of the MC season presented an exciting scenario for Noble. His employer, Mississippi College, was set to play his former college home, Mississippi A&M, in the season opener for the Aggies.

The site of the game was Aberdeen. The tilt was billed as the centerpiece of the Monroe County Fair. The subplots were endless. Noble was an Aggie legend in multiple sports. How would he handle coaching against his former coaches and some of his former teammates?

For two quarters, the game was essentially a stalemate. On the second half's opening kick, Mississippi College's Frank Anderson broke free for a 90-yard touchdown return. The extra point try failed.

Later in the quarter, Hale pushed the MC lead to 13-0 on a 40-yard jaunt. The conversion was good.

Coach Hayes and the Aggies finally got on the board in the fourth quarter when Noble's backfield mate from a season before, Otto

Schwill, plunged to paydirt. A&M's comeback fell short, and Noble won his first game against his alma mater.

As Hale and others returned to Jackson by train, they were met at the depot by Mississippi College students who carried them on their shoulders to the parking lot where their automobiles and a brass band were waiting.

Once back in Clinton, a celebration lingered long into the night. President Provine even dismissed Monday morning classes.

Noble's squad continued their tough play the following week in Tuscaloosa. A very physical game saw Alabama star offensive lineman Dexter Hovater, one of three brothers to start for the team, break his left leg in the first quarter.

Mississippi College turned back Alabama three times inside their 10-yard line to keep the game close. Goree Johnson finally broke through to break the scoreless tie. The extra point was missed, and Alabama held a 6-0 lead.

Late in the second quarter, Anderson burst into daylight with an 80-yard scoring scamper to pull the Collegians even with the Crimson. The extra point was good, and MC took a 7-6 lead into the halftime intermission.

Ultimately, Alabama's All-Southern quarterback Cecil Creen ran for a score off the left side for a fourth-quarter touchdown. The try after was good, and Alabama held on to win 13-7.

Week four sent MC to Baton Rouge to take on LSU. The Collegians made that trip south without Anderson, who was injured late in the win over Alabama. They needed him as the Tigers won 50-7.

The losing streak reached three games when MC fell to Tulane at the Jackson fairgrounds, 13-3. The headline wasn't the final score. The game had to be called early due to a fight.

Throughout the game, both teams were a bit chippy. The officials reportedly had to break up several skirmishes between the two teams. Things finally got out of hand, and punches were thrown. The root cause was alleged to have been profanity spewed by the Tulane players.

Not ready to turn the other cheek, the ministerial students on the field and in the stands were ready to roll. Hundreds of Mississippi College students stormed the field to join the fray as the two teams came to blows. The fight was broken up, and the game was called.

The war of words continued between the two fan bases with emotionally penned letters to the editor of the state's newspapers.

Noble stayed out of the barb trading and focused on his team. There had been an ugly incident involving his squad, but his program was mired in a three-game losing streak. The ultimate eraser in sports is to win and win big. That's exactly what Noble did, lest anyone regret hiring him as the MC head coach.

On Monday, November 7th, MC traveled to Hattiesburg's Kamper Park to take on Mississippi Normal College, now named the University of Southern Mississippi.

Known as the Normalites back then, the college team from Hattiesburg was downright pitiful. Normal lost their season opener to Meridian High School 31-0.

With Anderson healthy and back in the Mississippi College huddle, they went to work and laid waste to Mississippi Normal 75-0. The two schools don't agree on the final score, but both admit that MC won going away.

The Southern Miss record book records that game as a 75-0 defeat, while MC lists it as a 90-0 win.

No matter what the official tally was from that day, it was sure to leave a mark. Much like the third and final game of the year, Normal lost to Spring Hill 87-0.

The Normalites didn't score a point that season and finished 0-3. Coach Avery Benjamin Dille, a former Mississippi A&M player, left at season's end for a position as a high school principal in Charleston, Mississippi.

Due to WWI and the challenges of putting a competitive team on the field, Normal disbanded its football program for two seasons.

Just three days after the cakewalk in Hattiesburg, MC hosted Louisiana Industrial, now known as Louisiana Tech University. The bloodletting continued.

The two teams battled to a scoreless tie in Ruston the season before, but that was before Noble had Hale and Anderson running downhill full of piss and vinegar after that fourth-quarter riot with Tulane.

The Collegians routed the visitors from Louisiana 47-0. The shutout streak continued the following Saturday with a 26-0 victory over Ouachita in Jackson.

Since that melee at the end of the Tulane loss, Noble's Collegians were beating people up. They were doing it on the scoreboard and within the rules of fair play.

Already assured of a winning season, Mississippi College had the opportunity to complete the Magnolia State trifecta and claim a state championship by beating Ole Miss.

That season, the Red and Blue won their first three games but fell into hard times shortly after. Against SIAA competition, Ole Miss lost five games in a row and tallied just three combined points in those defeats.

Mississippi College was the favorite, and Noble hadn't forgotten about the nonsense that Ole Miss officials had attempted to rain down on his former mentor, Billy Chadwick, over the cancellation of the 1912 rivalry game on Thanksgiving day.

Despite their recent meager scoring efforts, Ole Miss jumped to a quick 14-0 lead over the Collegians. A pick-six in the first quarter, a 40-yard run in the second, and a pair of successful conversions made it appear that it wasn't Noble and MC's day.

Before the half, MC got on the board with a Hale touchdown run. The extra point made it a 14-7 game. A blocked punt led to a Collegian safety to draw MC closer at 14-9.

The second half belonged to Mississippi College as they scored 20 unanswered points and a 36-14 victory. The win was the second straight for the Collegians over Ole Miss.

Like Bible, the man Noble replaced, Dudy went 6-3 in his first season as the head coach of Mississippi College.

While college football was still a relatively new sport, Noble did some remarkable things in his one season in Clinton. He was the first Mississippi College coach to beat Mississippi A&M and the second to beat Ole Miss. He is the only MC football coach to beat State, Ole Miss, and Southern Mississippi in the same season.

Chapter 7

A Journey into "Hell"

The fallout from the "Ringer-Gate" scandal, which led to Ole Miss's ouster from the SIAA, was still felt years later. The recovery process took some time. There is probably nothing that Rebel folks hate more than bad press, especially when that media coverage involves their misdeeds. Ole Miss has always been about image. It isn't a recent phenomenon.

When the hammer fell, the guilty parties fingered were high-ranking members of the Ole Miss administration. The scandal went to the chancellor's office but touched all the decision-makers connected to the plot. Coach Nathan Stauffer, charged with playing ineligible players during the 1911 season, never coached college football again. Stauffer elected to return to his native Pennsylvania to set up his medical practice.

Coach Leo DeTray, who took over the Ole Miss football program after the SIAA suspended Stauffer, didn't survive the Fletcher eligibility cover-up in 1912. Three years later DeTray accepted a post coaching football and basketball appointment at Knox College in Illinois.

In two seasons there, he won five football games. After three unsuccessful stops as a college coach, DeTray went into the oil business and never returned to college coaching.

Chancellor Andrew Kincannon left after the spring semester of 1914. He resigned from his position at Ole Miss and took over as the administrative head of the Memphis school district. Former Mississippi Superintendent of Education Joseph Neely Powers succeeded Kincannon.

Rebel athletic director William Driver was hired shortly after the SIAA penalty came down but left Oxford just one year into the Powers' era for a post at Texas A&M. Perhaps the move was political and an attempt to curry some favor with the SIAA.

Still, Powers hired Fred Robins to head up the athletic department and coach the football team at Ole Miss. Robins was a star quarterback and halfback at Vanderbilt before taking over as the head football coach at Mercer.

Many within the Ole Miss fanbase felt that Dr. Dudley and the rest of the SIAA leadership, who were Vanderbilt alums, had a bone to pick with the Rebels. Perhaps they took an "if you can't beat 'em, join 'em" approach when they hired Robins.

Robins' tenure in Oxford lasted just two years. Between 1915 and 1916, his Rebel football teams won five combined games and went winless against the SIAA competition. The Memphis *Commercial Appeal* dubbed the 1916 season "the most disastrous football season that Ole Miss has ever experienced." The campaign ended on a six-game losing streak. Robins couldn't continue, so he resigned.

Whether forced out or the product of personal reflection, it all means the same thing—Ole Miss needed a new football coach. Chancellor Powers targeted Dudy Noble to resurrect their program and run the athletics department.

Noble made a name for himself in that one year at Mississippi College, even claiming a win over Ole Miss, which he despised. Using the powers of persuasion, a promotion, and a much bigger checkbook than MC had, Powers lured Noble to Oxford with promises of patience and higher pay.

Before moving to Lafayette County, Noble had some unfinished business at A&M; he still needed to graduate. Legend has it that one of the required courses Noble needed to complete after his athletic career had ended was a math class that he had hoped to avoid.

After meeting with his academic advisor, Noble was informed that the mathematics course was a requirement for his studies to earn his degree. The posted grades in the class were a seesaw affair. At times, Noble did pretty well, and other times, not so much. Passing the class and earning the associated college credits came down to the final.

The exam consisted of four problems students should solve using various formulas taught during the semester. About halfway through the timed test, a dejected Noble walked to the front of the class and laid his test booklet on the professor's desk.

No, he hadn't aced the final. Instead, Noble scrawled on the front of his answer sheet, "I don't know a dam one of them." When grades were posted a few days later, Noble was awarded a B for the course. Surmising that a mistake had been made, Noble saw the professor. After he explained to his instructor that he hadn't even completed one of the questions on the final, the professor cut him off.

"Mr. Noble, I would have given you an A if you had spelled damn correctly," the professor said. CR "Dudy" Noble graduated from Mississippi A&M with his B.S. Degree in General Science. While listed as a member of the 1916 class, Noble officially graduated in the summer of 1917, according to his academic records. Now a Mississippi A&M alumnus, Noble went to work coaching baseball and football at Ole Miss.

While Noble had more dollars in his pockets, he wasn't dealt much of a hand on the gridiron. The average weight of the Rebel players was about 160 pounds, which was light in the britches even for that day and time. Complicating matters even further, no M-Club letterman returned for the 1917 season. The lack of girth and experience showed.

Noble's first game as the Rebel head man ended in a 0-0 tie against the Jonesboro Aggies, now the Arkansas State Red Wolves.

Week two ended with a 52-7 thrashing at the hands of LSU. Ole Miss's lone score came on a pick-six long after the game had been decided.

After an open date, the beatings continued as Alabama shut out the Rebels in Tuscaloosa, 64-0. Three games into his Ole Miss tenure, Noble hadn't found a way to get his offense into the end zone.

The dam finally burst against Mississippi A&M. The Aggies had a fine team that year in their first year under Coach Stanley Robinson.

Ole Miss scored two touchdowns in the game but fell 41-14. Those two touchdowns were the most that any team scored on A&M all season. The Aggies went 6-1.

The offensive futility for the Rebels continued in a 69-7 blowout at the hands of Sewanee.

In the season finale, Noble earned his first win at Ole Miss with a 21-0 decision against his previous team, Mississippi College.

The Ole Miss yearbook recounted, "Without a single 'M' man around to build a team, Coach Noble had to take a squad of green, inexperienced men and mold them into a coordinated, fighting machine. All this took time; the season was almost over before the Red and Blue struck its stride.

"But even with this great handicap, the team, under the great generalship of Coach Noble, upheld the honor of Ole Miss on all occasions."

Noble posted a 9-1 record on the baseball diamond the following spring. That .900 winning percentage remains the benchmark for winning in the history of Ole Miss baseball.

The lone loss in that 1918 season came to A&M in a 7-3 affair in Columbus, Mississippi. The Aggies and Rebels played four games that year in four different locations. Ole Miss won three of them.

There is a bit of a caveat to those games. A&M had to push back a pair of games when a spell of ptomaine poisoning ran through the team, sidelining a half dozen Aggie players. The record books won't tell you that. They tell you who won and lost; in this case, Ole Miss won.

Noble took a few more knocks on the football field when the fall rolled around. Ole Miss played just four games during the 1918 football season, and the schedule featured an anomaly as the Aggies and Rebels played twice.

The season got off to a disappointing start as the Rebels lost to a military team based out of Payne Field just outside of West Point, Mississippi.

A long pass set up the game's only score as Payne Field won 6-0. As time expired, the Rebel defense huddled inside their own 10-yard line, trying to prevent another score.

Noble's offense found its footing on a muddy field against Union a week later. The Rebels celebrated a 39-0 win. It proved to be their lone victory of the season.

After an open date, Ole Miss traveled to Starkville to take on A&M. The offensive prowess shown against Union wasn't evident against the Aggies. A&M did what they wanted and quickly took control of the game.

The Rebel running game couldn't get going, so Noble resorted to several forward pass attempts in the second half. Nor by air, by land, or by sea could Ole Miss mount an offensive drive of any merit. A&M won easily by a score of 34-0.

The return game rematch took place on December 7th in Oxford. A much more competitive game was played.

A&M scored two touchdowns in the first half but missed one of the conversions. The Aggie defense made that lead stand up over the final two quarters to win 13-0.

The 1918 season is the lone season in the history of the long-standing series between the two schools to feature two games. Noble is the only coach on either side of the rivalry to suffer two defeats in a year. Chances are that distinction will last forever.

When the spring semester began, Noble tried his hand at coaching the Ole Miss basketball team. The Rebels hadn't had an official men's basketball coach since the 1912 season when By Walton led them to a 10-2 record.

Following Walton's departure, Ole Miss went 0-7 the following season, with five losses against YMCA teams.

The program withered but experienced a resurgence during the 1916-1917 campaign that saw the Rebels post an 11-7 mark. The program was disbanded a year later due to student involvement in World War I.

Noble was charged with rebuilding interest in the sport, but the task proved extremely difficult. Games were hard to come by. The Rebels only played three and lost them all. Two of those losses came to Mississippi A&M.

As the preparations for the 1919 baseball season began, Noble had to recruit students to be a part of the varsity program.

The class sports programs flourished under Noble's supervision. In fact, on March 3, 1919, the *Jackson Daily News* shared, "Under the direction of Coach Noble, more interest has been created in class athletics than under any other athletic director who has been here."

Ole Miss Baseball needed several of those class athletes to fill holes in its varsity roster. Only a handful of lettermen returned from the previous year's team that nearly went undefeated.

Ace pitcher, Dick Field, who beat A&M three times in 1918, was gone, as was all but one hurler from the season before. Graduation hit the squad hard.

A full schedule was promised that featured games against Alabama, Illinois, LSU, Mississippi A&M, Mississippi College and others, but only four games appear in the Ole Miss record books.

Somehow, somewhere, there is a discrepancy in the record-keeping as the April 3, 1919 edition of the *Oxford Eagle* has full accounts and box scores of games against Illinois printed.

Pitcher Alphie Carney is credited with a win over Illinois in the season opener, striking out five and walking just one. Ole Miss is reported to have won that game 7-4, though it isn't listed in the record books.

Illinois is credited with an 8-7 win in game two of the three-game series. Ole Miss dropped the rubber game 1-0 thanks to an unearned run in the third inning.

Mysteriously, this entire series is omitted from the Rebel record books. That is not to suggest mischief on anyone's part but to point out that old-school records are often incomplete.

The same fate befell the records for the Millsaps series with Ole Miss that took place April 9th, 10th and 11th. The Rebels swept the series, winning 17-2, 8-2 and 7-0.

Noble's 1919 team was 4-2 at this point in the year despite what the official records indicate.

The record books for Ole Miss and Mississippi A&M match for the four games played against each other during Noble's final season in Oxford.

On Thursday, April 17, 1919, the Aggies overcame a two-run deficit to tie the game in the fifth. A two-run blast by A&M catcher S.K. Womack in the sixth was the difference in the 4-2 affair.

In the Friday rematch, Ole Miss got off to an early lead. The Rebels led 2-0 after four innings of play.

A&M Pitcher J.N. White came through with a two-out RBI single that plated a pair of Aggie runs to make it a game again. Ole Miss answered with a solo shot from Rebel first baseman Rodney Sisk. Things got a little interesting in the eighth when White touched home again on an RBI sacrifice fly to tie the game at 3-3. Ole Miss got a pinch-hit RBI single in the bottom of the eighth, which proved to be the winning run.

When the series resumed in Starkville during May, the Aggies held a record of 11-6. A pair of losses to Alabama likely cost A&M a share of the SIAA championship.

The Aggies did their part to end the season on a winning note. In game one of the two-game bill, Ole Miss made 11 errors. Future Aggie Major Leaguer Hughie Critz came up a home run short of hitting for the cycle in the 7-3 victory. Critz was 3-for-4 on the day, scoring three runs.

Carney was back on the mound for the Rebels in the series and season finale. Things started on the right foot for Ole Miss with three early runs in the second to take a 3-0 lead.

The zeroes kept mounting on the scoreboard with Carney on the bump, but A&M finally broke him. A&M stole six bases in the game and got timely hits in the fifth and sixth innings to cap the scoring at 5-3 in favor of the Aggies. A&M and Coach Stanley Robinson ended the year 13-6 overall and 6-4 in league play.

It appears Noble finished his second season as the Rebel skipper with a 5-5 overall record unless there are some more games out there unaccounted for in the official record book.

While it has been reported for over 100 years that Noble posted a losing baseball record in his final year at Ole Miss, the evidence clearly shows that is false.

There was media chatter before the 1919 season about Ole Miss playing games with Alabama and LSU, but neither of those schools reported any games being played that year with the Rebels.

Once the school year ended, Robinson moved from Starkville to Clinton to take over the Mississippi College football program. Dudy Noble moved back to Starkville as an assistant football coach and the head baseball coach.

Noble later characterized his time in Oxford with the famous quote, "I already know what Hell is like; I once coached at Ole Miss."

Chapter 8

Back Home to Stay

In 1920, Dudy Noble returned to Starkville to champion the Aggie baseball program. After the better part of three years in Oxford, Mississippi, Noble was headed home.

His time at Ole Miss was largely unremarkable. In his two seasons as the Red and Blue football coach, Noble went just 2-7-1. Rebel football was a mess when he arrived, but Noble did little to improve the situation.

He was replaced by R. L. Sullivan, who returned to the United States after serving in WWI. After completing his duty tour in France, Sullivan arrived in Oxford to revive Ole Miss football.

A season later, Sullivan was running the entire athletic show for the Rebels. Though not credited in the University of Mississippi record books, Sullivan is listed in the Ole Miss yearbook and referenced in numerous media accounts as the head baseball coach in the few years following Noble.

In the Ole Miss baseball media guide, the 1920, 1921, and 1922 seasons are officially listed as an era with "coach unknown." Still, the evidence clearly shows that Sullivan was the Rebel skipper until the 1923 season when Pete Shields was named head coach.

No matter the quality of record keeping at Ole Miss back then, one thing was sure: Dudy Noble was no longer on the Rebel payroll. While no official statement exists to announce Noble's ouster, the win/loss records suggest that Ole Miss athletics needed a fresh start. They thought they had it with Sullivan.

Noble returned to Mississippi A&M, the site of his glory days as an athlete. The folks in Aggie town received the move with enthusiasm.

The 1920 baseball season was expected to be a rebuilding year. A&M returned just four starters from a team that went 11-7 in 1919.

Perhaps the most significant losses were first baseman Jimmy Alexander and shortstop Mark Lee. While Lee graduated with a degree in electrical engineering, Alexander elected not to return to college.

After the fall, Alexander was voted team captain for the 1920 squad. After his unexpected departure from the program and school, his teammates named third baseman Hughie Critz captain in Alexander's place.

Critz was a little on the smaller side but swung a big bat and was known for his defensive prowess at the hot corner.

Heading into the season, pitching was a big concern as few veteran arms returned for "twirling" duty.

As spring practice wore on, a sophomore right-hander named Monroe Mitchell emerged as an arm Noble could count on.

Mitchell had talent and excellent baseball bloodlines. Known as "Mitch" by his baseball teammates, Monroe was the nephew of former Aggie greats Bennie and Willie Mitchell.

The Mitchell twins were seniors on the 1909 baseball team that earned A&M's first-ever SIAA league championship.

Playing for Coach Dolly Stark, Bennie was the team captain, but Willie was the team's brightest star. The two alternated on the mound and played left field when the other toed the rubber on game day.

During that 1909 season, Willie tossed the first perfect game in school history. That game may have been the closest thing to perfection that a pitcher at any level has ever thrown.

In a 1-0 defeat of LSU down in Baton Rouge on April 11th, Willie struck out 26 of 27 hitters. The final Tiger batter of the day pushed a routine ground ball out to second. "Mack" McCargo fielded it and threw to first to end the perfect game shutout.

Mitchell went the distance, allowing no hits, no walks, no runs, and only one batted ball in fair territory. It was a dominant performance of epic proportions.

Bunny Hearn, who transferred from Elon to A&M, also occasionally relieved the Mitchell twins.

With 22 wins in 26 tries, that Aggie team was as good as they came. A&M outscored their opponents to the tune of 122-41. Nine of those runs allowed came in the season opener. Aggie pitchers combined for six shutouts in the season's final seven games, with the Mitchell twins doing much of the heavy lifting.

While Monroe Mitchell had little experience when he suited up for Noble in 1920, he had the baseball pedigree to suggest that he could be a big-game guy.

Noble's first season started against the same opponents he had the last two years at Ole Miss, Illinois, in a strange twist of scheduling fate. To avoid the Midwest's cooler conditions, the Illini program scheduled a tour of the South that included stops at Alabama, LSU, Mississippi A&M, Ole Miss, and others.

A couple of competitive games occurred between A&M and Illinois, but Noble's Aggies came up on the short end of both with scores of 5-3 and 3-2.

The Aggies bounced back to even their record with a doubleheader sweep of Mississippi College on Saturday, April 10th.

Roy Lyons shifted out to leftfield after some defensive struggles the week before at first base. Lyons' positional replacement at first, B. D. Holmes, ripped three singles in a 6-3 win in game one of the twin billing with Mississippi College. Critz scored a big blow for the Aggies when he belted a triple to put the game away.

Game two was all about Mitchell. He went the distance and helped his effort with a pair of hits. In the eighth, Mitchell scored the game's lone run in a 1-0 pitcher's duel.

A week later, in a doubleheader with Howard, now known as Samford, the quality pitching continued, but the opening series' infield errors reared their ugly head once more.

William Davis Ratliff, "Stewball Lefty," Stovall pitched a masterful game, but a half dozen errors prevented a shutout. Despite the defensive miscues, the Aggies hung on to win 3-2.

In game two, Mitchell was again on his game and took a 1-0 lead into the ninth. Due to an error in the final frame, Howard forced a tenth inning. The Aggies wound up on the downside of a 2-1 decision thanks to two unearned runs.

Alabama drove west to Starkville for two games on April 23rd and 24th. The Crimsons had won at least a share of the SIAA title in the previous three seasons.

Noble and the Aggies had posted a 3-3 record in their first six outings, but A&M hadn't played any team with the talent of Alabama.

Mitchell was the winning pitcher, scattering six hits over nine innings in the 4-1 opening victory. The offensive hero of the day was Aggie catcher Cotton Klindworth, who hit his second home run of the season to aid in the day's scoring output.

Game two nearly went the Aggies' way as well. The *Starkville News* noted that Claude "Heck" Russell pitched well enough to win, but errors led to a come-from-behind victory for Alabama, 3-2.

A&M earned a split and could play with anyone in the South on any given day. The Aggies needed to clean up some defensive play, which could lead to a winning record.

Brimming with confidence after the Alabama series, A&M hit the road to Nashville for their first road games of the year against Vanderbilt.

The Wednesday game saw the Aggies come out swinging. A&M plated three runs in the first inning, which gave Mitchell plenty of margin to work with.

Vandy climbed back into it with a pair of runs in the fourth. The Aggie defense aided in one of those runs, which was par for the course, but it proved to be the only error charged to A&M on the day.

The Commodores committed four errors, and one of those in the seventh opened the door for Critz to come around and score the fourth and final run of the game. The closing score read 4-2 in favor of Noble's Aggies.

A&M had grown accustomed to winning game one, but the real challenge lay in taking game two to complete the sweep. Such was the case when the Aggies and Commodores resumed the series.

Russell was back on the bump and picked up his first support run in the second when the Aggies strung together a few hits to make it 1-0.

Critz and Lyons scored a pair of runs in the fourth to push the lead to 3-0. With two outs in that inning, Russell came through with a clutch RBI single of his own for what proved to be the winning run.

A&M added insurance runs in the fifth when Klindworth connected for a two-run homer that landed beyond the right field wall.

Ahead 6-0, Russell needed to throw strikes and hope his defense could stand tall behind him.

According to the *Nashville Banner*, Vandy scored a pair of runs in the seventh on a bizarre play. A batted ball bounced over third and got lost under the bleachers. The Commodores were awarded a home run. With a man already on base, what should have been a ground-rule double instead became a two-run dinger.

Russell gave up one more run in the eighth inning of the conventional variety and ended the scoring at 6-3. The series had two games to none in favor of A&M.

The Aggies seemed ready to turn the corner, but that optimism proved short-lived. A trip to Birmingham for the two-game rematch with Howard saw the pitching and defense fail. A&M dropped both games by 8-5 and 7-2 scores.

The goodwill with fans built up with the sweep of Vanderbilt was quickly erased.

In the season's final week, A&M was set to play four games against Ole Miss. The Rebels were a fine ball club pushing towards a possible SIAA title. While the Ole Miss record books have several games omitted, it was an exemplary year of baseball in Oxford.

The only thing that stood in the way of the Rebels' first-ever league championship was the farm boys from A&M.

The first pair of games were played in Starkville at Hardy Field. Mitchell drew the start for the Aggies in game one, which was typically bad news for opponents. That theme persisted in this match-up as well.

A&M scored their first run without the benefit of a hit. "Pee Wee" Howell reached base on a throwing error and then went to second on a ground ball out off Mitchell's bat.

Klindworth grounded toward the hole at short, and Howell sprinted for third. The Ole Miss shortstop made the stop and tried to throw Howell out. The attempt proved faulty, which allowed Howell to score as the ball rolled free near the home dugout.

A&M bunched together three of their five hits on the day in the sixth inning. The net result was two more runs to make it 3-0 Aggies.

While the hometown squad was making good use of their hits, Mitchell was dealing. He had to work out of a bases-loaded jam in the third and a two-out threat in the eighth, but the Aggie starter kept a clean sheet.

Mitchell scattered five hits in nine shutout innings that saw him strike out a dozen Rebels.

Game two had a nightmare of a start for Ole Miss. A&M batted around in the first inning and scored three runs to race out to a 3-0 lead. Noble elected to employ a little small ball to put some pressure on the Rebel defense.

After Klindworth opened the home half of the inning by reaching on an error, Noble elected to bunt him to second. Lyons successfully got the sacrifice attempt down. Rather than take the out at first, Ole Miss starter A.B. Carney tried to force Klindworth at second, and the ball rolled into the outfield. Both runners moved up a base on the error.

Suddenly, the Aggies had two men in scoring position. Rather than take their hacks at it, Noble had the following two players, Critz and centerfielder D.G. Clayton, lay down bunts.

The move struck a tense Ole Miss defense by surprise. Both attempts were successful, and a run scored on each. Critz came around to score on a Holmes RBI single. A&M loaded the bases and seemed ready to blow the game wide open, but Carney got out of the inning without further damage.

Those three runs were all Russell would need. The hard-throwing hurler allowed five hits over nine innings and struck out four in the 3-0 shutout.

Even though that second win fell on a Tuesday, a hearty celebration broke out. Not only had the Aggies won a pair from their longtime rivals, but they had also seriously damaged any hopes of Ole Miss winning the league title.

An impromptu parade began in downtown Starkville, and locals and students cheered the players along as they marched down Main Street and onto University Drive, where even more well-wishers awaited. The ensuing celebration lasted long into the night.

While A&M wasn't in contention for a championship, they did their best to play spoilers. Ole Miss struck back in their two home games to keep their slim title hopes alive.

Back in Oxford, the Rebels won a pair of one-run affairs by 4-3 and 5-4 scores. Critz had a solid couple of games, even blasting a home run to give A&M a brief lead in the second inning of game one.

Ole Miss officials tried to claim that they were the rightful SIAA champions. The 1921 Ole Miss yearbook even printed that claim.

When the dust settled, the Rebels were denied the title even though their only two conference losses came to A&M. According to the *Birmingham News*, the rub was that Ole Miss didn't play a single league opponent outside of their home state other than Vanderbilt.

The case for the Rebels was that they posted a 19-game winning streak before losing to A&M.

Several teams had a right to claim a share of the title, but the SIAA awarded a split championship to Alabama, Auburn, and Georgia Tech. Despite having an incredible season, Ole Miss didn't share in the post-season spoils. It may have been a different story if they hadn't lost in Starkville. It was a measure of revenge for Noble.

When the SIAA released its all-league teams, no Ole Miss player was selected. A&M had a handful.

Clayton was the lone Bulldog to receive a first-team selection.

Klindworth and Critz were the second-team catcher and third baseman, respectively. Although just a sophomore, Mitchell earned third-team honors as a pitcher.

Klindworth and Mitchell still had some big things ahead of them in Starkville, but Critz was done in an Aggie uniform.

Despite his speed, glove, and consistent bat, Critz was initially passed on by Major League clubs. As a result, he sought to prove himself in the Cotton States League.

After four years of toiling in relative obscurity, Critz was picked up by the Cincinnati Reds in 1924. Critz finished second in the 1926 National League MVP balloting two seasons later.

Critz played for part of seven seasons with the Reds before he was traded to the Giants, where he finished his career.

In 1933, Critz helped the Giants win the World Series. In game one of that championship series, Critz scored what ended up being the winning run against the Washington Senators on a Mel Ott single.

Long after his playing days were over, fans of the Reds, in a 1962 balloting process, voted Critz the greatest second baseman in franchise history. He was later inducted into the Reds' Baseball Hall of Fame.

Critz was the first big leaguer to play for Dudy Noble at Mississippi A&M. Critz would have plenty of Aggie company in pro ball in the years ahead.

Chapter 9

The Grassroots of a Coaching Legacy

As the SIAA men's basketball tournament was being played in February of 1921, trouble was afoot on the southern sports landscape. Nearly half of the teams in the 30-member association were planning their departure.

At issue was the one-year rule. The larger schools in the SIAA favored all first-year players having to sit out their first years as newcomers. The prohibition even applied to transfers as covered in what was deemed the "migratory" rule.

In addition to the concerns about freshman eligibility and transfer regulations, there was money. Even in the infancy of conference athletics, some schools used monetary inducements to recruit and poach players.

These same concerns that have been discussed for over a century are being discussed now. It's a complicated matter today, and it was even more complex when league leaders met at Atlanta's Piedmont Hotel to discuss the formation of the Southern Conference.

Schools like Howard, Mercer, Millsaps, Mississippi College, Oglethorpe, and others needed those first-year players to field competitive teams. They were adamantly against the rule and worked to derail its implementation at the SIAA annual convention in Gainesville, Florida.

A rift between the league schools began, and plans were made for the supporters of the measure to form their own conference.

Dr. Steadman Vincent Sanford, the director of athletics at the University of Georgia, was chosen to be the first commissioner of the Southern Conference.

One of the tenets of Sanford's platform, in addition to the one-year rule, was more uniform scheduling. Many SIAA schools would play mostly non-conference opponents and just a handful of league games. Sanford wanted a more level playing field.

Another concern among Southern Conference would-be defectors was an SIAA rule that prevented league baseball players from participating in summer leagues that afforded them some modest compensation. The SIAA planned to stand firm on that legislation, while the Southern Conference saw no issue.

After all sides said their peace, 14 schools, including Mississippi A&M, bolted for the new league. Joining the Aggies as charter members were Alabama, Auburn, Clemson, Georgia, Georgia Tech, Kentucky, North Carolina, North Carolina State, Tennessee, Virginia, Virginia Tech, and Washington & Lee.

The vote came down just weeks before the college baseball season began. Contracts had been signed and schedules finalized. Rather than scramble to throw together a last-minute change of plans, the decision was made to play the 1921 baseball season as previously scheduled.

As practice began, Noble reportedly had over 75 players come out to make the team, hoping to earn a varsity letter.

Noble's A&M squad was expected to be good as some talented regulars returned, including catcher Cotton Klindworth. Before the season began, the Aggie players voted him the team captain.

Mitchell and Stewart returned to shore up the pitching duties during the 21-game schedule. A newcomer, Kinard "Fresh" Austin, from Jones County, Mississippi, was also a part-time pitcher and outfielder, though just a freshman.

The Aggie nine was talented and flush with great baseball nicknames. Readers are aware of the exploits of all-conference catcher Klindworth, but the rest of the starting lineup possessed equally appropriate diamond-naming designations.

There was "Judge" Little at third, "Pee Wee" Howell at short, "Rat" Boyd at second, and "Lefty" Rawls at first. The A&M outfield was patrolled by Hearne "Ty" Cobb of Crossett, Arkansas, "Nub" Howard, and "Freshman" Fowler.

Just for fun, the Aggies even had a reserve infielder called J.C. "Collar Button" Halliburton.

Offensively, things were a challenge at times. The Aggies posted a 13-8 record but only outscored their opponents 77-72.

When the final standings were posted following a 6-5 win over Mississippi College, the Aggies earned a share of the league baseball title.

Klindworth was named all-conference for the second straight season. He, Flower, and Little all hit over .300 on the year.

With his first hardware as a college coach under his belt, Noble sought to build on the successes of the first two seasons. In addition to developing the talent on hand, the Aggie mentor needed an influx of young players to create a sustainable program that wasn't just a one-year sensation.

Noble targeted a shortstop from Ellisville, Mississippi, who went by the name of Buddy Myer. Named after his father, Charles Solomon Myer, and born to his mother, Maud, Myer created a buzz down in the "Free State of Jones."

Pro scouts were already aware of him and hoping to get him to opt for pro ball instead of college. Due to his age and the fear of putting a teenager on the road to face the trappings of adulthood, Myer's parents directed him to go to college.

Myer had options but elected to spend his college career playing for Noble. The two shared similar upbringings and were known to be relentless competitors. Myer was noted as well-mannered off the field, but an absolute savage on the field, fueled by a desire to win that was largely unparalleled.

In his first season in Starkville, Myer supplanted starting shortstop Pee Wee Howell, a two-year varsity letter winner. Howell slid over to second to make room for Myer in a talented infield filled with veterans.

A road trip to LSU opened the 1922 season. Not only was Myer in the lineup, but Noble also had the freshman hit clean-up.

The Tigers led 5-4 after seven innings in a game that saw the teams combine for 25 hits. A&M took the lead for good in the top of the eighth when Rawls came through with a two-RBI single to push the Aggies ahead 6-5.

Myer polished off a three-for-four day with the coup de gras in the top of the ninth. With the game still hanging in the balance, Myer launched a three-run home run to deep center field to put the Tigers away 9-5.

A&M came up just short of the sweep in game two. The Aggies held a 3-0 lead but surrendered four runs in the seventh. A&M pulled even in the eighth, but LSU walked it off in the ninth to win 5-4.

After a pair of splits against Spring Hill and Illinois, the Aggies rattled off a streak of six wins and one tie. During that run, A&M played Wisconsin for the first time in program history.

Another program first came when the Aggies faced off against Texas in a two-game series at Hardy Field in Starkville. The two squads split the two games, but the series said something about Noble's group. The Longhorns had won the Southwest Conference seven straight seasons entering the match-up. A win against Texas was undoubtedly something to crow about even back then.

Another pair of failed sweep attempts followed against Oglethorpe and Alabama before the Aggies and Rebels got together for the four rivalry games.

A&M took game one in Starkville against Ole Miss with a score of 4-0. Monroe Mitchell was masterful, allowing just three hits and recording nine strikeouts. Not a single Rebel made it to second base in the contest.

The second game of the series also went the way of the Aggies, with Austin throwing a no-hit shutout of the Rebels in a 2-0 game.

Myer went 2-for-4 on the day with a double. He also played a nearly flawless game defensively, participating in eight putouts.

Game three saw Mitchell labor a bit, but he managed to post seven zeroes on the scoreboard as the Aggies took a 5-0 lead into the bottom of the eighth.

The Rebels touched Mitchell for three runs in their next-to-last bat, but Ole Miss could get no closer. A&M hung on to win 5-3.

The fourth and final meeting of the season between the two rivals took place on Saturday, May 21st. Runs were hard to come by, and it took two extra innings to settle the squabble.

A&M drew first blood in the fifth inning when Klindworth reached base on an error. Despite his heft, Klindworth was a fine base runner and was a threat to steal. He nabbed second base to get himself into scoring position.

Tip Parker came through with an RBI double to give the visitors a 1-0 lead.

A pair of miscues by Myer led to a tie game in the eighth, but the deadlock was short-lived. Lefty Rawls hit a solo blast in the top of the ninth for what looked like the game's final salvo.

It appeared that Austin would once again stymy the Rebels with a no-hitter, but a solo shot with two down in the ninth brought the game even at 2-2.

Not to be outdone with heroic feats, Rawls led off the 11th with a solo home run of his own to give the Aggies the lead for good at 3-2. With that one-run victory, A&M completed the four-game sweep and set themselves up for a chance to win the league for the second straight year, if they could win against Alabama.

Game one of the final twosomes saw Mitchell throw a one-hit shutout of the Crimson. For six innings, Alabama ace Robert Hinton matched Mitchell.

A&M scored all they needed in the seventh when Klindworth cleared the bases with a triple that drove in Rawls, Mitchell, and Howell. Klindworth came around to score on a mishandled grounder from "Izzy" Turner. The net result was a 4-0 lead that Mitchell maintained through the game's final outs.

The title chase went down to the final day of the regular season. It proved to be a winner-take-all event.

It looked like Alabama would rain on the Aggie parade early on.

Alabama scored in the top of the first on a triple and an RBI sacrifice fly.

A&M pulled even in the bottom of the inning when Myer came around to score on a solid single from Parker to make it 1-1. Pitching took over from there until the seventh.

Alabama retook the lead under circumstances similar to those in the opening frame. A triple was followed by an RBI single to break the tie at 2-1 in favor of the visitors.

Just as they had in the first, A&M answered right back. A big inning appeared to be in store as the Aggies loaded the bases but could only manage a single run on a sacrifice fly off the bat of Fowler.

Through 11 innings, Alabama starter Lee McMillan, a native of Greenwood, Mississippi, allowed seven scattered hits. While the Delta boy was up for the challenge, one must surmise that he was pitching on fumes.

It was the last game of the season. There was no tomorrow. Noble even gave the ball back to Mitchell in relief of Austin midway through the contest. Both teams were throwing everything they had in hopes of winning a championship.

The game remained deadlocked into the 12th. Mitchell kept Alabama off the scoreboard in the top of the inning. A&M hoped to walk it off in the bottom half.

Both teams struggled to string anything together in the latter innings, but Lefty Rawls found a McMillan offering to his liking and laced a triple into centerfield. The Aggie fans roared in anticipation of the winning run touching the Hardy Field home plate. They would have to wait, at least for a bit.

Mitchell followed with what amounted to a swinging bunt back to McMillan. Rawls retreated to third, and Mitchell beat it out at first. Now the Aggies had runners on the corners and Myer stepping into the batter's box.

Buddy Myer had been a catalyst all season. With the season and title on the line, McMillan opted to make another Aggie beat him and walked Myer.

With the sacks full and the air ripe with emotion, McMillan stepped on the rubber in the jam of all jams. The fans felt it as Judge Little dug in for the biggest at-bat of his life.

As McMillan wound up and fired that dusty pearl homeward, Rawls broke from third. The crowd roared with anticipation as Little squared to bunt. Yes, bunt.

The ball met the bat and found safe haven in the sacred green grass of Starkville just as Rawls slid across the plate. The Aggies had done it. They walked off Alabama for a conference title on a squeeze play.

Mississippi A&M ended the season with a 16-6-3 record, winning six straight. In the two games at Tuscaloosa, the Aggies scored just four runs, losing one game and tying another. Redemption was sweet in Starkville as the fans rushed the field to celebrate a second consecutive championship.

A&M's favorite son had returned to campus and again made Aggie baseball a Southern power. It took Noble's mentor, Billy Chadwick, nine seasons to win two conference titles. Noble did it in just three.

Various media scribes around the South released their All-Southern baseball teams, and nearly all selected Klindworth as their catcher.

Mitchell also received some post-season accolades after his best season as a college player, which saw him strike out close to 100 hitters.

A season later, Mitchell was in the big leagues as a member of the Washington Senators. "Mitch" worked as a reliever on the same pitching staff that claimed Major League Baseball Hall of Famer Walter "Big Train" Johnson as its ace.

Although he never reached the Big Show, Klindworth also made it into pro ball. The former Aggie captain began his minor league career with San Antonio of the West Texas League before bouncing around the Cotton States, South Atlantic, and Tri-States leagues.

In five minor league seasons, Klindworth had 337 hits, 50 of those were doubles. He hit seven home runs and legged out 11 triples. Following the 1927 season with the Meridian Mets, Klindworth hung up his spikes.

Klindworth later said at a campus ceremony honoring Noble, "His achievements and his success rests not in his great record but in his ability to teach boys and men."

Perhaps emboldened by his success on the baseball diamond, Noble elected to try his hand at coaching football again. When the Aggies hit the field in the fall of 1922, Dudy Noble led the charge.

They started well enough, with A&M defeating the Panthers of Birmingham Southern 14-0.

George McGowan connected with Bill Clark on a 20-yard touchdown strike to open the scoring. McGowan handled the extra point.

The tension of the contest subsided in the fourth quarter when Curtis Cameron of Meridian plunged in for the second touchdown of the day. The point after was good, and the Aggies were 1-0.

Game two ended in a scoreless tie with Howard. According to the *Vicksburg Herald*, McGowan broke a finger in the first quarter and missed the rest of the ball game. The final whistle sounded with the Aggies at the Howard five-yard line.

Week three saw the Aggies travel to the Jackson fairgrounds to battle Ole Miss in the annual rivalry game. During his time as the Rebel head football coach, Noble was 0-3 against his alma mater. This situation was very different, as Noble was on the winning sideline.

A 19-point second quarter proved to be the difference in the ball game, even though it went down to the wire.

Aggie fullback Gene Barnett scored three touchdowns. Media accounts of the game reveal that Barnett played with two injured shoulders and had sponges underneath his shoulder pads to protect his frame from further injury.

Ole Miss rallied in the fourth and pulled to within six at 19-13. The Aggie defense stood tall and turned the Rebels away on their final offensive possession. A&M got the ball back and salted away nearly all the remaining time. The final play was a punt back to Ole Miss with no time left.

The win was the 10th straight for the Aggies in the series with Ole Miss. On a strange note, Dudy Noble coached four rivalry games between the schools, and A&M won all four.

A week later, the Aggies played their first true road game of the season when they traveled to New Orleans to take on Tulane. It appears the A&M offense never got off the train, as Tulane won 26-0.

The offensive woes continued the next week as A&M had to battle from behind to force a 7-7 tie with Ouachita Baptist. Late in the game, the Aggies forced a fumble 30 yards from paydirt. McGowan engineered a scoring drive that ended with Clark sprinting in from four yards out for the score. McGowan converted the extra point to bring the game to a draw.

A&M and Tennessee met in Memphis on November 11th for their Southern Conference game. McGowan led the Aggies down the field and came away with a field goal to give A&M a 3-0 lead.

That three-point kick was the lone Aggie score on the day as Tennessee cut through the A&M defense like a knife through butter in a 31-3 blowout.

Noble won his final game as a head football coach the following week at LSU. In a game filled with turnovers, the Aggies emerged victorious, 7-0.

In the fourth quarter, A&M broke the scoreless tie on a drive that decided the ball game. McGowan completed a long pass, putting the Aggies in business deep in Tiger territory. Barnett ran off tackle to get into the endzone to secure the road win.

A&M returned home to face an undefeated Drake team that had allowed 20 points on the season. A&M did little to hurt Drake's season defensive scoring statistics in a 48-6 loss at Scott Field.

The Bulldogs from Des Moines, Iowa, returned home with an unblemished final record, while A&M had one more game to play.

Many around Starkville would have been fine had the season ended against Drake, but it didn't.

Alabama was playing well and playing with purpose. Crimson head coach Xen Scott had been diagnosed with cancer before the season. Scott pushed on and coached the team from start to finish.

In his final game as a college football coach, Alabama defeated Mississippi A&M 59-0. Scott resigned at season's end to address his health concerns. He died in 1924 at just 41.

While Noble lived on, the blowout at the hands of Alabama was the last game he coached as a varsity football headman.

Noble made three stops as a football coach: Mississippi College, Ole Miss, and Mississippi A&M. In four seasons, he turned in a record of 11-14-3. While a football star player, his accomplishments as a football head coach were less than stellar.

Chapter 10

Building a Baseball Brand

With varsity football coaching officially behind him, Noble focused on taking Aggie baseball to a new level. With back-to-back conference titles under his belt, Noble had turned A&M into a regular contender for some big things in a short time.

Looking to defend their position in Southern League baseball, the Aggies returned to work. The good news for all who cheered for the program was that several regulars returned for the 1923 season.

The centerpiece of it all was star shortstop Buddy Myer. The Ellisville, Mississippi native was a dependable bat and a shutdown infielder.

Myer wasn't alone on the Aggie infield. Lefty Rawls returned at first base and was voted as the team's captain.

Nub Howell made the move from reserve outfielder to the everyday second baseman.

Sophomore Robert "Bump" Peel of Waynesboro, Mississippi, won the starting job at third, and Cecil Brunson, last year's backup catcher, earned the right to replace Cotton Klindworth behind the plate.

The 1923 season began with a pair of losses at home against Illinois. While the current Bulldogs hadn't faced off against the Illini in over 20 years, the two programs were one-time regular opponents.

In 1913, A&M and Illinois met on the diamond for the first time. Once Noble was hired in 1920, he scheduled annual meetings with the visitors from Champaign through the 1931 season.

As April opened, so did A&M's Southern League schedule. The year's second series saw A&M and LSU meet in Brookhaven and McComb on back-to-back days.

The Aggies took both games by a combined score of 11-2. LSU managed a run in each game.

The good fortune continued when A&M returned to campus and

took down Millsaps by 6-2.

Noble's Aggies pushed their winning streak to five games after a two-game sweep of Wisconsin.

Tennessee bested A&M 3-0 in a pitcher's duel, which was decided by errors. Volunteer ace Ben Cantwell scattered four Aggie hits in the shutout. Three defensive miscues plagued Aggie starter Kinard Austin.

Bump Peel committed a pair of errors, and Izzy Turner misjudged a fly ball that fell for a base hit, leading to another run.

A&M got their revenge a day later, with an 8-4 victory.

The match-up series with Georgia was one of great interest. In 1922, both teams had a claim to the Southern League title. A&M was awarded the outright championship. Noble even offered to play a series against the Athenian Dawgs, but the two sides couldn't agree.

Travel issues delayed Georgia's crack at the Aggies by a day, forcing a doubleheader. Hundreds of spectators waited alongside the A&M coaches and players for UGA's nine to arrive, but they couldn't reach Starkville until dusk.

Ticket holders went home unsatisfied as the opening game was postponed. Bragging rights would have to wait another 24 hours. Among those waiting in vain was Georgia shortstop DeLacy Allen, a Mississippi native.

Allen had been home visiting family and planned to join the team when they arrived in Starkville. Like the other interested observers, he spent much of his time getting hot in the Mississippi sun for no reason.

In game one of the twin-billing, Georgia Bulldog coach Bill White elected to start Cliff Pantone for the first time on the season. The last two seasons, Pantone had been one of the Bulldogs' best hurlers. Arm trouble had kept him off the mound through the first half of the 1923 season.

Pantone pitched seven scoreless innings before A&M finally got to him. Before the Aggies chased Pantone, Georgia had built a 5-0 lead. A home run by Pantone was a part of the offensive effort.

A&M sent Pantone to the showers with two down, three runs

home, and the bases loaded in the home half of the eighth.

White called on Bill Munday to put out the fire, and he did for a while, fanning the final hitter of the eighth.

In the ninth, Munday committed the cardinal sin of late-inning relievers. He walked the leadoff man, and the baseball gods were watching. Peel followed with a single that led to an RBI and a two-base error.

Georgia clung to a 5-4 lead, while the Aggies had the tying run at third with no outs. White turned to Andy Chambers in favor of the fading Munday.

Chambers entered the game and struck out Brunson, Howell, and Stringer to end the game.

The day's second game was an outstanding pitching duel, with A&M starter Austin outpitching Georgia's George Clark, in a 2-1 affair.

Austin allowed two hits in the game, with the only run charged against him coming in the first. A&M tied the game in the third and scored what would end up being the winning run in the fourth when Clark walked a man with the bases loaded to force home Myer.

Ultimately, the two teams, considered the best from the previous season, split their series. No club could claim superiority over the other.

On a side note, the *M-Club Book of Athletics* records that the two games took place on April 18th and 19th, but they were both played on the 19th as a doubleheader. The second game was called in the bottom of the eighth due to darkness.

A week later, A&M played the Florida Gators for the first time. The Aggies crushed Coach Lance Richbourg's team 10-0 and 9-0.

Now 9-4 on the season, Noble's squad prepared for their first two games in the rivalry series with Ole Miss.

Under the direction of first-year head coach Pete Shields, the Rebels were having a fine season. The Ole Miss record books report that they turned in an 18-3-1 season. Included in those 18 claimed wins are three games that Ole Miss actually lost to Dudy Noble and Mississippi A&M. The Rebel baseball media guide shares that Ole Miss swept all four games, but the newspaper accounts of the day provide evidence that isn't the case.

Game one was played on April 30th in Oxford. In front of what the Memphis *Commercial Appeal* reported as "the largest crowd to witness a game at Ole Miss in several seasons," A&M scored two in the first, four in the seventh, and two in the ninth to defeat Ole Miss 8-1.

The second game of the two meetings at Ole Miss also went the Aggies' way, with a score of 9-5.

Headed into the late innings, the Rebels led 4-1, but some shoddy defense led to a reversal of fortune and eight runs for the Aggies.

The two wins in Oxford improved A&M's record to 11-4.

The Aggies split a series at home against Alabama and were then swept by Vanderbilt. A road series in Tuscaloosa also ended with a 1-1 result, which brought the A&M season mark to 13-8.

Two more dates with Ole Miss remained on the slate, and both were played in Starkville.

There was little offense in either game. The Rebels won game one by the score of 3-0 and A&M won the final contest 3-1. The net result was a 14-9 overall record for the Aggies, who posted a 3-1 win/loss mark against Ole Miss.

The year ended without a Southern Conference title for the first time in three years for either team.

The season also changed the life of Buddy Myer. Pro baseball scouts flocked to baseball diamonds around the south to see Myer play. Some tried to woo him away from Starkville and get him to sign a pro contract.

The Washington Senators came to what amounts to a handshake agreement with Myer to sign him once his time at A&M ended. His mother, Minnie, valued education and wanted Myer to earn his degree before chasing his Major League dreams.

While not officially signed to a pro contract, Myer returned for one final season on Dudy Noble's team, and what a season it proved to be.

Kinard Austin returned as the team's pitching ace. Most of the infield was back for another season. The most significant loss was that of first baseman Lefty Rawls. Veteran reserve Fred "Spark Plug" Corley filled that vacancy created by Rawls' graduation.

Nub Howell was voted the team captain and helped lead a lineup of six returning batsmen.

The experience at the plate showed in game one as A&M trounced LSU in Baton Rouge 14-5. Noble's troops pounded out 21 hits on the day, including a round-tripper off the bat of Myer.

A statement was made, but that robust total proved to be the high mark for the Aggie offense of the year.

A&M's trek through south Louisiana included a stopover at Tulane for two games that the two teams split.

The home opening portion of the slate featured a series with Tennessee. The first match-up brought long-standing Volunteer ace Cantwell back to the mound. A&M managed six hits off of him, including another home run from Myer in an 8-0 victory.

Myer was also an offensive star in the second game with an RBI triple and a pair of runs scored in a 6-4 decision.

A&M dropped a nail-biter to Wisconsin in the next game 4-3. Once again, Myer led the offensive charge for the Aggies with three of the team's eight hits.

It had been a wet trip south for the Badgers, who had two games rained out against Alabama and one against A&M. Travel concerns prevented a doubleheader against the Aggies as Wisconsin had to board a train bound for the Windy City to open Big-10 play against the Chicago Maroons.

Noble's Aggies also drew a Big-10 opponent, Illinois, in their next pairing. The Illini roster featured Howard Edward "Red" Grange of football fame, who patrolled center field. Grange posted an 0-for-2 day in the 6-3 Aggie win. A&M starter Johnny Johnson was wild, striking out 15 and walking 10.

Grange is one of the most decorated American athletes in college sports history. In 1923, the man called the "Galloping Ghost" led Illinois to a football national title. He earned three All-American honors as the greatest football player of his era. In the fall of 1924, Grange was named the first-ever unanimous All-American football selection.

In the series' first game with Mississippi A&M, Myer drew headlines, and Grange served as a footnote. With two singles in the contest, Myer upped his season average to .480.

Grange sat out his second game day in Starkville as Illinois rallied to win 7-3. The Illini plated four runs in the 10th inning to gain the final separation required to walk away the winners. Now 5-3 on the campaign, A&M welcomed the defending Big-10 champion, Michigan Wolverines, to town for the first meeting between the two schools in any sport.

The Aggies prevailed in game one 11-4 and recorded one of the first triple plays in school history with a 4-3-6 official scoring listed in the box score.

A&M benefited from 14 walks in the game and a hit batter. Lefty Bolton went the distance for the home team, striking out a dozen.

Michigan got their revenge the following day by throwing strikes and playing clean defense behind starter Homer Stryker, 3-1.

Stryker, a WWI veteran, was a medical school student, older than many of his college baseball peers. Once his time at Michigan was over, he created several medical devices that revolutionized orthopedic care.

If someone has a broken foot or leg, a rubber heel designed by Stryker has probably aided their mobility. When that broken bone healed, a Stryker oscillating saw likely cut away the cast that protected it.

With 10 games under their belt, A&M hosted Vanderbilt on campus for a league series.

In the last few games, Myer had been slumping. Rather than dropping him in the order, Noble moved him to leadoff. It was a curious move, but one that paid off.

In the opening game against the Commodores, Myer led the way with a 4-for-5 day as the Aggies rolled 10-2. The A&M shortstop was just a home run away from the cycle.

Austin struck out 10 Vandy hitters on the day, allowing just four hits and single runs in the fourth and sixth innings.

The Aggies had split their two previous series but earned a sweep against Vanderbilt. Myer started heating up and proved to be a rally starter once again, hitting at the top of the order. The 6-2 win featured a pair of triples from Myer, including one to open the gate to a two-run first inning.

At the midway point in the season, A&M was 8-4 and in the thick of things for the title chase. Three of their losses came from nonconference opponents from the Big 10.

The Mississippi A&M Aggies and the Alabama Crimsons had been among the best southern collegiate teams in the years leading up to the 1924 season. With both teams playing well, the expectation was that the winner of the rain-shortened series would take complete control of the Southern League standings.

Alabama scored a pair of runs in the first and another in the third inning to take a 3-0 lead into the fifth. The Aggies managed to load the bases and pose its first real offensive threat on the day. Izzy Turner came through with a hit that scored Austin, but Myer was gunned down at the plate to preserve the Alabama lead at 3-1.

The teams traded runs in the seventh, and Alabama scored an unanswered run in the eighth, bringing the score to 5-2 in favor of the Crimsons.

Not willing to go down without a fight, Myer tripled in the ninth and scored on Clay Hopper's single. A&M had the tying run at the plate and could draw no closer.

The loss was a tough one for the Aggies to take. They had plenty of time to stew over it as game two, set for 4 PM the next day, was rained out. A&M's hopes for revenge would have to wait.

The final two games of the series took place in Tuscaloosa. To deny the Crimsons the chance to pave their path toward a conference title, the Aggies would have to do something they had never done before: win two at Alabama.

Alabama took a 1-0 lead in the second, but that advantage was short-lived. Peel and Johnson singled to open the third inning. A sac bunt moved both up into scoring position. Dutch Amsler tripled to send both home and give the Aggies a 2-1 lead.

In the fourth, Brunson added to the A&M tally with a solo home run that the *Birmingham News* reported was the first home run to clear the fence at Alabama in two seasons.

A patented Dudy Noble squeeze play plated Turner in the sixth to push the visitors ahead 4-1. Alabama wouldn't go quietly. The "Capstone Kids" rallied for four in the home of the sixth to retake the lead.

As all great games go, this one was back and forth until the end. A&M tied it in the seventh and took a 6-5 lead on a passed ball in the ninth. Alabama battled back to force extra innings with a run in the ninth.

A&M finally took the lead for good in the top of the 10th when Bump Peel tripled in a pair of runs. Alabama got the tying runs on base in the bottom of the frame, but Johnson pitched through it and left them stranded for an 8-6 victory.

The season's final meeting between the Aggies and Alabama got off to an odd start. Myer laced a base hit back toward the middle to open the game. According to the *Birmingham News*, both Alabama middle infielders were knocked out after colliding with each other trying to field the baseball and record an out.

Officials stopped the game so that both players could get medical attention. After several minutes, the tandem was revived, and both elected to stay in the game despite being a little woozy. They were ball players.

Myer came around to score the first of four runs that the Aggies strung together during the first four innings. Lefty Bolton held Alabama down while the offense was putting runs up on the board.

Alabama finally touched home in the sixth, but that was all the talented southpaw allowed. A&M scored a single run in the seventh and ninth to put the game away, 6-1.

They had done it. The Aggies had gone to Alabama, taken both games, and put themselves in a commanding position to win the league.

A&M rolled through games with Auburn and Mississippi College by a combined score of 14-1 to earn three more wins.

The winning streak reached seven games after the Aggies took both games in Starkville against the Ole Miss Rebels.

In the first of four games, the Oxford-based program took a 2-0 lead in the later innings. In the eighth, Nub Howell tripled and scored on a ground ball out to the right side by Hopper to make it 2-1.

A&M tied the game in the ninth after a Turner triple. A passed ball allowed him to score, much to the delight of a standing-room-only crowd.

The Aggies nearly plated the winning run in the 10th following a Myer triple, but he was stranded on base.

Another strange occurrence happened in the bottom of the 11th on a double from Dutch Amsler. Corley was hit by the pitch to put two men on with no outs.

Brunson pulled a ground ball through the right side, but it hit Corley on its way to the outfield. As a result, Corley was correctly ruled out. Brunson took Corley's spot at first.

It wouldn't be Magnolia State baseball without something weird happening in a huge game.

The game went final and into the record books as Peel walked it off with an RBI single through the hole at short to make it 3-2.

In the final home game of the season, A&M jumped on Ole Miss early and never looked back.

Myer led off the game with a single and came around to score the first run. Another was added before the first inning was over to make it 2-0.

In the sixth, Myer hit what is believed to be the first grand slam in school history to push the Aggies ahead 6-0. When the day was done,

Myer was 3-for-5 with two runs scored and four RBIs.

The Rebels scored a pair in the fifth and seventh innings, but Austin made the lead stand up with a 6-4 final. The Aggies were inching closer and closer to another league title under Noble.

Game three saw the two teams meet in Oxford. A tremendous pitching duel ensued, with Ole Miss winning 2-1. A&M was held to just two hits. One was an RBI single from Peel in the seventh to open the Aggie scoring, but A&M couldn't string anything else together. "Dit" Briggs did the honors for Ole Miss pitching a gem.

Rebel coach Pete Shields called on Briggs again the next day to see if he could baffle the Aggie hitters for a second day. The decision proved to have disastrous consequences.

Myer led off the game with a double, which got the offense rolling. A&M put together four hits in the first inning, chasing home three runs to take a 3-0 lead.

Incredibly, Briggs went the distance for the second straight day, but the outcome was much different.

The Aggies scored three more runs to make it 6-0 in the eighth. Ole Miss scored a pair in the home half of that inning but went quietly in the ninth to lose 6-2.

With the win, A&M completed their conference schedule atop the Southern Conference league standings with room to spare. The Aggies were 12-3 against league opponents.

The only thing left to play for was a mythical state championship against Mississippi College. A&M won that, too, by splitting those final two games with the Choctaws.

In just four seasons as the Aggie head baseball coach, Dudy Noble had won three conference titles in four seasons. He built his beloved alma mater's program into the undisputed Diamond Kings of southern baseball.

Noble had grand plans for the next season but would have to navigate through it without his star shortstop, Buddy Myer.

True to his word, Myer worked to honor the promise he made to his mother to earn his college degree before beginning a pro career. Myer sat out the remainder of his time at A&M to work on his studies. He graduated in 1925 and started his time in pro baseball.

Myer put together a 17-year pro career, mainly with the Washington Senators. Two of those seasons earlier in his career were spent with the Boston Red Sox and the rest with Washington.

In 1927, the Senators traded Myer away straight up for Topper Rigney. Later in life, Myer said that he believed the rationale behind the trade involved a dispute with Tris Speaker—one of the greatest players of all time.

Two seasons later, Washington wanted Myer back. Boston made them give up five players to get him.

Back where he belonged, Myer was the American League stolen base leader in 1928. He won the AL batting title and was named a Major League All-Star for the first of two times in 1935.

Myer retired from pro ball in 1941. While he was never named to the MLB Hall of Fame, he is the first Mississippi A&M baseball alum ever to receive a vote for induction.

Chapter 11

Going From Hunter to Hunted

Now known as the top southern baseball program in the college ranks, Mississippi A&M began to draw interest from programs outside the regular playing footprint for games.

Yes, the Aggies had played some Big-10 programs that traveled south for early games to avoid the cold weather conditions of the Midwest, but Noble was ready to take the A&M baseball show on the road.

Playing other top teams from different conferences gave the Aggies a chance at credibility far beyond the opinions of southern sports scribes. Yes, Noble's clubs had proven to be good locally, but some wondered how good they were nationally.

Noble aimed to find out.

The 26-game 1925 schedule was the most ambitious in school history. Gone were the days of playing Birmingham Southern, Howard, Millsaps, and Oglethorpe. The A&M program was growing, and Noble sought out more robust competition.

When Noble was a player, the teams rarely left the state of Mississippi. When they did play across state lines, the travel involved taking on programs from border states.

College baseball grew as a sport, and A&M grew along with it. Noble took the Aggie baseball program to the state of Texas for the first time in 1925. To make it worth their financial investment, A&M was set to play six games against three Texas college programs in under a week.

The season-opening series had the Aggies playing in Waco, Texas, on Baylor's campus, which had won the Southwest Conference (SWC) title in 1923.

Baylor winning the league was a rarity in those days as the Longhorns of Texas ruled the SWC.

In 1924, led by legendary coach Billy Disch, the Longhorns won the conference championship for the 11th time in 12 seasons. Texas went 29-1 that year, and their only loss came to Baylor.

The final stop on the Aggie Baseball train tour would be to Dallas to take on Southern Methodist University (SMU). The Mustangs were coming off a disappointing 1924 season under Coach Ewing Freeland.

Freeland played both baseball and football at Vanderbilt before going into coaching. In 1921, Freeland coached his only football season at Millsaps. He was affectionately known as "Big Un" because he weighed just over 200 pounds.

While Noble scheduled aggressively that season, he had confidence in his club. He had reason to be optimistic with some experienced bats returning.

The outfield returned with Dutch Amsler in left, Clay Hopper in center, and Izzy Turner in right.

Brunson and Corley returned in the infield, but some spots had to be filled. Bump Peel, Buddy Myer, and Nub Howell were gone.

After pre-season training and scrimmaging ended, Noble named Carter "Red" Bates as the man at the hot corner. "Speck" Loewer succeeded Myer at short and H. Hartzog at second. The three varsity newcomers were all-stars on the freshman team the previous season. The squad's biggest chore was finding someone other than "Lefty" Bolton to pitch. Bolton was one of the top pitchers in the South and carried the glory of a pair of nicknames. "Mutt" was his usual name around the clubhouse, but his proficiency as a left-handed pitcher made Lefty a fitting moniker.

Noble loaded up a 15-man travel roster and boarded the steam engine locomotive for their westward journey on Saturday, March 21st. The Aggies caught the train to Memphis, where they made a connection to Dallas. The final leg of the trip took them to Waco to play ball.

Within that travel party was Pickens "Pick" Noble, the younger brother of Coach Dudy Noble. According to The *Waco Times-Herald*, Pick was a potential starter. Hopper had missed the last two weeks of pre-season practice due to illness. Perhaps Noble was playing possum because Hopper did indeed make the trip.

In game one, with two outs in the opening inning, Corley cracked a deep drive to center and managed to sprint around the bases for an inside-the-park home run to give A&M a 1-0 lead. Baylor managed to tie it in their turn at bat on an error by Loewer.

The game remained nip and tuck through the middle innings. A&M plated three runs in the fifth, but Baylor answered right back with two of their own to keep the game tight at 5-4.

Baylor starter Lefty Stallings gave way to reliever Jake Freeze in the fifth, which proved to be the turning point in the game. Stallings only gave up a pair of hits, including the home run to Corley, in his four innings on the mound. Freeze walked four and gave up one hit in his first inning.

Freeze remained in the game, and the Aggies feasted. The big blow came in the seventh when Tuner hit a three-run bomb to center to push the lead out 7-3. An error-filled eighth by the Baylor defense allowed A&M to put the game away with three additional runs.

The Bears rallied for one in the eighth, but the game went final 10-4 in favor of Noble's Aggies.

Bolton went the distance for A&M, striking out a dozen, walking five, and scattering eight hits.

In the first inning of game two, the Aggie bats picked up where they left off, and the Baylor defense did, too. After the Bears booted an inning-ending double play ball, A&M loaded the bases on a Turner single. Corley cleared the deck with a triple that sent three runs home. Corley touched home shortly after on an RBI single from Loewer.

It was 4-0 Aggies before anyone even got hot.

Baylor gave their fans something to cheer about by scoring three in their half of the opening inning.

The score remained 4-3 until the fifth when A&M picked up an insurance run on a passed ball.

In the sixth, Baylor pulled within a run at 5-4, but a two-out error led to the tying run. A slow dribbler was pushed out toward second. Hartzog flipped it to first base in time, but Corley dropped it.

The runner from second never stopped hustling on the play and rounded third, looking to score in the moment's confusion. Corley recovered with time to throw him out, but the throw sailed off target, and the run scored, evening the game at 5-5.

In the seventh, a pair of walks provided some trepidation for the Aggies, but two quick outs followed. Just when it seemed A&M might wiggle off the hook, a clutch hit up the middle gave Baylor a 6-5 lead that they never relinquished.

With the split, the Aggies showered and prepared for the next leg of the journey to Austin, Texas, to take on one of America's best programs in their backyard.

The pitching match-up in game one of the two-game series with the Longhorns featured lefthander John Lewis "Jack" Crigler of A&M and right-hander Ben David Allen of Texas.

The *Austin American-Statesman* reported that "the game was viewed by an overflow crowd that threatened to invade the diamond."

Texas raced out to an early 3-0 lead, which delighted that large contingent of local baseball fans. The Aggie bats got cracking when it seemed like they were done.

A&M outscored the Longhorns 8 to 1 in the remaining frames thanks to four home runs. Corley sent two round-trippers out of the yard to atone for his errant play the day before. Amsler and Loewer also connected on big flies to lead the hit barrage.

In the ninth, Crigler managed to get two outs but left the game with the bases loaded and the tying run at the plate. Noble called on Bolton to close the game. Once on the bump, ole Lefty struck out the final hitter on three pitches to earn the save in the 8-4 win.

Looking to earn the Austin sweep, Noble sent Bolton back out for the start in game two. A&M trailed 2-1 after four but broke through in the fifth.

Turner cleared the bases with a three-run double. Later in the inning, Corley hit another towering shot to left for three more runs.

Up 7-2 and with Bolton on the hill, one would expect the Aggies to cruise to an easy victory. That expectation would prove faulty.

Bolton was touched for six runs in the home half of the fifth as the Longhorns retook the lead at 8-7. Rather than pull him, Noble elected to stick with his ace despite the tough inning.

A&M pushed five more runs across before the game went final, including one on yet another Corley home run to win 12-8. Bolton calmed down after his trouble in the fifth and didn't allow another run the rest of the game.

While both wins in Austin were team efforts, Bolton and Corley proved to be the headliners. Bolton was deemed "certainly of Major League caliber" by the *Austin American*. During the series finale, Corley accounted for six of the dozen runs driven in, going 3-for-5 with two dingers, a triple, and three runs scored.

One suspects that those connected with Texas baseball may have escorted Corley to the train station to ensure he left town before doing any further damage.

The final two games proved to be a fitting end to an exciting trip for the A&M Aggies. The highlights from the two-game series with Southern Methodist University (SMU) read Maroon.

For those two meetings in Dallas, Noble's club won by a combined score of 11-5.

The first game saw A&M get out to a 2-0 lead in the first, but the Aggies found themselves trailing 4-2 after three innings.

Thanks to three hits from Brunson and Hartzog, the offense rallied to outscore SMU 4-0 over the balance of the game to secure a 6-4 victory.

Game two featured a pitching gem. This time, Crigler was on the bump. He struck out four and allowed just one run on three hits in the 5-1 win. Two of those hits and the lone run came in the eighth inning.

"Greaser" Stuart was the hitting star that day, collecting three of the Aggies' 12 hits and touching home three times out of the two-hole in the order.

One never knows when it's their last time, but that final game against the Mustangs on March 18, 1925, was the last time Mississippi A&M ever played SMU on the baseball diamond.

Following the 1980 college baseball season, the SMU administration decided to drop their baseball program.

On another side note, the *M Book of Athletics* confuses the order of the two games played at SMU and records an incorrect score of 6-0 in game one.

Newspaper accounts of those two games confirm that they were played on March 17th and 18th, respectively, with A&M winning 6-4 and 5-1.

The Aggies had proven themselves as they boarded the train from Dallas back to Starkville with a 5-1 record. A&M baseball wasn't just good for around here. Coach Dudy Noble's squad was a good baseball outfit, no matter the competition or playing locale.

Noble had taken a risk, but like most great competitors, he wanted to play the best competition possible. The trip to the state of Texas legitimized the claim of A&M being the best outfit in southern baseball and prepared the team for another title defense.

Before the Aggies got into league play, they had to handle a four-game campus invasion by Illinois and Wisconsin.

Against Illinois, A&M earned a split. Lefty Bolton easily mowed through the Illinois order, scattering six hits and allowing three runs in a complete game.

Bolton got all the run support he needed in a four-run second, but the Aggies kept tacking on in the 11-3 win.

Game two went the way of the visitors. Illinois jumped out to a 7-0 lead, but it was a fight. The Aggies scored in each of the final five innings.

It appeared a comeback win was in the cards when Hopper hit a solo shot in the seventh and then a three-run blast in the eighth to make it a one-run game heading to the ninth.

A&M got the tying run aboard with a leadoff single from Loewer, but the next three hitters went down on strikes to close out an 8-7 win for Illinois.

After two days of rest, the Aggies returned to the field to host Wisconsin. The Badgers had posted modest winning seasons in the last four years, but they played very few games outside of their southern scheduling.

In the first game of the twosome, Crigler looked poised to turn in a complete game shutout. The youngster had his way with Wisconsin for eight innings.

Loewer belted a triple and a home run to pace the offense that charged out to a 7-0 lead headed to the ninth.

Crigler ran out of gas for a bit, and Wisconsin took advantage, sending four men home in the inning. Just when it seemed that Noble would have to pull him, Crigler found just enough juice to close out the 7-4 win.

Game two didn't include any such dramatics. Bolton didn't start the game, but after A&M took a 2-0 lead, Noble pulled out his ace. In the final six innings, Bolton struck out 11 and allowed just two hits. Dutch Amsler led the offense with three hits on the day in four plate appearances.

The Aggies were 8-2 heading into conference play. While every game counted, many considered the nonconference portion of the schedule to be "pre-season." The truth was, league play was all that mattered.

There was no NCAA tournament back then. No one dreamed of going to Omaha. Teams were defined by what they did within their conferences. While what A&M did through the first 10 games of the 1925 slate was historical, the season would be remembered based on the remaining 16 contests.

The home series with Tulane needed to end with two wins, but the two teams split them. There was still plenty of baseball left to be played, but losing that second game to the Greenies was something the team would regret later.

As was the case in recent years, the series between Alabama and Mississippi A&M would likely determine the Southern Conference championship.

Unfortunately for A&M, the Crimsons took three of those four games. The Aggies were in a hole that was about to get deeper.

For the first time in the history of the series, A&M and Ole Miss agreed to play five times. Both teams would retain their regular two home games, but a fifth game was added in Greenwood, Mississippi.

Why Greenwood? The two teams were invited to play to help celebrate the opening of the Yazoo River Bridge on May 8th after the two games in Oxford.

In game one of the match-ups against Ole Miss in Oxford, A&M came out on the short end of a 3-2 pitcher's duel with the Rebels, but the game wasn't without controversy.

In a battle of aces, Bolton and Whittington slugged it out. Bolton gave up several hits on the day but managed to work his way out of trouble, getting 13 strikeouts.

The game started well enough, with A&M scratching across a pair of runs to take a 2-0 lead. Ole Miss tied it up with two of their own in the fifth. The game remained deadlocked until the 10th. The Rebels nearly won it in the ninth, but the potential winning run was thrown out at the plate.

In the bottom of the tenth, Whittington laced one down the first base line that the umpire initially called foul. According to *The Clarion-Ledger*, after Aggie catcher Cecil Brunson said the hit looked fair, the umpire changed his mind and ruled it a fair ball. Whitting strode into second base with a double.

A single from Harden Wood, yes, Harden Wood, allowed Whittington to come around and score the winning run. The overflow Mother's Day weekend crowd in Oxford went home happy.

On Sunday, the Maroon mothers had their chance to celebrate the exploits of their baseball-playing sons.

A&M scored four in the first inning, including Hartzog's three-run inside-the-park home run. Ole Miss's pitching posted zeroes the rest of the game, but their offense couldn't match their effort.

The Rebels got things going in the fifth, but Noble turned to Bolton with the bases loaded and a run home. An error allowed two more runs to score, but Bolton got out of the inning and closed the game. A&M won 4-3.

Despite all the fanfare, the Greenwood game was almost not played. Ole Miss didn't record a hit or hit a single ball out of the infield in a rain-shortened game that went only five innings. The Aggies won 3-1 to take a two games to one lead in the annual series.

The series shifted back to Starkville, and with it came an outstanding pitching performance by A&M's Jessie Stringer. Throughout nine innings, Stringer allowed five hits and one run long after the game had been decided.

Hartzog was again the hitting champion for the Aggies, going 3-for-4 and scoring three runs in the 7-1 win.

Unfortunately, the second game in Starkville was rained out. A thunderstorm poured on what was reported to be the biggest crowd at Hardy Field to date, over 2,500. That was terrible news for a suddenly hot Aggie team pursuing Alabama.

The Aggies aided in their cause by taking a pair of lopsided wins against Kentucky. The 1925 season was the first-ever meeting between the two schools.

Down the stretch, Noble had the club playing well. They couldn't afford to let up if they had any hope of winning another Southern Conference title.

A couple of gaudy scores were recorded when the Aggies hosted LSU. A&M won game one, 10 to 4.

Game two brought an offensive explosion led by Clay Hopper. He had one of the finest days at the plate in the program's history, going 5-for-5 with three home runs in a 17-6 shelling of the Tigers.

The season ended on a nine-game winning streak by taking the final pair of games against Mississippi College. Despite the late-season hot streak, the Aggies finished behind Alabama in the league standings. There was too much ground to make up, and Alabama was too good.

While Noble didn't have another title to celebrate, the 1925 season proved to be the winningest in his long career as the head baseball coach in Starkville. The Aggies went 19-7 overall and proved once again that they were one of the finest baseball clubs in the South.

Chapter 12

The Chadwick Era Comes to a Tragic End

Noble had established an impressive baseball program during his first six years as the Aggie skipper. However, his one year as the A&M football coach in 1922 was largely forgettable. His passion and expertise lie in baseball, and football may not have been his preferred sport. That isn't to say that football was totally out of his life. For much of the 1920s and into the early 1930s, Noble served as an assistant coach, mainly working with the freshman team.

Though the official nickname of the Mississippi A&M athletics teams was the Aggies, the first-year footballers were labeled the Bull Pups. Even in those early days when the Aggies had a live mascot at various sporting events, an English Bulldog was used.

Noble's Bull Pup squad ran the same schemes that the varsity used, so when they competed with the real dogs, they were well-versed in the playbook and concepts the team ran.

In 1923, the Pups went 3-0-1 and didn't surrender a single point the entire year. The final game on the schedule that season ended in a scoreless tie with Alabama.

A season later, Noble served a stint as a varsity assistant on Coach Earl Abell's staff. Abell's Starkville tenure lasted just two years, and both seasons ended with winning records.

Despite posting a couple of solid seasons at A&M, Abell elected to return to his alma mater, Colgate, as an assistant in 1925. Three years later, he was promoted to head coach there.

When Abell left, Tulane assistant coach Bernie Bierman followed. With a new varsity staff in place, Noble returned to his freshman football duties, where he remained for several years and led the baseball program.

While Noble remained a constant in A&M athletics, a turnover cycle continued regarding Aggie football.

Bierman lasted just two seasons before he left to take the head coaching job at Minnesota.

Interestingly, A&M athletic director Billy Chadwick tried to hire Bierman before he landed on Abell in '23. Chadwick wrote a letter to Bierman to gauge his interest in the position. Still, the former Minnesota All-American halfback opted to join the staff at Tulane alongside his longtime friend Clark Shaughnessy.

After Abell left the program, Chadwick made another run at Bierman. This time, Billy got his man. At Tulane, Bierman worked part-time with multiple sports and sold bonds on the side just to pay the rent. Chadwick was willing to pay him enough so that he could focus on coaching basketball and football.

Two seasons after accepting the job at A&M, Bierman got the call to come home and returned to being a Golden Gopher again. He penned a few words about his decision in his life story. An excerpt ran in *The Minneapolis Star*.

"I spent two years at Mississippi A&M—1925 and 1926. Football was at a pretty low ebb at that school when I took charge. The athletically minded boys who turned out were pretty small. We played stiff schedules each year, and the lack of size among the candidates was a distinct handicap."

Over those two seasons, Bierman's Aggies turned in a combined 8-8-1 record.

Bierman's final game on the A&M sideline was one to remember, but not for good reasons. The Aggies had reeled off 13 consecutive wins against Ole Miss from 1911 until 1926.

A blocked extra point was the difference in a 7-6 game. Once the final horn blew, the Rebel fans in attendance rushed the field and tore down the goalposts at Scott Field. A riot ensued, and many a wooden chair was sacrificed that day by the Aggie faithful to defend the honor of good old A&M.

The *Clarion-Ledger* writer who recapped the game was undoubtedly a fan of the Ole Miss team. The nameless scribe wrote a recap worthy of inclusion in Mad Magazine that ended with the following closing: "A sixteen-year-old dream was realized when the University won the game this afternoon, for not since 1910 has a Red and Blue eleven triumphed over one wearing the maroon moleskins."

The students who ran the A&M student newspaper, *The Reflector*, alleged that the column was likely written years ahead of time and just waiting for publication.

If so, the paper the text was typed upon had likely yellowed, waiting out multiple seasons for its day in the sun.

Chadwick hired John W. Hancock, a former star lineman at Iowa, to replace Bierman. After his playing days, Hancock worked as an assistant coach at Colorado Teacher's College, now known as Northern Colorado.

Bierman's departure also put the basketball program in flux. When A&M issued a release naming Hancock the head football coach, Ray Dauber was brought in to handle hoops and the track program and serve as one of Hancock's football assistants.

The new-look gridiron staff became the first to lose an Egg Bowl. After the melee that ended the '26 season, the two schools agreed to introduce a rivalry game trophy in hopes of calming the tensions between the two schools.

After over a decade of dominance, the Aggies were on a losing streak in the series. The futility against the Rebels continued throughout Hancock's tenure.

His first season in Starkville ended with a 5-3 record, and the Aggies were competitive even in defeat, but it was downhill from there.

Two losing seasons followed, with the program bottoming out in 1929, winning just one game, a 6-0 snoozefest over Mississippi College.

Dauber didn't fare much better on the hardwood. His first season at the Aggie helm was good, with A&M going 13-7 and posting a 10-1 record in league play. The team finished second in the Southern Conference, so hopes were high.

Those expectations proved to be misguided. Dauber followed up that debut season with 8-15 and 5-8 campaigns.

Angst among the Aggie fanbase was prevalent. Baseball, however, was Noble's true shining glory through those seasons of wither. While Noble wasn't winning titles, he was still fielding winning teams.

A&M won more than they lost in every season from 1926-1929. The 1929 season produced the lowest win total since Noble's first season as the Aggie skipper with a 9-6-3 mark.

With all three major sports trending in the wrong direction, many alums pointed at Chadwick as the culprit. His football hires wouldn't stay, and his recent basketball hire wasn't producing. Even the great Dudy Noble was seeing a decline in productivity on the diamond.

Every great story has a villain, and most painted Chadwick in that role. The buck stopped with Chadwick, and a very vocal fanbase made their concerns known to college and governmental leaders.

Governor Theodore Bilbo controlled the purse strings for A&M and every other state-funded institution of higher learning in Mississippi.

Bilbo was a colorful character. A staunch democrat and a devoted segregationist, Bilbo won the Governorship and served his first term from 1916 to 1920.

A native of Juniper Grove, Mississippi, Bilbo earned his college degree at Peabody in Nashville and then graduated from Vanderbilt Law. He was also a confessed member of the Ku Klux Klan.

After working in private practice in Poplarville, Bilbo went into politics, winning a seat in the state senate before winning an election to be the Lieutenant Governor during Governor Earl Brewer's four-year tenure.

Once Brewer's term was up, Bilbo won the voters' approval to succeed him. Despite his failings, Bilbo did some important things the first time. He established a state highway system and outlawed public executions.

An unsuccessful campaign to serve in the United States House of Representatives followed his first term as Governor.

While Bilbo was making a run at national politics, his Lieutenant, Lee Russell, sat in the top seat of state government as Mississippi's 40th governor.

Russell, an Ole Miss-educated lawyer, was admitted to the bar under a diploma privilege that didn't require him to take the state bar exam. That was a common practice nationwide and was used as a recruiting tool in Oxford.

While graduates of other law schools nationwide had to pass the Mississippi state bar exam, Ole Miss law school alums didn't. This practice continued in the state of Mississippi until 1981. Mississippi was one of the last states to abolish the privilege.

Bilbo and Russell were both named in some shady shenanigans in 1922. Russell's former private secretary and stenographer, Francis Cleveland Birkhead, filed a $100,000 federal lawsuit against Russell, charging him with "seduction and breach of promise."

Birkhead alleged that she had become pregnant during an affair with the Governor and that she underwent an abortion procedure that prevented her from bearing children.

Bilbo was summoned to testify in the case in the spring of 1923 but failed to appear. Oxford-based judge Edwind Holmes didn't take kindly to the former Governor, who evaded his responsibilities in the case and charged him with contempt.

Holmes levied a $100 fine and a 30-day jail term. It may have seemed like political theater, but Holmes' judgments were unwavering. Bilbo reported to the Lafayette County jail, where he laid his head for ten days. The sentence was reduced, but not before a strong message had been sent.

It's important to note that the case against Russell eventually fell apart, and he was exonerated. He described it as an attempt at blackmail and revenge after he targeted some insurance companies for what amounted to antitrust violations.

When Bilbo was released from the clink, he announced he was running for Governor again. While he failed to win enough ballots in 1923, incredibly, he won re-election in 1927 and began a second term in 1928.

Midway through that term, Bilbo enacted a sales tax in the great state of Mississippi, making it the first state in the country to have one.

That same year, 1930, Bilbo threw his weight around with the state institutes of higher learning. Since state tax dollars funded schools like A&M and Ole Miss, Bilbo felt he had a say in how they should be run.

In hindsight, it's evident that sufficient checks and balances weren't in place to stop him as he took some tyrannical steps in a vulgar display of power.

One of the first items on his higher education agenda was the relocation of Ole Miss from Oxford to Jackson. Ole Miss students came to a near riot and burned Bilbo in effigy.

While that prospective relocation effort failed, Bilbo made sweeping changes just because he could in what became known as the "Bilbo Purge."

Numbers vary depending on what account one may read. Still, the *Clarion-Ledger* shared that over 300 faculty members and the school presidents at A&M, Ole Miss, and the Mississippi State College for Women had been terminated due to the whim of a madman.

A&M and Ole Miss may have been bitter enemies in many respects, but these moves forced the two schools to work together as allies in a collective attempt to survive.

In a July 4th speech, Bilbo declared, "I asked the legislature to create a director of higher education. They refused to do it, so I am acting as director."

Due to the shake-up, Ole Miss lost its accreditation from the American Association. Bilbo scoffed, "Ole Miss is 400 times better than ever before."

The Rebels weren't the only ones losing prestige and money. At the time, Mississippi A&M received $340,000 a year in federal funding.

The Secretary of Agriculture notified Bilbo that those funds would be withheld due to some of his questionable actions.

Bilbo arrogantly told the media, "We will operate as long as possible without federal aid, and then all can quit at once."

Mississippi A&M President Buz M. Walker was given the heave-ho in a political coup fueled by ego.

Hugh Critz, the father of Aggie baseball star Hughie Critz, replaced him. The elder Critz was also an A&M diamond alum, having played second base on one of the first Aggie teams.

In a letter written to John Wendell Bailey, who compiled both editions of the *M Book of Athletics*, Critz shared his emotions about being elected and finding out about the deep cuts to the A&M faculty.

"The legislature convened in Jackson early in 1930, and very shortly thereafter, I was advised that Dr. A.B. Butts or I would be elected as president.

"The following day, Friday, I received a telephone call to report to the New Capitol building at my earliest convenience. I left at once for that destination.

"Upon my arrival, I was ushered into the presence of the Board of Trustees, who told me they had elected me president and Dr. A.B. Butts as vice president.

"I went back to my work to inform my superior that I had been elected president of Mississippi A & M College.

"Either that afternoon or the next morning, I was given a typewritten list of employees and was assured that none of them would be elected. The law did not specify that the president should nominate. The Board of Trustees had the legal authority to discharge any or all employees.

"I did not attempt to hide the fact that I had received such a blacklist. I was besieged by day and called by telephone at night until 12 o'clock, starting again about 4 a.m. It seemed they all expected to find me at home about midnight and at the early hour in the morning.

"I walked out on the street and happened to meet the Governor, and he gave me an additional list, and that upset us greatly as we did not know who would be discharged in addition to those on the list."

Critz didn't share that A&M athletics director Billy Chadwick's name was on that list. After nearly 22 years of faithful service, Chadwick was out.

Chadwick poured the building blocks of what fans of Mississippi State enjoy today. He was the first to invest in athletic fields and suggested that college athletics could be a growing enterprise. Chadwick also encouraged all students to play at least one sport to keep their minds sharp and their bodies fit.

While the run at the end of his tenure on the fields and courts of play hadn't been stellar, Chadwick deserved a better exit. His time may have been nearing an end, but to have his termination come so viciously was terrible form.

Because of his popularity within the A&M campus community, a push was made to find some way to keep him within the Aggie family. Chadwick left athletics and went to work as the school registrar at his previous salary.

The move proved temporary as Chadwick left A&M after about a year and never worked in athletics again. Instead, he went to work on a debit insurance route for Lamar Life Insurance Company. Chadwick would set up policies and collect monthly premiums from his insured clients as part of that job.

On June 6, 1934, Chadwick was out on his route in Raymond when he was struck by a truck driven by R.R. Bush of Learned, Mississippi, who had fallen asleep at the wheel. A man named W.L. Swinney was a passenger in the truck driven by Bush.

The two men sought aid for Chadwick after the collision and were able to locate Dr. Robert Lee Hagaman of Raymond. Despite the good doctor's efforts, Chadwick died on the way to Baptist Hospital. He was just 50.

A year later, a Hinds County jury ruled against Chadwick's widow, Margaret, who had filed a lawsuit seeking $50,000 in damages due to the accident. She received nothing more than a broken heart.

Chadwick left behind six children: Eugene, Chester, Elizabeth, William Dean Jr., Catherine, and Lindsey. His body was laid to rest in Odd Fellows Cemetery in Starkville.

On March 3, 1969, Margaret passed away at the age of 82. She never remarried. She was buried alongside Billy less than a mile from the Mississippi State campus.

In a loving tribute to the life, legacy, and memory of the man the Aggie students affectionately called Chad, the Bryan Athletic Department Building on the Mississippi State campus overlooks Chadwick Lake.

Chapter 13

The New Boss

After Chadwick's unceremonious termination and before his untimely death, Mississippi A&M needed a new leader in athletics. As documented, all three major sports were trending in the wrong direction.

While the carnage rested upon the state colleges severely, perhaps the Aggie athletic department experienced the greatest sense of trauma.

Football coach John Hancock and basketball coach Ray Dauber went out the door with Chadwick. While Chadwick was respected, Hancock was jeered by Aggie fans who had grown sick of losing on the gridiron.

After some political wrangling, Bilbo's leadership team and the Board of Trustees offered Dudy Noble the opportunity to continue as the baseball coach and pick up the responsibilities of running the athletic department and coaching the football team.

Before accepting the post, Noble was mentioned in connection with the head baseball coaching job at Alabama. With the dramatic upheaval in the Mississippi college job market, everyone faced an uncertain future.

Noble stood in the employment serving line with an empty bowl. Unlike many of his former co-workers, he had some options to consider. He was going to be fed. It was simply a matter of which ladle he chose to accept.

With his wife, Elizabeth, to consider, Noble opted for the bigger job and check. Another perk of the new gig was a fine residence near the Mississippi A&M campus entrance.

It seemed like a win/win for Noble. He could improve his financial situation and aid his alma mater in her time of dire need. Aggie athletics needed a leader to right the ship. Noble believed he was the man to do it.

A football staff had already been assembled. Christian Keener "Red" Cagle and Russell Crane would serve as varsity assistants, and former baseball and football star Cotton Klindworth would coach the freshman footballers and assist on the baseball side.

Crane was asked to coach the line, and Cagle the backfields on offense and defense.

Just before the season began, Noble had misgivings about returning to the sidelines as the Aggie head coach. The new responsibilities of running the entire athletic department were proving to be a bit of a chore.

After consultation with President Critz and the Board of Trustees, Noble was given the go-ahead to name Cagle as the varsity headman.

Cagle was a former Army football star permitted to resign from military service, freeing him from his obligation after his expected graduation from West Point. Cagle never saw that commencement take place, as he was essentially expelled.

Football wasn't the only factor in Cagle's decision. In his junior year at West Point, in a clandestine wedding, Cagle took the hand of Marion Munford Haile of New Roads, Louisiana. In those days, cadets weren't permitted to marry. Due to violating the War Department's rules, the decision to relieve Cagle of any further military obligations was likely easy.

The matter was still not entirely over just because the Army said so. Many Aggie alums were disappointed with the decision to hire Cagle after he appeared to show a flaw in his character by flaunting the Army's rules on marriage.

Dissenting voices attempted to get former A&M President Walker to withdraw the contract extended to Cagle. With Walker now out of power, the mob clamored for relief from Critz. The newly installed President was unwavering in his support for Cagle.

Critz told the *Clarion-Ledger*, "Unless they show something that would reflect on Mr. Cagle, I am in favor of him. I shall not investigate unless some objection is raised. I think Mr. Cagle's coming is a great thing for A&M."

Despite Critz's endorsement, Cagle's lone season in Starkville was an unmitigated disaster. He left the program before the campaign ended to accept a contract to play pro football.

A&M dropped the season's first three games to non-conference opponents Southwestern (TN), Millsaps, and Mississippi College.

The first Cagle win came in Jackson against LSU 8-6. As a Louisiana native, perhaps the game against the Bayou Bengals meant a little more to him.

Shutouts at the hands of NC State and Tulane followed. Another embarrassing loss came against Henderson State in the final out-of-league game.

Cagle's last game as the Aggie head coach was a 7-6 win over Auburn in Birmingham. Perhaps the trick was to play a team called the Tigers on a neutral field.

The day after the win over Auburn, Cagle traveled to New York to begin his professional career with the Giants. Critz granted him a release from his two-year contract with A&M, which opened the possibility of inking a new deal with New York.

Cagle had a game to play, and the Aggies did, too, the Battle for the Golden Egg. Ole Miss won the game easily, but it wasn't a great Rebel team. The 20-0 contest was the lone conference victory of the 1930 season for Ole Miss, which finished 3-5-1.

The strange year continued for A&M athletics; the 1929-1930 basketball season saw the Aggies play all 13 games on the schedule on the road. The team used the Starkville High School gymnasium to practice while what was known as the Tin Gym was under construction.

While the venue was mostly finished, the termination of Dauber and the craziness that came along with all the sudden changes at A&M, the difficult decision to cancel the basketball season was made. No team was fielded for the 1930-1931 season. The Aggies failed to hit the hardwood for the first time since WWI.

After leaving Starkville, Dauber landed at Western Reserve in Cleveland, Ohio. His stay there was short as A&M lured him back to campus. Dauber was charged with restarting the hoops program and coaching football and track.

It was an interesting move, considering that Dauber had been a part of declining seasons with football as an assistant and basketball as the head man. The move spoke to the desperation the A&M administration felt at the time. In many respects, their hands were tied as they operated under the mercy of Bilbo and his lackeys.

Bilbo was a bully with power, but he was about to learn a valuable lesson at the hands of one Dudy Noble.

As the 1931 fall semester began, word spread around the A&M athletics department that Bilbo had cut the operating budget in half. Those fresh restraints would have crippled every effort that Noble made to move the sports programs forward. Rather than sit around, he acted.

Noble cleared his calendar for the day and drove down to Jackson, Mississippi, to confront Bilbo in person. As he entered the state capital, he was told that Governor Bilbo was away on state business but was expected to be back in the building before the end of the day.

Rather than return home to Starkville, Noble sat on the steps outside the capital to await Bilbo's return. He waited and waited and waited.

Just as the day was set to end, Bilbo appeared with a couple of his staffers in tow. As he reached the top of the steps, Noble asked him if it was true that he had cut A&M's athletic operating budget.

As Bilbo stammered and tried to explain that specific changes had to be made, Noble grabbed him up by his coat and pushed him against the wall, and said, "If you ever do something like that again, I will kick your ass."

You can take the ole boy off the farm, but you can't take the farm out of the boy. What a sight to see! Noble had accosted the Governor of Mississippi steps away from his office in the capital, all in defense of Mississippi A&M.

Perhaps it was a moment of clarity that settled in that made him realize he might go to jail, so Noble left. He got back into his car and drove back to Starkville. The business day was over, so Noble went home to spend the evening with Elizabeth.

When Noble returned to the athletics department, a telegram awaited him. Bilbo had restored the full budget. In fact, he increased it.

Despite having the expected resources and then some, it was a challenging year in sports that academic year. Football went 2-6 and didn't win a single Southern Conference game. The Aggies lost the Egg Bowl again. It had been six years since A&M had tasted victory over Ole Miss on the football field.

Basketball went 5-10, Noble's baseball program went 12-9 overall and 8-5 in league play. While the diamond hadn't been as kind as the earlier years of Noble's tenure, it was the only sport Aggie fans could count on despite more modest results than they were accustomed to.

1932 was pretty much the same as the year before, except you could add baseball to the list of fan frustrations as Noble posted a losing year for the first time in 13 seasons at the helm.

There were two significant changes. Mississippi A&M was now Mississippi State College, and the Aggies were now known as The Maroons.

Shortly after Bilbo's second term ended on January 19, 1932, a measure was introduced to officially change A & M's name. With it, the school chose to change its nickname.

The truth is Mississippi A&M had outgrown its original moniker. It was no longer just an agricultural and mechanical school. With more business, engineering, and science programs available, Mississippi State College fit the growing institution.

Mississippi Governor Martin "Mike" Conner signed the bill into law on February 15, 1932.

More change was on the horizon as the Maroons were about to

change conferences for the second time in school history.

Following the 1932 football season, 13 members of the Southern Conference flew the coup and formed the Southeastern Conference.

Alabama, Auburn, Florida, Georgia, Georgia Tech, Kentucky, LSU, Mississippi State, Ole Miss, Sewanee, Tennessee, Tulane, and Vanderbilt were the league's charter members.

While there were some minor issues to quarrel about, geography was the driving force behind the split. The move made sense as the Southern Conference had grown too big, and it was difficult for Western teams within the league to travel through the mountains to take on the easternmost teams near the coast. It made life easier for both schools and fans.

Dauber didn't continue with the Maroons football program as the team entered a new conference and era.

Ross McKechnie was the new man to champion the Mississippi State College football program. A former Washington Husky football player, McKechnie left the program following the 1917 season to enlist in the Army.

After WWI ended, McKechnie remained in the military service and coached and played on several military teams. Before accepting a post in Starkville, McKechnie had some success with the West Coast Army squad, even beating Cal and San Francisco.

In 1932, McKechnie helped instruct the ROTC at Mississippi State College; a season later, he was leading the football team, too. The move also allowed Noble to run the athletic department without the encumbrance of returning to football, rumored to be the case before McKechnie's appointment.

Like the hiring process that brought Dauber back to Starkville, state government officials handled the decision to grant the job to McKechnie. Governor Conner established a state college athletic board, and those individuals had the final say in who was and wasn't hired.

While McKechnie had experience with the game of football, he had never coached a down in college. Yes, he played collegiately, but running the show was a completely different story. It seemed to be a hire of convenience in the same vein as Dauber's earlier selection.

1933 proved to be a challenging year for State on and off the athletic fields of play. Noble had his detractors, and his job security had some ebb and flow. The calls for change in Mississippi State athletics are ever-present. It's a tradition as old as the school itself.

A vocal minority wanted Noble replaced as the director of athletics and wanted the "good ole boys" out, even if that meant a change in leadership for baseball. Some of those addicted to the pain of unnecessary change had the ears of some on the state athletic board. As a result, times were tense in the house of Noble. He was even replaced as the freshman football coach by Goat Hale, who he had coached at Mississippi College.

Dauber coached the basketball team with a heavy heart during that phase of athletics. Just after Christmas 1932, Dauber's parents died in a car accident. Dauber found his parents' automobile crashed on an icy embankment. He tried in vain to get them to medical professionals in time.

State went 6-13 in hoops and finished 12th in the SEC standings. Dauber eventually resigned and accepted a position at Tulane, coaching basketball and serving as a football assistant.

Baseball had a bit of a rebound, posting a 10-5 record and finishing second to Georgia in the SEC standings.

The Great Depression was in full swing, so fewer games were scheduled to save money. State only took two trips out of state that year to play at Alabama and LSU.

Football turned in a 3-6-1 record, with a win over Sewanee as the lone SEC win. Another year, another Egg Bowl loss.

There is one rather humorous anecdote about the 1933 season. When Noble contacted Auburn about the two schools playing for the first time in three seasons, Tiger head man Chet Wynne declined in a way that got Noble's dander up.

Noble told Wynne, who also served as Auburn's AD, "You needn't put on such airs. You coach at a cow college just like I do."

As the year ended, there were rumors about Noble taking over the Maroons basketball program, but in the end, Hale was given the job. His first season, 1934, showed some promise, which was an encouragement that good days lie ahead.

It appeared that the turnaround in baseball was complete, as Noble and the diamond program won 11 of 16 games on the schedule.

Football remained a burr under the Maroons' saddle. State went 4-6 and failed to win a single SEC game. McKechnie's squad scored a combined 12 points in SEC play. It wasn't working.

Like the Dauber years, McKechnie failed to bring gridiron success to campus. His two seasons as the head coach of the Maroons ended with a 7-12-1 record. State won one SEC game and lost both Egg Bowls.

After the 1934 season ended, the winds of change once again blew through Starkville, Mississippi. McKechnie was out as head coach, but that wasn't the only change in Maroon athletics.

Mississippi State College had to turn things around with football. The program had recorded seven straight losing seasons dating back to John Hancock's first season in 1927.

The Maroons needed a football savior. To land him, the powers that be would have to pay him and pay him well. Sick of losing on the gridiron, the Mississippi State administration, led by Duke Humphrey, would have to push for a more significant commitment.

Some of the coaches Humphrey approached were high-dollar men with impressive resumes. They also had considerable salary demands. To secure the right coach, the athletic department's structure had to be changed.

A high-profile coach would want control and not just over football. Big-name coaches wanted to have some say in finances. Many of them wanted to be an AD in addition to coaching football.

Noble had served in the post for four years primarily out of necessity, but he also liked the position. While his hands were tied in the hiring process, he became a good business manager. Noble's decisions as AD brought State out of the red and into the black.

There was money to spend, but Noble wouldn't be the one to spend it moving forward. No, Humphrey would care for football because football took care of everything else. Under the right circumstances, Noble would have to step down for the betterment of football and athletics.

That is exactly what happened. Noble was out as AD and back to coaching the baseball team. While he still had some work to do within the administration and physical education departments, Noble would no longer sit in the big chair and make the big calls—at least, not for a bit.

Chapter 14

A Major Change

As Mississippi State College President Duke Humphrey sought out a new football coach, his previous one, Ross MacKechnie, hadn't officially resigned. While it was evident to many that change was needed, in late December of 1934, MacKechnie was still on the payroll.

In a significant turn of events, Humphrey and MacKechnie unveiled their football plans at a crucial social gathering at the prestigious Robert E. Lee Hotel in Jackson, Mississippi. This gathering, attended by influential alumni such as Ransom Aldrich, marked a pivotal moment in the new football coach's decision-making process.

Aldrich was a farmer from rural Benton County, Mississippi, and a former Dudy Noble college classmate. The 1915 A&M graduate knew people, how things fit together, and Mississippi State College.

More to the point, Mississippi State folks knew him and trusted him. In 1934, Aldrich was the state alumni president. In the years ahead, he would become the President of Mississippi Farm Bureau.

Aldrich orchestrated the meeting in the capital city and played a pivotal role in the decision-making process. This summit, attended by the school and its major donors, aimed to establish a common ground for the future of football in Starkville, highlighting the significant influence of the school's alumni in shaping the program's future.

One can only guess how Humphrey and MacKechnie felt on their drive back to campus, but just one of them would be invited to football functions moving forward. Following several days of discussion, the Aggie alums issued a vote of no confidence in MacKechnie despite his desire to stay on.

Under the guidance of influential program supporters, Humphrey embarked on a mission to find a new football coach. Unlike his predecessor, Critz, Humphrey had more authority in the decision-making process. While the state college athletic board still had to give their final approvals, steps were taken to grant school officials more autonomy, reflecting the school's commitment to improving the football program.

Several names surfaced associated with the vacancy, and all had ties to the military. Humphrey was making some inquiries with the War Department to see if a deal could be struck to bring a promising coach to Starkville to run the ROTC program and change the trajectory of the football program.

LSU's former headman, "Biff" Jones, was a popular name in the wind. Jones had gotten sideways with Louisiana politician Huey P. Long, and his walking papers were drawn up shortly after.

While Jones technically resigned, he was pushed out of Baton Rouge like a barge on the Mississippi River with the Louisiana fat cats piloting the tugboat.

Despite three winning seasons and a share of the Southeastern Conference championship back in 1931, Jones had worn out his welcome on the bayou. His name was quickly dismissed as a potential candidate for the job at Mississippi State, and he wound up at Oklahoma.

A name popular with alums was Stanley Robinson. He coached the Maroon and White football team from 1917 to 1919 before departing for Mississippi College just as Noble returned to Starkville from Ole Miss.

Robinson had modest success at MC before heading to Mercer for three seasons. After things didn't work out at Mercer, Robinson landed back in Clinton, coaching the Choctaws again. His name was familiar, but he didn't have the resume Humphrey was looking for, so he never emerged as a serious candidate.

The final two names on Humphrey's list were Garrison "Gar" Davison and Ralph Sasse. Davison followed Sasse as the Army football coach and had put together a pair of solid seasons with the Cadets.

Davison had one final year of service at West Point, which was undoubtedly part of Humphrey's discussions with the War Department.

Humphrey elected to go with Sasse and brought him to campus for a visit to discuss taking the reins of a football program hungry to win.

Once the two men reached a handshake agreement, Humphrey detailed his hiring plans to the interested alumni, who once again convened at the Robert E. Lee Hotel in Jackson. Alums lauded the hire, and Humphrey was praised for handling the search.

On Monday, January 21, 1935, the Mississippi State Alumni Association voted unanimously to endorse Sasse as the Maroons' next coach. With a signed contract and the support of the fan base behind him, Humphrey succeeded in fine fashion.

Sasse became the highest-paid football coach in the school's history, and he had the resume to support such a financial commitment on behalf of the college. Mississippi State had landed a big fish. It was national news.

In addition to being a war hero, Sasse was a winner on the football field. In three years coaching the Army squad, Sasse posted a 25-5-2 record, never losing more than two games in a season. His first team in 1930 won nine games.

One of Sasse's first orders of business was to keep MacKechnie on staff. Some may question the wisdom behind such a move, but a man who helped defeat Nazi Germany and commanded the 301st Tank Battalion wasn't the kind of fellow to go through life letting his ego get in the way.

Sasse felt that MacKechnie's knowledge of the returning roster would be valuable. Both men's ability to make it work says something about them.

Joining MacKechnie on Sasse's first staff were D.W. Aiken (ends), Frank Carideo (kickers), George Pillow (centers) and John Stokes (line). MacKechnie coached the backfield. Goat Hale stayed on to handle the freshman team.

In addition to expanding the new coaching staff, Sasse hired a team physician, Dr. W.H. Wendler, for the first time in school history.

The hope was that Sasse could find some Maroon magic and turn things around quickly in Starkville. That hope was realized.

In the first game of the Sasse era, running back Ike Pickle helped lead the team to a 19-6 win over Howard. Media accounts of the day remarked on how improved the team looked over the previous years.

Sasse expected a real tussle when he took the team to Vanderbilt for week two.

State had 14 first downs to Vandy's 6, and the Maroons forced three turnovers. State end Chuck Gelatka blocked not one but two kicks in the game. One of those special teams plays resulted in a safety to give State a 2-0 lead.

One play made the difference in Vanderbilt's 14-9 win. Pickle deflected a third-quarter Commodore pass, but not enough to end the play. A Vandy player snatched it from the air and took it the rest of the way for a score.

A week later, the Maroons blasted Millsaps by the score of 45-0. Sasse pulled the first team in the second quarter and let the reserves handle the rest of the blowout victory.

With a 2-1 record, State was ready to travel to Tuscaloosa for a match-up against the defending national champions, Alabama. The previous season, Bama went undefeated, capping the season with a win over Stanford in the Rose Bowl in front of nearly 85,000 fans.

Not only was the Crimson Tide a national power, but tradition was also on their side. The gridders from Starkville hadn't won in the series since 1914, when Dudy Noble was a junior player.

In the years that followed that rare win, the guys in maroon and white scored 34 points in those dozen clashes with Alabama. It hadn't been pretty.

Rather than roll with the usual ground-and-pound offensive approach, Sasse surprised Alabama by going to the air.

On State's second drive, Charles "Pee Wee" Armstrong whipped the ball around left and right with short precision passes. The Tide was stunned. Sasse even dialed up a trick play with a double pass that saw the ball wind up in the hands of Pickle, who scored. The extra point was good, and the Maroons jumped ahead 7-0.

Sasse wasn't there to put up a good fight. He was there to win. Following an Alabama fumble at their 35-yard line, State went right back to work and scored in just two plays. The PAT was no good, but it was 13-0 before the popcorn vendors made their second rounds through the stands.

On the ensuing drive, the Maroons picked off a pass to thwart a possible Alabama score. State couldn't string anything together and was forced to punt. Pickle dialed up a 64-yard kick that was downed at the Alabama one. The Maroon defense stood tall and forced a punt. State took over at the Alabama 34-yard line.

After a short drive, the Maroons were back in the endzone following a short run from Pickle. The conversion was good, and Sasse's State squad silenced Denny Stadium.

Alabama finally got on the board in the third quarter when they blocked a punt and returned it for a score. The extra point capped the day's scoring at 20-7 in favor of State. It was the first loss for Alabama in Tuscaloosa since 1928

The Maroon defense was outstanding on the day, allowing just 198 yards of offense and no points.

Mississippi State hadn't recorded a winning season in seven years, but the Maroons had shocked the college football world with a decisive win over the defending champs.

The wins kept coming. The Maroons slid by Loyola and Xavier in back-to-back road games by 6-0 and 7-0, respectively, to improve their record to 5-1. State was for real, and they were about to prove it once again.

Due to Sasse's connections with the Army, the two programs agreed to meet for a game at West Point, which has proven to be the only meeting between the teams in program history.

Army was 4-0 on the campaign, allowing just eight points all season. The match-up also provided fans with a showdown between Duke

Humphrey's two finalists for the head coaching gig in Starkville.

After winning at Xavier, the Maroons pushed on to New York to prepare for the bout at West Point.

Just like at Alabama, State set the early tone. Pickle did most of the grunt work in the run game on a 73-yard drive to get the football deep in Army territory. The initial score came on a four-yard dive for glory from Bill Steadman. The extra point was good, and the Maroons had an estimated 20,000 fans fidgeting nervously.

The game remained largely at a standstill until the third quarter. Future Heisman Trophy runner-up Charles "Monk" Meyer connected with Clinton True on a 50-yard plus touchdown pass. The conversion was successful, and the game went to the fourth quarter, tied at 7-7.

With the game and glory on the line, Mississippi State took over around their 20-yard line. Armstrong mixed in the short passing game and some well-timed runs to pick up a pair of first downs.

Just as Army began to play closer to the line, the Maroons took a shot. Armstrong dropped back to pass and let it loose. Fred Walters from Laurel, Mississippi, ran under it, shook a man, and then sprinted for the score. The conversion failed, but the Maroon defense made the 13-7 score standup.

Army may have had all the best rifle training in the world, but the East Coast media scribes dubbed State the "sharpshooters."

While the win was glorious, it took a toll on the roster. Despite Dr. Wendler's hard and attentive work, State was severely handicapped as it headed to Baton Rouge to battle LSU.

Playing mainly with reserves, the Maroons fell behind 28-0 before they could score and find an answer on defense. State managed two touchdowns to make the score look more respectable, but the team got whipped 28-13.

The Tigers went on to win the SEC and appear in the Sugar Bowl. The team was led by first-year coach Bernie Moore, who was promoted from within to replace Biff Jones.

State bounced back to shutout Mississippi Teacher's College

(Southern Miss) 27-0 and Sewanee 25-0.

The Egg Bowl loomed large, as the winner was likely headed to a bowl game. There were just four at the time: the Orange, the Rose, the Sugar, and the Sun.

Ole Miss had a fine team that season and entered the rivalry game with eight wins to their credit, just like State. While many years have featured a game between teams on unequal footing, this Battle for the Golden Egg had more significance.

In a somewhat sloppy game filled with penalties and roughhousing, Ole Miss struck first on a drive essentially riding the shoulders of running back Ray Hapes. Brother Clarence did the honors from two yards out to lift the lid on the day's scoring. The extra point was good, which made it 7-0.

The Ole Miss defense stood firm through much of the game, but the Maroons finally got humming in the fourth. The big play on the drive was a 43-yard pass from Armstong to Walters to get inside the Ole Miss 20-yard line. Two plays later, Steadman galloped into the end zone.

With a chance to tie, Armstrong's point after touchdown was no good. State needed a defensive stop and one more scoring possession to claim sole custody of the Golden Egg for the first time since it had been introduced into the rivalry.

State kicked off, and disaster struck. Hapes got loose and returned the kick 90 yards for a touchdown. The extra point was good, and it was 14-6, Rebels.

One can barely imagine the frustration those coaches and players must have felt as they watched the jubilation at their expense firsthand in Oxford. Foiled again, the Maroons headed back to Starkville without the Egg.

State traveled home empty-handed and without a post-season invite. Ole Miss went to The Orange Bowl. Just when you think the story may be over, it takes another turn.

Enlisted military men were to be banned from coaching at civilian institutions.

Humphrey shared with the media and the Mississippi State family that Sasse would return for the 1936 season, but he could make no assurances beyond that.

While Sasse enjoyed his first year in Starkville, he made no bones about where his allegiance lay.

"This is strictly up to the War Department," Sasse told the *Clarion-Ledger*. "I go where I am assigned. Naturally, I'd like to stay at Mississippi State.

"I like the school, the boys, and I like football coaching, but the Army is my career. I am first and last a military man. My assignment was as head of the ROTC unit at Mississippi State.

"I feel that in no way did football coaching interfere with the military work.

"When Mississippi State sought my transfer, I accepted because I considered it a challenge in a way. A challenge to see if I could improve the football team, help the college.

"They'd been a bit down in football and I wanted to see if I couldn't bring them up. I hope I've succeeded to some extent.

"You know, I want to keep on coaching there and I expect to. I'd like to finish the job; carry the objective I've set for myself."

With that news hanging in the air, the Mississippi State fans, who had enjoyed a tremendous season, had to hold their breath.

The War Department later provided some transparency that cleared the way for Sasse to remain in Starkville. State contracts were just one-year deals back then, so the new Maroon and White savior was inked by Humphrey without any hesitation.

Sasse was soon in the headlines for another reason.

Ole Miss received the Orange Bowl bid and headed down to Miami to prepare to take on Catholic University. The Rebels lost the game 20-19 but felt undermined.

Sasse and his wife, Kathryn, were vacationing in Key West and enjoying some sunshine at the Army Recreational Center. The Rebels suggested that if Sasse could be an Army man, he could also be a covert Catholic asset.

Former *Clarion-Ledger* sportswriter Purser Hewitt spoke with Sasse about the brouhaha once everyone returned to Mississippi.

Sasse told Prewitt that Catholic head football coach Dutch Bergman was a longtime friend. The two had previously discussed possibly scheduling a football game against each other for the 1936 season.

Sasse also said that the family vacation had been planned long before either team was invited to the Orange Bowl.

The Maroon coach did his best to suggest that he didn't advise Bergman on how to beat the Rebels, but one must wonder about the validity of that claim.

It would be far from the first time two coaching friends shared some scouting information. If Sasse had a rooting interest in the game, one would have to believe it was on behalf of Catholic and his pal, Bergman.

Devoid of evidence but full of piss and vinegar, Ole Miss folks cried foul and suggested that Sasse had acted improperly by even meeting Bergman at the racetracks for an adult beverage, catching up, and taking in some horse racing.

No one knows what Bergman and Sasse talked about or what information they shared, but the situation put the Rebels in a tizzy.

If Sasse needed a welcome to the rivalry moment, this was likely it. The first-year State coach had done some incredible things, but the Golden Egg remained in Oxford. One has to wonder how the mountain out of a molehill nonsense may have motivated Sasse and put the Rebels squarely in his crosshairs in the years ahead.

Chapter 15

A Shock to the System

With football enjoying unprecedented success and more good fortune on the horizon, Dudy Noble was tending to baseball, leading the P.E. department, and doing some bookkeeping in the athletic department.

One may wonder if he felt frustrated being essentially set aside as athletic director, but he didn't. Noble loved Mississippi State. He wanted to do his part and do what was best for the school. That meant he had a more minor role for almost three years.

His primary focus was baseball, and the Maroons were winning on the diamond. The 1935 Maroons played an All-SEC schedule against just three opponents. State had a home-and-home series with Alabama, LSU, and Ole Miss.

There were no train trips to Texas or jaunts to the eastern part of the league. A dozen games were played against the Maroons' three regular rivals. One got washed out due to the weather, but it was a good year.

Pee Wee Armstrong proved to be as good a pitcher as he was a quarterback. Another outstanding State athlete forgotten like the sands in the hourglass, Armstong was a real dude.

Grady Perkins also proved to be an arm that Noble could count on as the Maroons began their quest for their first-ever Southeastern Conference title.

April featured four games against LSU. In the final meeting between the two schools in 1934, State touched Tiger pitching for 25 runs, setting a new school record for runs scored in SEC play.

LSU went to Starkville for the first home series of the State season but went only to go home with two defeats. When State returned to Baton Rouge, the Tigers tried to return the favor but had to settle for a split. The Maroons scored a season-high number of runs in the 16-2 victory.

State took their 3-1 record on the road to Oxford for a pair of games on May 4th and 5th. The Rebels, or Flood as they were called at times, didn't have a good year for Coach Tad Smith. Ole Miss went 0-for-10 in SEC games, including the four against State.

The Maroons took the twosome in Oxford by 12-2 and 6-0 scores. The return games in Starkville ended 4-0 and 2-1 in favor of State.

Between those two rivalry series, the Maroons split with Alabama in Starkville. State won game one, 6-3, but was shelled in the second, 17-0. It was a humiliating defeat.

The title chase was expected to go down to the season's final day, with the Maroons and Crimson Tide playing a pair in Tuscaloosa.

Alabama entered the final fight ahead of State in the SEC standings. Alabama could win the league title for the second straight season with just one win. While State could win it with two wins in Tuscaloosa by earning the tiebreaker over the Tide, winning three of the four games.

The stakes were high, and the territory hostile. The two teams had been thorns in each other's sides since Noble joined the league as a coach. More times than not, the battle of U.S. Highway 82 determined a champion.

When Coach Tilden Campbell turned in his lineup card, Alabama star pitcher Lee Rogers drew the starting assignment. Rogers had just one defeat on the season, which came earlier in the year in Starkville when State touched him for six runs in a 6-4 win.

It paid the Maroons to be cautious, but they needn't be scared. They had seen Rogers. They understood the southpaw's talent but knew they had beaten him before.

Grady Perkins was the counter for State. Perkins was the winning pitcher in the victory in Starkville in the first game of the series between the two teams. Noble decided that if it wasn't broken, why bother fixing it?

Perkins pitched well in the rematch, scattering seven hits and allowing two runs. That is a winning line in most games, but Rogers limited State to one run on three hits. Alabama won the game and the league title for the fifth time in 10 seasons.

The second scheduled game in Tuscaloosa was rained out. It was all academic, anyway. There was no chance of the Maroons catching the Tide. The season was over, with the Maroons recording a 9-3 mark and a second-place finish in the SEC standings.

Noble had to work hard to get the 1936 Maroons up to snuff. Nine Maroon regulars, including his top two hurlers, were gone. Making a run at anything that resembled a special season was expected to be a real chore.

With the ability to schedule some nonconference opponents, Noble added Minnesota and Purdue to the slate. Both the Golden Gophers and Boilermakers made their first-ever trips to Hardy Field. Outside of those newcomers, it was the usual suspects on the schedule.

State went 8-5 on the year and turned in a 6-4-1 record in conference play. The year's highlight was taking all four games from the hated Ole Miss Rebels.

The season finale sent joy through Starkville as the Maroons defeated Ole Miss 13-10 to clinch the season sweep. There was some good news for the Oxfordites. After three years of SEC play, they finally won a game against a league opponent when they knocked off Alabama 2-1.

Sasse assistant coach Carideo took charge of the Maroon basketball program after some restructuring in the athletic department. Carideo fueled the first winning SEC season in program history in the spring of 1936 with a 9-5 record in conference. The team finished 11-6 overall.

Things were trending in the right direction for State in all sports. Sasse's arrival brought a renewed sense of optimism. His retention, thanks to the Army, helped usher in some unbridled exuberance ahead of the 1936 football season.

Sasse won a school-record eight games in his first season. Maroon fans were wondering what might be possible in year two.

The season started well enough, with blowout wins over Millsaps and Howard. Neither team scored on the State defense.

The Maroons likely snuck up on an overconfident Alabama team in '35. They wouldn't have the same luxury in '36. The Tide had the game circled, but Sasse's bunch was primed for the challenge.

Alabama hosted the game in Tuscaloosa for the fourth straight year. The 1936 meeting was one of 11 in a row played between the two schools in Denny Stadium.

Just as they were a season before, The Maroons were ready for the Crimson Tide. In a tightly contested defensive game, the lone score came on an 83-yard fake punt from Alabama in the second quarter. The Tide held on to win 7-0, but it was clear that State wouldn't be a pushover from now on if Sasse roamed the sidelines.

State whipped Loyola in Meridian at Ray Stadium 32-0 to bring their record to 3-1.

A week later, the Maroons traveled to Dallas to take on eventual Cotton Bowl champion TCU. The two battled to a scoreless tie.

Sewanee was the next victim, and what a victim they proved to be. State rolled over them 68-0. The Maroons had played six games, and none of their opponents had scored a single point against the State defense. The lone score came on special teams.

Seventh-ranked LSU broke the Maroon defensive scoring streak the following week when they won 12-0.

Like the Alabama series, State played down in Baton Rouge in back-to-back years. It was worse than that. The Tigers hosted the game in Louisiana 26 times in a row. All but two of them were in Baton Rouge.

One wonders about such arrangements, but Maroon officials sold home games regularly to help fund the athletic department. Some SEC teams offered State more money to make the trip than they would've made by hosting a football game at Scott Field.

November 21st brought Ole Miss back to Starkville. A lot had happened since the two schools had met on the football field. The Maroons were battling for their first-ever bowl game, while the Rebels hoped to avoid the SEC cellar.

Of course, there was also the bad blood that came to a boil in the south Florida sun from the previous year when Sasse and his family were seen consorting with Ole Miss enemies before their New Year's Bowl game loss to Catholic.

The Rebels had one of the best path pavers in the country in Bruiser Kinard. The issue for Ole Miss was that the road to victory had been mostly gravel. That isn't to suggest the Rebels put together an arduous schedule of games. Ole Miss only contracted four SEC games and had already lost the only two they had played when they got to Starkville.

Ole Miss coach Ed Walker told the *Clarion-Ledger* the week of the rivalry game that he felt his Rebels had been in the Maroon crosshairs all season long.

"State seemed to have but one idea in mind when it carded games for this fall, and that was to lick Ole Miss," Walker whined.

It would be fair to say that the Rebel headman knew what was coming. The statement described each man in maroon as near superhuman and among the best in the country at their position, including quarterback Pee Wee Armstrong, whom Walker described as "one of the three best passers in the nation."

Armstrong had been nursing an ailing shoulder he hurt against LSU in the days leading up to the Egg Bowl. Many wondered if he would suit up. He did, but he played sparingly. Bernie Ward took most of the snaps.

State ran some no-huddle offense and sped down the field to score first on a short run inside by Steadman. The extra point was good, which gave the Maroons a 7-0 lead.

Ole Miss got on the board in the third quarter on a 20-yard Dave Bernard touchdown catch—the point after was no good after a muff by the holder. The miscue allowed State to cling to the lead at 7-6 heading to the fourth.

State's first score in the final quarter was set up when Gelatka alertly jumped on a fumble at the Ole Miss 16-yard line. A play later, Pickle was in the end zone. The extra point made it 14-6 Maroons, but they weren't done.

Following a trade of turnovers, State got the better end of the deal and posted another rushing touchdown. The kick was blocked, bringing the score to 20-6 in the home team's favor.

Emotions ran high, and Sasse fell victim to the sentiment as well. Armstrong entered the game for just one play when State got the ball back with just minutes to play. With a grimace on his face, Armstrong let the pigskin fly downfield. The pass was complete for a 57-yard touchdown. It was the coup de gras. State won its first Egg Bowl, 26-6.

Duke Humphrey walked out to the 50-yard line as the game went to the final. Ole Miss Chancellor Alfred Butts met him there with the Golden Egg in tow. Mississippi State held the prized trophy in Starkville for the first time for a full calendar year.

While the regular season typically ends with the rivalry football game these days, State still had a pair of games to play back then. They would trudge on without Armstrong, who had torn ligaments in his throwing shoulder, under center. Dennis Cross took most of the snaps in the remaining two games on the schedule.

Cross led the Maroons to shutouts of Mercer and Florida to end the regular season 7-2-1.

With their second straight winning season under Sasse, State was in the bowl conversation. The Maroons were a deserving squad, but there were some last-minute discussions about where, when, and who they would play.

The initial rumors had State headed to the Cotton Bowl, but things changed. Tennessee declined an invitation to the Orange Bowl, so officials in Miami extended an invitation to the Maroons.

Orange Bowl chairman Keith Phillips made the matter formal on December 8, 1936, when he announced that State and Duquesne would square off in Miami.

At long last, a Maroon and White football player would have plans for the holidays other than heading home for Christmas with the family. Mississippi State was going to a bowl game.

The return of Armstrong buoyed their chances of winning in South Florida. Though not fully healthy, State's regular starter under center was healthy enough to play and not handicap the offense.

Armstrong led the team on an 80-yard march on State's first scoring drive, mainly through the air. Connections to Gelatka and Steadman helped move the chains and keep the drive alive. Once inside the red zone, the Maroons called on Pickle, who delivered a seven-yard touchdown run. The extra point was no good.

The Dukes answered back with a pass-heavy drive that ended in the endzone. Their point after was true, and State trailed 7-6.

Armstrong and the Maroons answered back before the half was over. A 16-yard completion from Armstrong to Walters pushed State back out in front as a 31-yard dash after the catch into open territory found paydirt. The extra point attempt failed again. Sasse's Maroons hit the halftime dressing room with a 12-7 lead.

The defenses ruled the second half. The Maroons even picked off four passes and seemed primed to put the game away late in the fourth.

With State defenders harassing him on every snap, Duquesne quarterback Boyd Brumbaugh had grown accustomed to giving ground. With the game on the line, the Maroons chased him back inside his 20-yard line in hopes of securing a sack or forcing an incompletion.

Brumbaugh evaded enough tacklers to find some ground, square his feet, and let it fly. The desperation heave was launched on a wing and a prayer. That prayer was answered as Ernest Hefferle ran under it and took it the rest of the way for a touchdown. State lost 13-12.

The season might not have ended as State supporters had hoped, but they had the Golden Egg and their first-ever bowl trip to brag about.

Sasse was inked for a third season, and hopes were high. Mississippi State fans had recently grown accustomed to winning football games and were hungry for more.

The Maroons opened the 1937 season with back-to-back shutouts of Delta State, 39-0, and Howard, 38-0. Football fever spread around the greater Starkville area.

For the first time since Dudy Noble was carried off the field by the Texas A&M cadets in his final college football game, Mississippi State played the Aggies. This time, the meeting occurred as part of the Rose Festival in Tyler, Texas.

There would be no similar acts of sportsmanship this time around. Texas A&M scored two touchdowns in the second quarter and never looked back. Sasse's offense never got on track and the Maroons fell for the first time on the season, 14-0.

Texas A&M wasn't the only former foe back on the slate. Auburn agreed to play for the first time since 1930. The Tigers dropped three straight games to the maroon-clad marauders from Starkville before discontinuing the series.

The two old "cow colleges" renewed the rivalry, and Auburn won going away 33-7.

State battled back to take down Florida 14-13 at Scott Field. The game had some late drama. The Maroons built a 14-0 lead in the first half and tried to play keep away the rest of the game.

The Gators finally had something to cheer about when "Moon" Mullins broke through the Maroon line, blocked a punt, and recovered it for a touchdown. The extra point made it 14-7.

After State stalled on offense, Florida mounted another scoring drive, with Mullins again doing the honors on a catch and run that ended in the endzone. The bad thing for the Gators was he missed the point after.

When it seemed the Maroons would survive without any more nonsense, State fumbled on first down following the ensuing kickoff. Florida recovered and had a chance to steal one, but the Maroon defense stiffened.

The Gators lined up for a potential game-winning field goal, but it was off target like that second extra point. State won despite doing its best to throw it back into the fire.

A week later, State traveled to Shreveport and battled Centenary to a scoreless tie to bring the season record to 3-2-1. What started as a promising season was beginning to fade.

LSU destroyed the Maroons 41-0 in Baton Rouge, killing nearly all the momentum from the Florida win. That loss had more far-reaching issues for State than just a football game.

In the days following the loss, rumors about Sasse's health circulated. On November 9th, a shocking development occurred: Sasse resigned.

While Humphrey stated that the partnership would end once the season did, Sasse was done. He never coached another down for Mississippi State.

As the shockwaves roared through the campus, the students responded in a way that those who love that cherished institution would expect.

Understanding the need for togetherness in the face of adversity, a grassroots movement began. Nearly 1,800 students marched to the athletic dormitory to support the Maroons' football coaches and players.

While those who cheered for the team dealt with the unexpected turn of events with heavy hearts, the players were hurting the most. Those true Maroon students pledged their undying support to those players as they tried to finish the season without their mentor.

"Colonel Sasse meant a lot to the student body and others on campus, but above all, he meant a lot to our team when it was up and also when it was down," team captain Bill Steadman said to the assembled mass. "He believed in hard, clean football, which he taught us and upon which we hope to finish the season, no matter how tough the going may be."

It was soon learned that Sasse had suffered a nervous breakdown and was no longer able to move forward as State's coach. He overworked himself trying to run the ROTC and lead the Maroons to a possible Southeastern Conference title.

Rather than throwing their hands up and quitting, all involved in Maroon football returned to work.

Coach John Stokes, the man Sasse had to have when he accepted the job, served as the interim coach.

Dudy Noble stepped up to assist his alma mater once again. Noble had been named freshman football coach earlier in the year after Goat Hale left for Ole Miss. Noble's Bull Pups went undefeated and unscored upon in that 1937 season, ending the year with a 20-0 win over Alabama. Earlier in the year, Noble beat the team he loved to beat the most, Ole Miss, 43-0.

When there is trouble in the family, the family sticks together. That is precisely what Mississippi State did. One had to expect that Noble, who always had a heart for Dear Ole State, would be in the thick of things when a crisis was afoot.

Fortunately, a struggling Sewanee team was up next on the schedule. While it wasn't a masterpiece in football execution, the Maroons worked to a businesslike 12-0 win.

Vowing to fight on for Sasse in hopes of providing some comfort for him as he continued to be under a doctor's care, State prepared for the Battle for the Golden Egg.

Not many gave the Maroons much chance to take down the Rebels in Oxford. While not a great team, Ole Miss entered the game with a 4-3-1 record. Coach Ed Walker's team also had revenge on their minds from losing the Egg a season ago. In a show of solidarity, the Rebel football team abandoned their razors nearly two weeks leading up to the game.

While Ole Miss was considered the bearded favorite, Walker looked to quiet down any chatter about a potential runaway win for the Rebels.

"I don't see why anyone would dope us to win," Walker told the *Clarion-Ledger*. "These Ole Miss-State affairs are always dog eat dog, and past performances never count for a thing. As I see it, the team that gets the breaks will win."

A massive crowd, including Governor Hugh White, was expected at Hemingway Stadium for the Thanksgiving Day game. The contest also served as senior day for Bruiser Kinard, an All-American. Kinard didn't want his last Rebel memory to be one where State left his home stadium with the Golden Egg.

The betting public may have counted the Maroons out, but those who made the trip to Oxford to squabble over the rivalry trophy didn't buy into that line of thinking.

Early in the ball game, the State defense put Ole Miss well behind the chains. As the Rebels tried to create some room to punt the ball away, George Carter exploded through the line and dumped Ole Miss halfback Parker Hall for a safety.

Just before the halftime whistle, the Maroons mounted a drive to produce the only offensive points of the day for either team. Steadman wouldn't be denied inside the five-yard line as he bullied his way in for the score. The extra point was good, putting State ahead 9-0.

State's defensive effort carried over to the second half. Ole Miss likely wouldn't have scored on the day without a crazy play that made it a game again.

Following a State fourth-quarter punt that rolled dead, James Goolsby failed to touch it down, which would have ended the play. The referee never blew the whistle, and Ray Hapes picked the ball up and returned it for a touchdown as the Maroon players left the field. The extra point was good, and suddenly, the outcome was questioned despite State dominating all day.

Later in the quarter, the Rebels nearly took the lead. Just as Ole Miss seemed to be taking control, Bob Hardison stepped in front of a Hall pass inside the State 10-yard line to save the day.

Ole Miss had one more final attempt to complete the comeback, but a dropkick attempt from near the State 30-yard line went awry, and the Maroons celebrated an Egg Bowl road victory in Oxford for the first time, 9-7.

With Sasse back in Starkville confined to his home, the young men he coached from next to nothing secured their third straight winning season and second Egg Bowl victory.

State fought hard the final week of the campaign but fell to Duquesne, 9-0. The game was deadlocked at 0-0 until the final minutes. The Dukes kicked a late field goal to make it 3-0. Just as the Maroons looked ready to march down and win the game, an interception led to the final score.

Despite that season-ending loss, there was pride in Starkville. Despite long odds and some trying emotions, those who represented the Maroon and White did so with dignity.

Those brave young men fought for each other, their fallen coach, fellow students, and Mississippi State's honor.

The Sasse era in Starkville was over on the football field, though he hung around to continue his work with the ROTC for a bit. His three teams at State posted a 20-10-2 record, though he wasn't on the sidelines for the final three games.

Sasse is an essential figure in Mississippi State sports history. He transformed the Maroons from SEC also-rans to contenders. While he never won a conference title, Sasse proved one could win in Starkville. He showed that fans of the Maroon and White could see some dreams come true. He changed so much and is to be remembered for it.

Of course, with Sasse out of Maroon sports, State needed a new football coach. They also needed a new athletic director, as Sasse had served in the role for two years, even if only by title. Colonel Paul Parker served in that capacity for the final year of the Sasse football tenure but was not retained.

Duke Humphrey had some big decisions to make. How could he top the hire of Sasse? Or could he? That remained to be seen, but he knew exactly where to turn to help keep the athletic department going in the right direction. He turned to Dudy Noble. Of course, he did!

Chapter 16

Back in the Saddle

With Noble back running the athletic department at Mississippi State, the search for a new football coach was job one. Humphrey would help lead the search, and rightfully so. His previous efforts ushered in one of the winningest stretches in school history.

One complicating factor was that Ole Miss was also looking for a new head man as Coach Ed Walker resigned following the 1937 season after eight years at the Rebel helm. The Walker era ended at Ole Miss with a 38-38-8 record. He went winless in SEC play in his final two campaigns.

Mississippi State made a valiant effort to bring back Bernie Bierman from Minnesota, but those attempts failed. Bierman won five national championships for the Golden Gophers and was later inducted into the College Football Hall of Fame.

Noble interviewed candidates at the American Football Coaches Association convention in New Orleans. Per tradition, every time State had a football coaching hire to make, Noble was rumored to be in contention. He quashed those rumors early in the hiring process.

Another popular name in the grapevine was Centenary head coach Curtis Parker. He was an avid pursuer of the job, but Humphrey and Noble elected to go in a different direction.

Vanderbilt assistant Henry Frnka was also connected to the search but withdrew from consideration just before a hire was made public.

On January 24, 1938, an Associated Press wire report announced that State and Ole Miss had ended their quests to find new football coaches.

The Rebels went with former Georgia coach Harry Mehre, who resigned after ten seasons in Athens.

State took a different path and welcomed LSU line coach Emerson

"Spike" Nelson as their new head coach. A former All-American lineman at Iowa, Nelson was a rising star in the SEC. His hiring brought a wave of optimism and hope, signaling a new era for the Maroons.

"I'm mighty happy to get this opportunity and I am most pleased with my contacts with Mississippi State people," Nelson told the AP.

Less than a month after his formal announcement as the new Maroon head football coach, Nelson spoke to the Mississippi State student body at an on-campus ceremony.

"I do not promise you a football team that will win all of it's games," Nelson said. "But, by the way the men are working in spring practice, I can promise you a football team that you can be proud of."

Noble also spoke to the crowd of State supporters, reminding them to remain vigilant in their support and to show humility in all things.

"It is important for the college to continue its commonsense spirit of winning without boasting and losing without whining," Noble said. "While we are all primarily interested in football, the so-called minor sports should not be neglected."

Emerson's first and only staff at State consisted of some familiar names. The one outsider, Shelby Calhoun, followed Emerson from Baton Rouge to Starkville.

Former Maroons' player Pee Wee Armstong, who went from playing to coaching, Frank Carideo, and Watkins Fatheree were holdovers from the Sasse staff.

The 1938 team was primarily young, comprised of sophomores and juniors. It was expected to be a rebuilding year as the program was at the end of the talent cycle.

A small cluster of young stars included quarterback Sonny Bruce, end Buddy Elrod, and halfback Jack Nix.

Coach Noble indoctrinated the sophomore class to blue-collar football as freshmen in 1937. They proved to be the foundation of a new era of gridiron greatness. It was a new look offense under Nelson and a new look head to toe. Unknown to many in the Mississippi State administration, the first-year coach ordered cardinal and gold uniforms rather than the traditional maroon and white. The Maroons were unrecognizable. That fashion faux pas wasn't well received by supporters or administrators.

Things started well enough for Nelson's squad on the gridiron. A 13-point third quarter pushed the Maroons ahead to stay in front of Howard in a 19-0 victory. Bruce, of Columbus, Mississippi, scored two touchdowns to pace State.

In week two, Nix proved to be the scoring star in a 22-0 shutout of Florida in Starkville. Bruce connected with Nix for a first-quarter scoring pass to make it 7-0. A field goal closed out a first half that saw the Gators earn just one first down.

Nix sprinted in for another score in the third from 15 yards out. The second team handled the grunt work the rest of the way. Elrod and the rest of the defensive unit held Florida in check all day, surrendering just three first downs.

Louisiana Tech traveled to Scott Field the following week and soon regretted getting off the bus. State ran for 358 yards and seven touchdowns in a 48-0 shelling of the opposition.

The Maroons were 3-0 and unscored upon. Maybe those new uniforms weren't so bad after all.

Emotions ran high as State traveled to Montgomery to tangle with the Tigers of Auburn. The two teams had met just 13 times heading into the '38 match-up, with the Tigers winning ten of them. State's three wins had come in the last four meetings, so there was some optimism about a potential victory.

Auburn took an early 7-0 lead, but State nearly pulled even just before the halftime whistle. Bruce connected with Nix for a big play that covered 67 yards and ended in the end zone.

Bruce converted the extra point try, but the attempt was nullified as an official had blown his whistle just before the snap. Some members of the Famous Maroon Band had wandered into the end zone as they assembled for the halftime show.

The play was ruled dead. Bruce's second attempt was no good, but it was a harbinger of things to come.

Auburn dominated the second half and went on to win 20-6. In the postgame press conference, Tiger head man Jack Meagher told the *Birmingham News*, "I thought we played our best game of the year. I was particularly pleased with the offense, and our line play for the third straight game was excellent."

State rebounded the following week on a road trip to Duquesne. The two teams first met in 1936 in the Orange Bowl and then agreed to a home-and-home series in 1937 and 1938.

The third time proved the charm for the Maroons, but it took some late heroics. The Dukes held a 7-0 lead into the third quarter. State scored and was in a position to tie, but the extra point failed. Bruce's backup, Harvey Johnson, was responsible for the score, a 39-yard run to glory.

The game-winning score also came from a second-teamer when Frank Chambers got loose on a 22-yard scamper. Once again, the point after was no good, but Elrod and the Maroon defense held on and shut out Duquesne the rest of the way.

Now 4-1, it appeared Nelson had the team playing well and was primed for a strong run through the back half of the schedule. State dropped the next four to Tulane, LSU, Centenary, and Southwestern (TN). The Maroons limped into the Battle for the Golden Egg with their tails between their legs.

Ole Miss was playing well. The Rebels were 8-1 and were set on revenge, having lost the last two Egg Bowls to State.

Future All-American and NFL player Parker "Bullet" Hall led the Ole Miss offense.

Hall scored the lid-lifting points on a short run. The extra point attempt was good, making it 7-0.

Ole Miss attempted to run a trick play in the second quarter with Hall being the receiver. As second-team quarterback Erm Smith targeted Hall, Nix stepped in front and returned the pigskin 87 yards for a pick-six. Bruce's attempt to tie the score was wide.

Bruce did his best to atone for that miscue after Elrod and the Maroon defense got a stop. Bruce fielded a punt deep in State territory and returned it 66 yards to set the offense up at the Ole Miss 23-yard line. The Rebel defense stiffened and turned the Maroons away to hit the intermission with a 7-6 lead.

State struggled to get much going in the second half, and a tired Maroon defense surrendered two touchdowns in a 20-6 loss.

With the season over and the Golden Egg back in enemy hands, State fans were unsettled. Nelson's name was Mud. The resentment of making a unilateral decision to change the team colors continued to linger.

Things came to a head at the end of January, just weeks after everyone returned from the holiday break. After meeting deep into the night, a decision was made that Nelson would be moving on.

Mississippi State officials released a statement to the media that said Nelson's resignation was accepted "because of an accumulation of problems, the course pursued was the best for all concerned."

Just like that, Nelson was gone, and along with him, his poorly received cardinal and gold uniforms. Legend has it that those unpopular duds were burned. They would make quite a collector's item if any survived.

Nelson shared in his part of the joint statement that some other opportunities had "opened for him," which was part of the decision. He packed up and left Starkville to be the offensive line coach at Yale. After two seasons, Nelson was elevated to the head coaching position, where he went 1-7. History shows us that Spike Nelson wasn't cut out to be a head football coach.

Mississippi State was in the market for a new head football coach. While Duke Humphrey led the previous two quests to find quality leadership, this time, the duty was placed squarely on Dudy Noble's shoulders.

State schools were granted more autonomy in coaching decisions. Things had changed a great deal since the Bilbo Purge. Rather than working as bean counters in addition to their coaching duties, athletic directors had the freedom to make more decisions.

Noble went to work on what proved to be an exhaustive search that yielded great results for State College football.

It was also a hiring process with many twists and turns involving some media reports that proved premature at best and dead wrong at worst.

State needed a winner, and they got one. Fortunately for the Maroons, the revolving door was about to be locked shut for a while. The new hire was the first to depend entirely on Noble's discretion. It provided quite a precedent for the hires to come, proving that the former Aggie athletic star had a keen eye for coaching talent.

Chapter 17

A Hire for the Ages

As Mississippi State embarked on its quest for a new gridiron coach in 1939, college football remained a localized sport in many respects. For those unable to attend games, the only lifeline was the newspaper accounts of their beloved teams, a stark contrast to the instant updates we enjoy today.

Radio coverage outside of metro markets was scant. With the signal and technology available, some major stations began calling games regularly in the 1920s. Still, those broadcasts weren't money-makers for schools.

WJDX of Jackson carried the earliest radio games for State football, but the schedule was somewhat hit or miss even with their resources.

There were no TV contracts, even in major metropolitan areas. When games between college programs began in 1869, they were, in many respects, a club sport. While things were more organized in the 1930s, those with TV sets still weren't able to watch their favorite teams compete from the comfort of their living rooms.

Undeterred by the lack of direct access, some programs ingeniously set up viewing parties. A telegram was dispatched after each significant play to a scorekeeper who would then announce the result to the eager observers in attendance, keeping the score on a metal board. As the team advanced down the field, a magnetic football would be slid to the appropriate yard marker, a creative solution that showcased the fans' unwavering dedication.

While there was plenty of fan interest and media reports, there were no media rights or lucrative revenue buckets for schools to dip into. All of that came much later.

It was an eat-what-you-grow arrangement. Schools had to sell tickets and solicit donations from alumni. Because the school relied on donors, many wanted a say in how things were run. Such was the case at Mississippi State.

Within days of Nelson's resignation, some State alums took it upon themselves to "assist" Noble with his coaching search. A group of central Mississippi donors invited Centenary head coach Curtis Parker to visit with them about the recent vacancy in Starkville.

Noble agreed to meet with Parker at the group's request once he had been wined and dined in the capital city. Many associated with the group felt that Parker was well qualified for the job and that it would be a rubber stamp deal. It wasn't.

Noble sat down with Parker but elected to interview some other candidates. Blessed with the gift of hindsight, Noble offered a courtesy interview to Parker as a favor to those fat cats in Jackson. He had his sights set much higher. It was a political move. Noble afforded the donors some say and even offered up some of his time to make them feel included, but ultimately, it was his decision.

In the February 23, 1938, edition of the *Greenwood Commonwealth*, Bob Upshur recounted a "second-hand" interview with Noble about the status of the coaching search.

"Who are the main prospects for the job, Mr. Noble?"

"We've got plenty of them," Noble replied.

"Have they all been interviewed?"

"Some have and some haven't."

"When do you plan to talk to the next prospect," the reporter questioned.

"Sometime after today and before football season."

"Where do you plan to go see him?"

"Roads lead out of here in every direction," Noble quipped.

"Well, who is going to be the new coach?"

"Probably be a man. Never can tell."

Noble was being coy, and rightfully so. Unknown to anyone outside the Maroon circle of trust, Noble was closing in on a big fish. It appeared that the stars were aligning for State to land one of the most successful coaches in the country.

Jock Sutherland was a former All-American player at the University of Pittsburgh and a pupil of legendary coach Pop Warner himself. Once his college playing career ended, Sutherland signed on to play with the Massillon Lions of the Ohio League.

His pro football career in the league, which ultimately became the NFL, was short-lived. In 1919, Sutherland accepted the head coaching position at Lafayette College.

During his five years with the Leopards, Sutherland recorded a 33-8-2 mark, including a perfect 9-0 season in 1921.

When Warner retired at Pitt, Sutherland was the obvious choice to replace him. In 15 seasons at his alma mater, Sutherland won 111 games and led the Panthers to four Rose Bowl appearances, winning one. Sutherland's teams racked up six national titles during his tenure. Many considered Sutherland a Pitt lifer, and he planned to be, but the administration had other ideas.

At the end of the 1938 season, Pittsburgh Chancellor John Gabbert Bowman decided to de-emphasize football, eliminating athletic scholarships and most of the budget Sutherland depended on to field competitive teams.

Bowman gutted the proud football program with one stroke of the pen and turned it into a laughingstock. Sutherland declined to stay on under those conditions, and the Panthers paid for the decision.

Mississippi State was ready to win and win big. Sutherland was the obvious leading candidate. As Noble and Sutherland's conversations became more serious, Duke Humphrey stepped in to assure both men that the College would find the resources necessary to turn the Maroons into a winning program just as they had done under Sasse.

On March 6, 1938, the *Clarion-Ledger* ran a story announcing the hire. "Jock Sutherland is coming to Miss. State College as head football coach," the report read.

The *Ledger* referenced a February 26th meeting between Humphrey, Noble, and Sutherland in Cincinnati and shared that the new Maroon man would be signing a five-year contract with a first-year salary of $13,500, which was $500 more than he was reportedly being paid at Pitt.

Things fell apart before a parade and an introductory press conference could be planned. The only snag that could have come up, did. In Sutherland's contract with Pittsburgh, he was required to give the school two years' notice before resigning. It appeared they planned to hold him to that.

"Because of circumstances that have developed at Pittsburgh after my resignation, I feel honor bound not to accept any coaching position as much as I would like to come to Mississippi State," Sutherland reportedly told Humphrey.

A disappointed Humphrey shared, "Sutherland was satisfied with the terms of the proposal which we submitted and was hopeful that the way could be cleared for acceptance."

The turn of events was devastating. A contract had been agreed to, and favorable news had been leaked to the media. Exuberance ran throughout the fanbase, only to be shot down by powers beyond anyone's control.

The usual rumors of Noble taking over as head football coach made the rounds again. Noble called the cadence during a handful of spring practices in February. Still, he had no plans to return to the sidelines.

Well-meaning but nosey alums again pushed for Centenary's Parker. The group even invited him back for a second visit. Only this time, Noble dodged a follow-up opportunity to interview him again.

Mississippi State passed on Parker for the second time in as many years. He coached one more season at Centenary before resigning to begin a career in Louisiana's booming oil industry.

No matter his reasoning, Noble had no plans to hire Parker at State despite the urging of some well-heeled donors. It was risky, but Noble bet on himself and his expertise. That wager paid off.

Noble was a huge fan of General Robert Neyland at Tennessee, so a drive to Knoxville was in order. Noble did gauge Neyland's interest in coming to Starkville, but the conversation yielded little. However, the meeting did lead to something significant for Noble and State, which were two names.

Noble's purpose in seeking Neyland's counsel involved some background on Coach Bobby Dodd, a Georgia Tech assistant and former Tennessee Vol player. Dodd played for Neyland from 1928 to 1930. He was a highly accomplished athlete in multiple college sports. Dodd was also a hot name in every Southern coaching search during his time as a Yellow Jacket assistant.

Neyland gave Noble the thumbs up on Dodd but shared that it may be difficult to lure him away from Atlanta. He also recommended another former player doing impressive things at West Tennessee Teachers College, now known as Memphis.

Allyn McKeen played for Neyland from 1925 to 1927. After his playing days, McKeen took over the freshman football team in Knoxville before moving to Memphis as an assistant coach and seeker of an advanced degree.

With one year of coaching on his resume, McKeen worked part-time as an assistant coach at West Tennessee and studied for his law degree. He was a practicing attorney and a promising young football coach.

Shortly after Mississippi State and others formed the Southeastern Conference, the SIAA sought to expand its membership. One of the new additions was West Tennessee.

The step up in competition proved to be more than head coach Zach Curlin could handle. His squad won just one game in the new league in two seasons. Curlin continued as the school's basketball coach, but new leadership was needed in football.

McKeen's first team at West Tennessee went 3-6. Four of those six losses were decided by a single score.

In 1938, the program recorded a perfect 10-0 record and won the SIAA conference championship. The season remains the only one in school history where the team was undefeated and untied.

McKeen had proven that he could win. He had the blessing of Neyland, whom Noble respected. It appeared to be a good fit. At just 33 years of age, McKeen was hired to coach the Mississippi State football team.

Making a move to Starkville with McKeen were former Volunteer standouts, Murray Warmath and Bowden Wyatt.

"We intend to put in a permanent system of football here," Noble told various media outlets at the time. "We're glad it's the Tennessee system.

"These men were highly recommended by Coach Bob Neyland of Tennessee and the other Tennessee athletic officials. We think we have the men who will build good football teams."

Spring practices resumed when McKeen and his two accomplished assistants hit town. His early impressions of the hand he had been dealt on the returning roster were favorable, but McKeen urged fans to be patient.

"We can't get a good line on individuals until we tee off for full-speed scrimmages," McKeen told the *Clarion-Ledger*. "It will take time for the players to get accustomed to the timing, rhythm, and speed required by the system we expect to use."

While Noble and the Mississippi State administration were pleased with a coaching search that included nearly 200 names of interest, some within the fanbase panned the McKeen hire.

Some suggested that he was too young and too inexperienced. The disappointment of the Sutherland situation tainted the next name, no matter who that proved to be.

When one is promised a steak dinner and gets pork chops served, there will be a level of disappointment. The chops may hit the spot but don't taste the same when their heart is set on a juicy ribeye.

McKeen had the approval of those who signed his paychecks, but he had some work to do to pass the muster of those who helped fund them. Noble took his brand-new football mentor on tour to assist in that effort.

Once spring practice and the semester ended, several alumni gatherings were organized, allowing fans to meet and greet their new coach, including one in May at the Heidelberg Hotel in Meridian.

One of the first summer stops occurred in Vicksburg at an event organized by Warren County Alumni President "Squatty" Hall at the local YMCA. Hall was a diminutive man with a ton of passion for State sports. He wore a coat and tie, slicked down part of his hair, and smoked openly at the table while seated next to McKeen.

"Mississippi State College will place a fighting football team on the field next fall," McKeen told a packed house, according to the *Vicksburg Post*. "A team of which alumni and supporters will not be ashamed.

"Though we are facing a difficult schedule, we will center our interest not only upon beating Ole Miss but other tough teams as well."

Before turning the microphone back over to Dudy Noble, McKeen spoke about the importance of home-grown players remaining in the state and serving as great ambassadors for their communities.

"We have our ups and downs at State," Noble told the crowd. "But believe our downs will eventually be converted to touchdowns. However, it will take time, work, patience, and the right kind of attitude."

There were stops on the Mississippi Gulf Coast, Jackson, Tupelo, and parts in between.

When the traveling party reached the Mississippi Delta, they were honored guests of the Greenwood Rotary Club. Noble and McKeen again requested patience.

"We hope to have a good team next year, but as of yet, I haven't seen the boys under fire," McKeen was reported to have said by the *Greenwood Commonwealth*. "We are not only building for 1939, but for 1940."

An alumni function even back then centered around facilities and requests for donations.

"Athletics at Mississippi State have paid their own way so far," Noble said. "While we have very good facilities, we are trying to improve them and hope to do so soon."

As the 10-game schedule was announced, there was a collective wince for supporters of Mississippi State football.

Outside of the season opener against Howard, there were few sure wins on the slate. Some wondered if McKeen would win a conference game in year one.

Week two had the Maroons facing Arkansas in Memphis in the second meeting between the two schools.

Road trips to Florida and Auburn followed before the Maroons returned home to face Southwestern Tennessee, a team that beat them the previous year under Nelson.

The final five games saw the squad travel to Alabama, LSU, and Ole Miss around home dates against Birmingham Southern and Millsaps.

"I had a fellow to ask me what were the tough spots in our schedule," McKeen told the *Clarion Ledger*. "My answer to him and anyone else, is look at that schedule. They all look tough to me."

Despite the perceived difficulty of the schedule, State went to work in week one against Howard. The Maroons were without star halfback Frank Chambers, so McKeen needed someone else to carry the rushing load. He elected to go with a two-pronged attack featuring Harvey "Boots" Johnson and Billy Jefferson.

The plan worked as Johnson and Jefferson ran wild in a seven-touchdown performance for the offense. Elrod and the State defense were especially stingy on the ground, allowing just one rushing first down in the 45-0 shellacking.

Against a heavily favored Arkansas squad that featured one of the top passing games in America, State caught a pair of breaks.

Chambers was back in action after recovering from an infection in his leg, and the rain fell and fell and fell. The slippery sod worked in the Maroons' favor as they sought to employ a ground attack.

McKeen dialed up some trickery on a fake punt from Chambers that ended 70 yards later in the end zone. The pass back on the extra point was muffed due to the slick football.

Arkansas tried to answer, but State's Hunter Cohern picked off a pass and rumbled 25 yards for another score. All told, Maroon defenders hauled in six Kay Eakin passes, with Jack Nix getting his hands on four.

The final score came when Johnson powered through for six. The extra point was good, and the score settled at 19-0. It was a major upset and one worthy of good press clippings. The Memphis *Commercial Appeal* ran a game recap on the paper's front page.

The kicking opportunities against Florida were more successful on dry terrain and warmer weather. State scored two rushing touchdowns and converted both points after attempts in a 14-0 victory.

One of the most significant moments in the game came just before the halftime intermission. Florida had a first-and-goal situation inside the Maroon five-yard line, but Elrod and the gang forced them to turn it over on downs just inches from the goal line.

Now 3-0, football fever was once again spreading through Starkville. A trip to Birmingham to play Auburn drew over 10,000 fans.

A controversial referee decision marred the game. Late in the second quarter, State put together a long drive that reached Auburn's 24-yard line.

State ran for eight yards on first down, setting up a second-and-two situation at the Tiger 16. The second-down pass attempt fell incomplete. McKeen called for a running play on third down, which went nowhere.

Just as State was deciding to go for it or kick the field goal, the officials signaled first down Auburn. Despite the protest from the State bench, Auburn was given the football, and the Maroons shorted a down. The game went to the half scoreless.

McKeen's group had their chances but kept fumbling the football. That sloppiness finally caught up with them after State fumbled the second half's opening kickoff, with Auburn recovering.

Auburn cashed in with a 30-yard touchdown pass. The conversion made it 7-0. State outgained the Tigers by nearly 100 yards on the day but kept shooting themselves in the foot by putting the ball on the turf. The game ended without another score.

The Maroons posted their fourth of six shutouts of the season when they blanked Southwestern Tennessee 37-0 on Homecoming.

A confident State team headed over to Tuscaloosa and Denny Stadium for another chance to turn back the Tide, and they nearly did.

Alabama scored on a short touchdown pass to take an early 7-0 lead, but the Maroons nearly answered right back before the half. Led by center Shag Goolsby, the State ground game went to work getting deep into Alabama territory.

McKeen elected to go for it on fourth down from the Alabama ten-yard line, but the Tide defense forced a turnover on downs.

It was nip and tuck the rest of the way, but neither team could score. Number 20 Alabama came away with a narrow victory.

State won in a 28-0 cakewalk over Birmingham Southern, with McKeen emptying the bench late in the game.

A trip to Baton Rouge followed, and special teams proved to be the difference. State missed a pair of extra points, and so did the Tigers. As LSU attempted a point-after to take a fourth-quarter lead, the Maroons blocked it to keep the game tied at 12-12.

State took the ensuing kickoff and began a march to gridiron glory. On fourth down from the LSU 16, State's Wilbur Dees connected on the winning field goal. The Tigers' final attempts to get anything going as the clock ran down proved futile.

The Maroons scored at will the following week at home against Millsaps. It was a 40-0 browbeating, and the third and fourth teams played the second half.

Ole Miss and the Battle for the Golden Egg awaited in the season finale. The Rebels entered the game with a 7-1 record. It was one of those years where the game mattered more than simple bragging rights.

It was also a chance for the Maroons, who had been thumped in Starkville by their rivals the previous year, to exact revenge.

Over 20,000 fans filed into Hemingway Stadium, making the 1939 Egg Bowl the most attended college football game in Mississippi history.

McKeen's offense had spent much of the year plowing opponents into the ground using a rough-and-tumble running attack. The first-year State coach tried to play against his own tendencies and came out throwing against Ole Miss.

Things went well for a few downs, but Boots Johnson threw an interception that Ole Miss captain Bill Schneller returned 32 yards for a score. The extra point attempt failed.

Following a second-quarter interception by Billy Jefferson, State tied the game at 6-6 on a short run from Johnson, who atoned for his earlier miscue.

In the fourth, McKeen returned to what State did best: overpowering its opponents. On the decisive drive, after a mix-and-match of runs and throws, Jefferson connected for a touchdown pass to give State the lead for good.

Just for good measure, the Maroons tacked on one final score. Following a stop by the State defense, Ole Miss punted for no yards. Two plays later, Boots Johnson was back in the end zone to cap the scoring at 18-6.

"Naturally, I'm pleased," McKeen said after the game. "Our boys were in fine condition and got stronger as the game went along; that's the payoff."

With the win, the Golden Egg was headed back to Starkville. In his first season as State head man, McKeen turned in an 8-2 record with two narrow losses to Auburn and Alabama.

A handful of plays prevented McKeen from winning an SEC Championship in his first season. Big things were coming for State—big things indeed, and they were coming soon.

Chapter 18

Champions

Heading into 1940, Mississippi State football was thriving. Dudy Noble's decision to hire Allyn McKeen earned him great respect among the Maroon and White faithful. Even some chronically negative critics chose to embrace optimism. The Maroons were performing well and showed potential for greatness. With a big season in 1939, McKeen and the new-look gridiron gang were ahead of schedule. An 8-2 record against a bear of a schedule had fans believing that more was possible.

When spring practice opened on February 12th, the team had considerable expectations. The freshmen reported first, and the full varsity, filled with returning lettermen, hit the field a few days later.

Despite the epidemic of football fever, McKeen did his best to temper expectations when he made the pre-season rounds to visit with alums.

"We have five or six teams just about in our class on that 1940 schedule," McKeen said, according to the *Clarion-Ledger*. "We are, under the law of averages, due to losing about as many as we win in well-matched games. If we're unlucky, we might lose four or five.

"Don't put too much pressure on our boys. Don't blame the boys unduly for the mistakes that they are bound to make."

The Maroons played the University of Florida in Gainesville for the second straight season. In 1940, the contest served as the season opener.

The Gators, led by first-year coach Tom Lieb, got things off on the right foot when they opened the scoring following a big special teams play. With State backed up, Gator end Fergie Ferguson blocked a punt. Florida took over at the Maroon 15 and scored a play later to take a 7-0 lead.

Just before the half ended, State had one of those moments that made it seem like it wasn't their day in the Sunshine State. The Maroons were in a first-and-goal situation but were turned away after four straight tries for a score were stuffed. The ball went over on downs after an incompletion from the two-yard line.

McKeen refused to lose and rallied the troops during the intermission. State scored 25 unanswered points to cruise to a 25-7 win. The Maroon defense dominated, holding the Gators to just seven yards rushing and three first downs.

The win over Florida left Boots Johnson hobbled. As State welcomed Southwestern Louisiana to Starkville, some questions about his health arose.

Johnson lined up at halfback on the first drive and helped orchestrate an 81-yard scoring drive to take a 7-0 advantage.

Jefferson plunged in from the one-yard line in the third quarter. The extra point try was no good, so State took a 13-0 lead into the final period of play.

With the game all but decided, Johnson re-entered the game and found John Black for a long catch and run to put the game away at 20-0.

Once again, State's defensive effort was outstanding, especially on the ground. Southwestern had -2 yards rushing and only earned one first down.

Now 2-0, the Maroons traveled to Legion Field in Birmingham to take on Auburn, the regular measuring stick. It had been a decade since State knocked off the Tigers, and many were convinced this was the year for a breakthrough win.

Johnson went to work early in this one and found Walter Craig for a 21-yard touchdown through the air. The extra point was good, and State had the lead.

Buddy Elrod and the Mississippi State defense kept Auburn off the field much of the day by mixing up their fronts and, thus, the Tiger blocking schemes.

Finally, with just under five minutes to play, Auburn put together their only significant drive of the day that found paydirt after a 73-yard possession. The extra point proved true, and the game was tied at 7-7.

State got the ball back with about a minute to play and nearly won. On the game's final play, Johnson hit "Blondy" Black for a 46-yard gain. With just one man to beat, Black tried to make a move to free himself but slipped and fell as time expired. State would have to settle for a tie.

The Maroons blew out Howard a week later 41-7 before making the trip to Raleigh, North Carolina, to battle NC State for the third time in school history.

State had to come from behind twice to ensure a victory. The Wolfpack took a 3-0 lead in the first and then led 10-7 at the break.

The second half was all Maroons as Black scored, and Granville Harrison found the end zone twice in the 26-10 win.

State's undefeated streak was in jeopardy the following week against a surprisingly tough Southwestern Tennessee squad.

Johnson and Harrison handled the scoring honors in the 13-0 victory. Still, one of the game's most significant plays came when the great Blondy Black ran down Winston Cocke from Clarksdale, Mississippi, on what looked like a sure kickoff return for a touchdown. With Cocke breaking into the open field, Black caught and slung him down at the State 20. The Maroon defense took over and preserved the shutout.

Now 5-0-1, State made its annual trip to Baton Rouge to play LSU. The Tigers planned to make someone other than Boots Johnson beat them. That strategy worked, but perhaps not in the way they had hoped.

Jefferson took over at halfback when Johnson needed a breather. Jefferson hit Craig for a 40-yard touchdown pass to draw first blood, 7-0.

Jefferson stayed in the game on the next offensive possession and tossed a scoring pass to Wilbur Dees to give State some breathing room. This time, the point after failed.

LSU scored early in the fourth to make it a one-score game at 13-7, but the Maroons had some killer instinct.

Jefferson threw his third touchdown pass of the day to put LSU away. This time, Jefferson connected with Harrison, who found the end zone. The extra point was good.

The State defense removed all doubt as the Tigers tried to climb back into the game. Harrison and Homer Jones came up with a big sack for a safety to cap the scoring at 22-7.

State rolled over a hapless Millsaps squad the following week 46-13. The Maroons went into the Egg Bowl with a 7-0-1 record. #11 Ole Miss was also playing fine football and prepared to invade Starkville with an 8-1 record. For the second straight year, both teams were putting together outstanding seasons.

Before a rain-soaked crowd, State took an early advantage 7-0 after Toxie Tullos banged in from short yardage.

The Maroons added a second score in the second quarter following an interception. State made quick work of the drive and found Black for a touchdown reception, but the point after was no good.

Down 13-0 at halftime, Ole Miss needed a stop. The Rebels kicked off to open the third quarter, and the game ended right there. Dees returned that kick down to the Ole Miss six-yard line. Boots Johnson took it in from there a play later. The kick was blocked this time, but with the score sitting at 19-0, it was time to start shining up the Golden Egg.

The Maroon defense picked off three fourth-quarter passes to preserve the victory and the shutout.

Ole Miss head coach Harry Mehre was gracious in defeat when speaking with the *Clarion-Ledger*, "They were just too good for us. Mississippi State is the best team we have played all season. They are too big, too strong, too fast for us."

Following the post-game handshake, McKeen told reporters, "I thought they played the finest game today that I have ever seen a Mississippi State team play."

The great Maroon revenge tour made its next stop in Tuscaloosa to play the #17 Alabama Crimson Tide.

State struck fast scoring before two minutes had elapsed when, who else, Boots Johnson put the ball into the end zone. The point after was good, and the Maroons led 7-0.

Alabama put together five drives deep into Maroon territory, but State turned them away each time with no points.

Charles Yancey proved to be the hero. With Alabama trying to mount a comeback, Yancey picked off a pass and returned it to the Tide 23-yard line. McKeen let Yancey finish what he started by calling his number on the next play from scrimmage. Yancey outran the Alabama defense to put the game away at 13-0.

Shortly after the game went final, Mississippi State accepted a bid to play Georgetown in the Orange Bowl.

The match-up boasted 38,301 fans in attendance, making it the most well-attended game in Florida at the time.

The Hoyas, coached by Jack Hagerty, had lost just one game in three years. Georgetown went undefeated in 1938 and 1939, suffering just one tie during that '39 season. Their lone regular season loss in 1940 came to eventual national champion Boston College.

As they had throughout the season, State struck first. The initial Maroon points came courtesy of a blocked punt. Hunter Corhern broke through the Hoya line and got in front of the kick that ricocheted skyward. State's John Tripson skied over the traffic and nabbed the ball midair for the score. The point-after was good.

Georgetown looked able to pull even, but a long pass play that settled at the State four-yard line was called back as an illegal forward pass. The Maroons held from there.

As the second quarter opened, State was on the move. On fourth down in the red zone, McKeen dialed up a pass play intended for Black. The attempt fell incomplete, but the Hoyas were flagged for pass interference.

Jefferson scored from two yards out. Sonny Bruce proved true on the extra-point attempt to make it 14-0.

The Hoyas scored on the next possession to pull within seven points, 14-7. Georgetown seemed to have made it more interesting later in the fourth.

An impressive drive got as deep as the Mississippi State six-yard line, but Buddy Elrod led the Maroons on a goal-line stand. The last play of the drive was an incomplete pass that sailed into the stands.

When the final horn sounded, Mississippi State emerged victorious as the Orange Bowl champions.

Georgetown outgained State on the ground and in the air in a game marred by several penalties. The squads evenly split 150 yards of infractions.

When the game reached the final, organizers and media criticized the officials. McKeen chose to take the high road.

"I'm too limp to say much," McKeen told the *Miami Herald*. "Georgetown was the toughest outfit we played all season. Jack Hagerty really has a fine team. It was a clean game, but I'm sorry that penalties played such a big part in the outcome.

"I believe one of our touchdowns and Georgetown's score were partially caused by rules infractions. That was a scrapping team if I ever saw one."

The game and the season were over. Mississippi State held the Golden Egg for the second straight season and an Orange Bowl Trophy.

That tie with Auburn cost State a share of the Southeastern Conference title. Tennessee went 10-0 and represented the league in the Sugar Bowl.

When the final Associated Press college football poll was released, Mississippi State was listed at #9.

That crop of young Bull Pups who cut their college canines under Dudy Noble's direction in 1937 turned in the only undefeated season in Mississippi State history in 1940 as seniors.

Many wondered what McKeen would do for an encore. The 1941 squad had some challenges replacing many of the top players from the previous season. Eight of the starting 11 had graduated, and 16 seniors left the program following the '40 football campaign. Yet, McKeen had some building blocks to work with for the '41 season.

Tackle Bill Arnold was as pure a path paver to ever suit up for Dear Ole State. Arnold's task that season was to open holes for the offense's focal point, Blondy Black.

As a sophomore, Black played second fiddle to Boots Johnson, but as a junior, it was Black's time to shine. Known as one of the fastest men in the Southeastern Conference, Black was a rising star on the gridiron and the track cinders.

When State opened the six-week spring practice sessions on February 13th, the Maroons' coaching staff had their work cut out. Expectations were high, but experienced returners were low.

As Noble, McKeen, and the football staff made the alumni chicken dinner circuit, there wasn't a lot of fiery rhetoric shared. McKeen was largely subdued, telling supporters that he would have a better handle on the quality of the team once he got into the fall.

On April 5th, the spring game was played at Scott Field. There wasn't a ton of fanfare surrounding the scrimmage, which signaled the end of spring practice. Some locals attended the game and gave Black rave reviews when the Maroons were able to block for him.

While some felt McKeen's third team would be as good as his 1940 Orange Bowl team, others expressed concern and steeled their nerves for at least a few losses.

As the dog days of summer gave way to the turning leaves of autumn, the prognosticators were set to put their forecasts to the test.

The '41 season opened with a dogfight against Florida. Both teams turned the ball over several times. State fumbled it away four times, and the Gators pounced on it each time.

The Maroons also threw a pair of interceptions, bringing their total number of turnovers to six. Fortunately for State, the defensive effort worked both ways, as Florida was held to just six first downs and less than 100 yards of offense.

Late in the fourth quarter, Florida was forced to punt. Black hauled in the punt and returned it 45 yards for the score. Those points were the only ones posted by either team, as State won 6-0.

Another slugfest that featured little offensive artistry took place in week two in Tuscaloosa against Alabama.

The two teams battled to a scoreless stalemate in the first half despite State controlling much of the time of possession.

In the third quarter, the Maroons scored mainly thanks to another strong play on special teams.

Homer Jones overwhelmed the Alabama line and got his hands on a punt, which he recovered at the Crimson Tide 23-yard line. Just three plays later, Billy Murphy connected with "Tut" Patterson, who made the reception at the three and leaped into the end zone. The extra point was good, 7-0 State.

Elbert Corley set up the second and final touchdown of the game when he snared an errant pass intended for Alabama All-American end Holt Rast for an interception and returned it inside the Tide's 10-yard line.

State cashed in three plays later when Black ran a sweep off the left side for the score. The conversion was good to cap the day's scoring at 14-0 in favor of Mississippi State.

Nearly 30,000 fans flocked to Baton Rouge to see McKeen's men battle with the Bayou Bengals. Another sloppy game with little in the way of offense ensued.

State had one promising drive that reached inside the LSU 10, but a fumble ended the possession. That was the closest that either team would come to scoring in a 0-0 tie. The *Shreveport Times* called the game a "major upset" in favor of the Tigers.

Week four saw Union come to Starkville for what amounted to a bloodletting. State led 21-0 at the break and then scored 35 points in the third quarter to cruise to a 56-7 win. Seven different Maroons scored touchdowns. Black had a pair.

In their first game of the year as a ranked team, #17 State took a rather workman approach and knocked off Southwestern TN by 20-6 to advance the Maroons' record to 4-0-1.

Auburn had been a thorn in the side of the State football program for years, but Blondy Black returned the favor when he got the chance.

Black outgained Auburn alone on the ground, rushing for 156 yards to 130 total yards for the opposition in a 14-7 victory, the first for #15 State over the Tigers since 1930.

Birmingham News sports editor "Zipp" Newman referred to Black as "the Blond Dragon" in his game recap.

The Maroons put their 21-game unbeaten streak on the line when they hit the road to take on undefeated Duquesne.

State looked like they would strike first, but Black fumbled at the Dukes' 11-yard line. The Maroons would regret not finishing that drive.

Duquesne went to work and picked up a big gainer on what was described as a "hidden ball" play. The descriptors of the day didn't paint the picture as if it was a ball truly hidden under a jersey, an old trick play dating back to the early days of Pop Warner. It may have been.

Duquesne added a third-quarter field goal to push their lead to 9-0. The final points of the 16-0 victory were recorded in the fourth quarter. It simply wasn't the Maroons' Day.

Back home, the boys in maroon and white got back on track with a 49-6 thrashing of Millsaps.

Once again, the Battle for the Golden Egg had bowl implications, but for State, the chance to win the SEC title hung in the balance.

Ole Miss was 6-1-1 on the season and a solid match for a State squad with the same record. The Egg winner would have bragging rights and be in line for a bowl trip.

The Maroons' only loss had come to a nonconference foe, so they were the lone team in the SEC to remain undefeated in conference play.

Like it had been much of the year against major football foes, State took part in a defensive struggle.

The lone touchdown of the game came in the second quarter.

Thankfully for those cheering for State College, the man crossing the goal line wore maroon.

After a short punt return, Collins Wohner found Kermit Davis for a 31-yard reception inside the Ole Miss 40.

A short running play followed, but excitement was on the horizon. State reserve quarterback Jennings Moates ran a quarterback sneak off left guard and broke free into the Ole Miss secondary, and 37 yards later, Moates was in the Hemingway Stadium end zone.

The Rebels nearly tied the game on a fourth-quarter touchdown catch and run, but the play was called back to the State 47-yard line because the receiver ran out of bounds.

From there, State stiffened and got the stop they needed to return the ball to their offense. Black salted much of the final quarter away but had to punt the ball back to Ole Miss with just over two minutes to play.

The Rebels attempted a drive for glory, but a long pass inside the State 20 was intercepted by Black, removing all hope for the Rebels and granting State its third straight win in the rivalry.

The game was a huge deal around the South and was syndicated in several states by over a dozen radio stations.

Ole Miss's loss ended its season. It was denied an invitation to the Orange Bowl.

Days later, McKeen signed a five-year contract to keep him in Starkville. Noble even ponied up raises and new deals for the entire staff.

Despite winning the SEC title, State didn't participate in a bowl game. Maroon officials had agreed to a road game with San Francisco on December 6th. Invitations for the postseason had to be extended before State's season ended.

It was a mistake, but some things that didn't involve football were about to change worldwide.

State dispatched the San Francisco Dons relatively easily. Black ran wild in the 26-13 win. In the post-game, Don tackle Doc Haley told the *San Francisco Examiner* that tackling Black "was like putting your face in a meat grinder."

Mississippi State's record was 8-1-1. The Maroons earned a #16 ranking in the final poll, a byproduct of not playing a bowl game. Despite winning the SEC title, voters largely snubbed State.

Following their win at Kezar Stadium in San Francisco, the State football coaches and players took a field trip to Los Angeles to finish their West Coast excursion.

After a trip to see Hollywood, many didn't return to Starkville for a long time. Soon after the team reached Los Angeles, the players learned of the attack on Pearl Harbor. Every able-bodied young man with a heart and a love for his homeland volunteered to join the service.

Following graduation, several Maroon football players traded in gridiron glory for service to Uncle Sam. Arnold and his close friend, Harold Grove, were among them.

WWII was raging. The United States had been drawn into it due to the cowardly attack on Pearl Harbor. There was a call to arms for Americans. State College men answered.

Chapter 19

Uncommon Men

Mississippi State football had experienced its zenith under Allyn McKeen. The Maroons lost just three games in the first three seasons with McKeen at the helm. The program won its first New Year's Day Bowl game and collected its first Southeastern Conference championship in football in 1940 and 1941, respectively.

With the world at war for the second time in just over three decades, college football paled in comparison. Still, the public clamored for more. Life went on in the United States, even with many of the nation's best and brightest fighting on the front lines to defeat Japan and Nazi Germany.

Quibbling over playcalling and rivalry games provided a much-needed distraction for a nation that waited with bated breath for a letter home from a soldier fighting for peace in the European and Pacific theatre.

College enrollment declined as young men elected to enter military service rather than enroll in college classes. With the decreased enrollment, the talent pool for college football grew somewhat shallow.

State was riding high and winning remarkably, but many wondered if the trajectory under McKeen was sustainable given the circumstances.

As the alumni events popped up around the state of Mississippi, McKeen became a little more reclusive. He was a well-liked coach who had taken the Maroons to heights never seen before, but McKeen grew tired of what took him away from campus and his team.

McKeen just wanted to coach football. The glad-handing and fake civilities of another dinner on the road bored him. He was responsible for doing some of that but opted out of those events when he could.

McKeen made an annual pilgrimage to Jackson to meet with central Mississippi donors. One of the most prominent figures within that group, and the entire Mississippi State fan base was Bob Sanders.

Sanders came from wealth but made plenty of his own as a textile manufacturer in Kosciusko. He was also a former Mississippi A&M quarterback who followed Noble's footsteps for the Aggies.

Also, Jackson Touchdown Club president, Sanders, was as well-heeled as they came. Sanders flew to games on his shiny red personal plane when State played football on the road.

Sanders gave a fortune to Mississippi State. His love for the school and its athletic programs was unsurpassed.

When Sanders wanted Dudy Noble, McKeen, and the football staff to break bread with him and his powerful friends, the Maroon contingent loaded up and made the trip.

Sanders was Mississippi State athletics' best friend at the time. When funds needed to be raised for various projects on campus, Sanders got a call. Not only would he write checks, but he would also influence others to do the same.

As a result of his support, the Mississippi State football function in Jackson became an annual event. McKeen might opt out of other "rah-rah" parties, but he showed up when it was time to put his feet under Sanders' table.

In January of 1942, McKeen returned to the Delta to meet with a group in Greenville. It was his first visit with that group since his initial goodwill tour after taking the job.

The Delta had power and some influential alumni. Staying in good graces with the state's agricultural leaders was essential.

Noble also made the trip, which gave him a chance to spend some time with his younger brother, Pick Noble, who was coaching the backfield at Greenville High School.

Over 100 State supporters gathered at the Greenville Hotel to hear McKeen and Noble speak. The stress of the war was evident throughout the country, prompting McKeen to suggest that college athletics could benefit all involved.

"Football benefits a man because it teaches him to keep fighting with a level head and to never quit," the *Delta Democrat Times* recounted. "The United States is a sporting nation and a competitive nation."

With a roster without many stars, the 1942 season looked to be a rebuilding one for McKeen. When asked about the challenge ahead, McKeen said, "We may be good losers, but we don't like it."

The season started well enough as the Maroons routed Union 35-2. In an example of silver lining hometown journalism, *The Jackson Sun* (Jackson, TN) headline read, "Union Collects Safety Off Southeastern Champions as Casey Out-Punts Maroons."

Lamar Blount was one of four Maroons to reach the end zone as State scored in every quarter. Blount had a pair of touchdown runs in the conquest.

Alabama got the better of State in week two after blowing open a scoreless game in the third when Tide star Russ Craft went for three touchdowns.

The Maroons avoided a shutout in the fourth with a touchdown pass that saw the point after fail. State earned just three first downs in the game. Blondy Black was held to a negative one-yard in the 21-6 defeat.

McKeen's offense sputtered the following week with a 16-6 loss to LSU. State got out early with a touchdown pass from Blount to "Tut" Patterson. The kick was wide, which kept the game at 6-0.

From there, it was all Tigers. LSU took a 7-6 lead into the half and added another touchdown and a safety in the second half to bring the game final.

Black wasn't mentioned prominently in the season's first three games, as he did his best to play through injury. The roster wasn't devoid of talent, but with Black less than 100%, it wasn't easy to get the train moving.

Now 1-2, State headed to Nashville to face off against #12 ranked Vanderbilt. Few gave the Maroons a chance to win, but Black was rounding back into form.

In the second quarter of a scoreless affair, Black fielded a Vandy punt and returned it deep into Commodore territory. Four plays later, Black plowed into the end zone to give State the lead.

It didn't take long for the Maroons to build upon the advantage. Raymond Ray jumped on a Commodore fumble on Vandy's side of the 50.

McKeen dialed up a double pass from Billy Murphy to Claiborne Bishop to George Varnado, who found paydirt.

In the second half, Jennings Moates scored on a quarterback sneak. Eagle Mautlich returned a Vandy punt 65 yards for a score. The capper came on a Robert Pillow plunge late in the fourth from one yard out.

The final score read: Mississippi State 33, Vanderbilt 0.

Despite having a 2-2 record, the Maroons entered the polls at #16 the next week as they traveled to Florida.

State drew first blood after Murphy hit Johnny Grace on a big gainer down to the Gator two. Murphy did the scoring honors to make it 6-0.

Florida pulled even at 6-6, but then Black took over and led State on a scoring drive that ended with a touchdown toss to Davis. The extra point failed, giving State a 12-6 lead as the teams prepared for the fourth quarter.

State added a pair of touchdowns in the final period to pull away. Florida scored a touchdown of no consequence to end the day's scoring at 26-12 in favor of the Maroons.

The win was the seventh straight for State over the Gators, the longest winning streak of the Maroon side in the long-standing series.

On Halloween, State, and Auburn met at Legion Field in Birmingham during a driving rainstorm. The rain was so severe in the first half that observers could not see who had the ball.

A break in the weather came in the third quarter. Due to the conditions, McKeen had ridden his running game much of the contest. When the chance came to strike through the air, the Maroons did.

Following solid ground gains, Murphy connected with Blount on a 15-yard touchdown pass. The conversion failed.

State held the Auburn offense to under 100 yards, all of which came on the ground. The Tigers had five rushing first downs and completed just one of a dozen passes attempted, which netted a loss of three yards.

The winning streak against SEC opponents continued a week later when State slipped by Tulane in front of a homecoming crowd of over 28,000 in New Orleans.

The game was nip-and-tuck and boiled down to a special teams mistake. Tulane was forced to punt deep within its territory. The Green Wave got the kick away, but it traveled only 11 yards.

State took full advantage and put Black in the game even though he was still battling some lower leg injuries. Black picked up a first down on his first carry. Fullback Charles Yancey followed with a chain-moving burst of his own. The drive ended with Blount plowing in for the game's only score.

The Maroons won 7-0 despite being rather sheepish at finishing drives. State had a chance to get some real separation following a 59-yard fake punt from Black, but the drive stalled.

State stepped out of SEC play the following week as they welcomed Duquesne to town for homecoming.

The Maroons took a 7-0 lead on a short Billy Murphy run off center. The rest of the half was a grind for both teams that couldn't generate any offense.

In the third quarter, the Dukes made a big stop and appeared in great shape to get a good field position following a State punt.

As the pass back to Black, who was in his own end zone, was completed, the Duquesne coverage team retreated to set up a return. As Black saw their backs turned, he took off behind them with the ball.

Before the Dukes realized what was happening, the fleet-footed Black had eluded them and sprinted 97 yards for a touchdown. The PAT was good, and State led 14-0.

Duquesne wouldn't go quietly. They got on the board with a one-yard run to cap an 85-yard drive that netted a touchdown. The extra-point try failed, but the game was still in question.

The Maroons answered right back in just a pair of plays. Kermit Davis made a great kickoff return to get the ball across midfield. A play later, Blount found a streaking Davis, who hauled the pass in and won the footrace to the end zone.

Sophomore George McIngvale got in the game late and scored a touchdown of his own to put the game away 28-6.

Since dropping back-to-back games, McKeen's men had won five straight while holding their opponents to a combined 18 points. State posted three shutouts in those five games.

The Battle for the Golden Egg approached. The 40th renewal of the rivalry saw the Rebels limp into the contest. Ole Miss was winless in the SEC and owned just two wins over Western Kentucky State and Memphis State on the season.

On the other hand, the Maroons felt better about themselves as they had strung together some impressive wins. Most expected McKeen to lead State to another rivalry win over the hated Rebels.

The Maroons saw a pair of promising first-quarter drives end with fumbles on the Rebels' side of the field. Ole Miss, led by freshman quarterback John "Sonny Boy" Shelby, scored first to take a 7-0 lead.

Black evened things up just before the half with a three-yard run that capped an impressive drive where he distributed the ball to a handful of playmakers.

State broke the 7-7 tie early in the third following an Ole Miss fumble on the second-half opening kickoff. The Maroons took over around the Rebel 25. Murphy connected with Blount to set State up at the Ole Miss one-yard line. Murphy pushed ahead for the final real estate to make it 13-7. The try after failed.

State pulled away early in the fourth on a Black touchdown run. The extra point was good, which pushed State ahead 20-7. That 13-point margin was short-lived. Ole Miss went right back to work behind Shelby, who had put the ball in the end zone. The PAT was no good, but the Rebels were within a touchdown at 20-13.

The Rebel exuberance lasted for about ten more seconds. Black, who ran a 9.6 100-yard dash, had tired of the competition and essentially ended it with a 95-yard kickoff return for a touchdown. The State lead swelled to 14 points at 27-13 with the extra point.

Shelby did his best to spark a comeback, but Bishop intercepted him, who returned it to the Ole Miss 12-yard line. Blount scored a play later. The conversion proved accurate, and State led in a "laugher" 34-13.

Black was the hero with three touchdowns in the game. The victory was the fourth straight for State in the rivalry with Ole Miss, making McKeen a perfect 4-0 against the Rebels.

In the season's final game, San Francisco made the return trip of the two-game agreement with Mississippi State. The site of the game was Crump Stadium in Memphis.

It was supposed to be a well-attended game, but Mother Nature had something to say. Rain soaked the playing surface and continued through the contest on a cold winter's day. Approximately 250 people attended.

The unsettled terrain wreaked havoc on the Don offense, featuring motion and quick dashes. McKeen's north and south running attack was better suited for the conditions, and it showed.

Blount scored with a short run to the end zone, capping State's first successful possession. As one would imagine, the point after was an adventure, barely getting off the ground.

Murphy got into the end zone in the second quarter to build what appeared to be an unsurmountable lead at 12-0.

State ran for 306 yards on the day. Seventy-six came on a thrilling Black run for a score in the third quarter. Miraculously the point after was good to bring the count to 19-0.

USF got on the board late to bring the game final at 19-7 in favor of the Maroons. A half dozen Dons were injured in the game due to the combination of the conditions and the three-headed ground assault of Blondy Black, Eagle Mautlich, and Spook Murphy. State attempted just one pass in the game, and it was completed for a 34-yard gain.

Despite an 8-2 record, State didn't get a bowl invite. There were still only five bowl games at the time. The Maroons finished fourth in the SEC and 18th in the polls.

Alabama, Georgia, Georgia Tech, and Tennessee were all in the top ten, and each got to play in one of the New Year's Day Bowl games.

In 1943, only five Southeastern Conference programs fielded teams. Some have suggested a lack of players, but that isn't true.

At Mississippi State, scrub and club football continued. Many players were too young for military service, so they remained in school and worked to improve at sports.

The state college board of Mississippi suspended all varsity sports for all instate colleges for what was expected to be the "duration" of the war in 1943. While the prohibition on college sports was expected, the official mandate came down in June following the end of the academic calendar.

Georgia, Georgia Tech, LSU, Tulane, and Vanderbilt continued their programs during the '43 season. Tech won the league championship, for whatever that's worth. They went on to play in the Sugar Bowl and defeat Tulsa.

That year, Vanderbilt didn't play a single SEC game, Georgia didn't win one, and the two Louisiana schools finished .500 in league play.

The only game that involved Mississippi State that year was an impromptu two-hand touch game in Miami, Florida. Football alums from State and Georgia Tech who were enlisted in the Army and Air Force played a game called the "Jeep Bowl" just for fun.

Eagle Mautlich played in that game. Jimmy Livingstone did as well and played barefoot. You can take the boys out of the deep south, but you can't take the deep south out of the boys. They were looking to settle some old college scores before they shipped off to fight a real war.

In many respects, the Jeep Bowl is important. The game lasted for a couple of get-togethers and never went to the final. It's surreal to consider that college-aged boys were taken right off the football field and thrust into a World War.

Before they left to face off with trained killers and madmen, they decided to play a football game on the beach in South Florida to feel like kids again. For many, it was the last football game they ever played. Some didn't make it back to school. Some didn't make it back to the States. Some didn't make it back alive.

They went from fighting for first downs to fighting Nazi and Japanese Imperialism, from grinding on the gridiron to stamping out genocide, and from battling foes from other schools to defeating pure unadulterated evil.

The task charged to those young men was an enormous burden. Considering the fate many of them faced, it causes the throat to close and the eyes to water. They were uncommon men.

Jennings Moates, the hero of the 1941 Egg Bowl, joined the Marines and trained at Paris Island along with Lamar Blount and Billy Murphy before deployment. Moates was later awarded a Purple Heart for his service and sacrifice after being shot by a Japanese sniper in Okinawa.

Some members of the State football staff were even pressed into military service. Murray Warmath and Bowden Wyatt enlisted and served as ensigns with the United States Navy.

While Dudy Noble had the business of Mississippi State athletics to attend, the war was also very personal. Noble's half-brother, Cary, was a U.S. Army's First Infantry Division member.

When the beaches were stormed at Normandy in 1945, the younger Noble was one of those with boots on French soil seeking to bring liberty to those engulfed in the war.

As the calendar flipped over to 1944, at least nine schools that made up the Southeastern Conference planned to play some form of football in the fall.

The three schools still considering their options were Florida, Mississippi State, and Ole Miss. The two Mississippi schools wanted to play but were at the mercy of the state college board.

The good news was that the tide was turning within the Magnolia State. State senators Linton Bryant Porter of Morton and Burton Ralph McMillan of Kosciusko led the charge to bring football back to Mississippi.

McMillan and Porter introduced a joint resolution to reinstate football in January 1944. Senator Oscar Wolfe of Ducan referred the matter to committee, and the wheels were in motion.

As the measure was being considered, Florida announced it would field a team that year, leaving State and Ole Miss as the only SEC teams without a firm commitment to play.

The resolution passed the state senate with just three votes of opposition—Senators William Fletcher Gore (Sturgis), H. Thomas Smith (Oxford) and Willie Coy Wallis (Ripley) all cast dissenting ballots.

"I vote no," Gore told the *Clarion-Ledger*. "As I could not get any enjoyment out of watching 4fs [inability to meet physical, mental or moral standards] push a football over the field while our sons are pushing Japs out of foxholes."

Complicating matters was a new man in the Governor's office and a freshly appointed state college board. Thomas Bailey was the 48th Governor of Mississippi and had to fill out his staff.

Despite widespread support around the state, the matter lingered. Call it red tape or just a question of doing the right thing; the measure was stuck in the big wheels of state government. There was some chatter during April that once the State College Board met in May, the proposal would be discussed officially.

On May 18, 1944, the Mississippi State College Board voted unanimously to reinstate football, allowing Mississippi State and Ole Miss to schedule games and resume varsity practices.

Just over a month later, Dudy Noble revealed that the Maroons would play a seven-game schedule for the 1944 season. State later added an eighth opponent just before the season began to serve as the opener.

With many of the players from the 1942 roster still on active duty, it was time for some fresh faces and new stars. The brightest of those newcomers was "Shorty" McWilliams. It didn't take long for the Meridian, Mississippi native to make an impact.

Week one brought a military team to Scott Field for the lid lifter. McWilliams ran for three touchdowns and played like a man among boys in the 41-0 shelling of the Jackson Army air base squad.

McWilliams proved he was more than a one-trick pony in a week two 56-0 thrashing of Millsaps. Once again McWilliams ran for three scores, but he also passed for another.

Arkansas A&M, now known as University of Arkansas at Monticello, served as the third opponent of the season. A&M was expected to serve as a solid measuring stick as they had several military men on their roster who were awaiting deployment. They proved to be no match for McWilliams.

State scored seven touchdowns on the day. McWilliams accounted for three of them, including a pair of long runs and a touchdown toss to Hal France.

The only saving grace for the Boll Weevils was they were able to score when the two previous opponents couldn't. State opened with a 28-0 lead and coasted to a 49-20 win.

Baton Rouge was the first travel destination of the season as the Maroons made their annual pilgrimage to LSU. There would be no kissing of the ring this go around, though.

McWilliams scored on a short run in the second quarter after passing the team down the field. The pass back was muffed on the extra point, so State took a 6-0 lead into the half.

State gained some separation in the fourth when McWilliams ripped off a 59-yard completion to D.B. Floyd just outside the Tiger ten-yard line to set up the final Maroon score. McWilliams took matters into his own hands and pushed his way into the endzone to give State a 13-0 lead.

The Tigers scored late and missed the point after. From there, State salted the clock away and shocked 25,000 LSU fans with a 13-6 win.

The 18th ranked Maroons headed to Memphis to play Kentucky on a neutral field. The Wildcats were just 2-4 on the season and heavy underdogs to State.

Kentucky fumbled seven times in the game, and the Maroons recovered each. The first two turnovers came in the opening minutes of the first quarter. State turned those two miscues into 13 quick points.

Just before the half, Doug Colson connected with Owen Moore for another score to make the halftime score 19-0 in favor of McKeen's Maroons.

McWilliams got on the board in the third period with a five-yard touchdown run. The point after was good to make it 26-0. McKeen emptied the bench in the fourth quarter as State extended its winning streak to five games.

Despite the win, the Maroons dropped from 18 to 19 in the polls. Poll voters were even clueless back then.

Auburn had been a tough out for State for years. Wins against the Tigers were few and far between. In 1944, the Maroons made the bus trip to Legion Field, convinced they were the better team and determined to prove it.

Fans of Auburn had plenty to crow about early as their team took a 7-0 lead on a Nolan Lang touchdown.

McWilliams struck from 76 yards out in the second quarter and evened score at 7-7 in the second quarter.

Auburn answered right back to retake the lead at 14-7 when Curtis Kuykendall turned in a big play of his own. Running off the right side, the Tiger star got loose for 69 yards and a score.

Just before the half, Colston capped a long State drive with a short run to paydirt. The extra point attempt sailed wide, and Auburn hit the intermission with a 14-13 lead.

State was set to receive the second-half opening kickoff, which meant Auburn had to kick it to McWilliams. That proved to be a mistake.

McWilliams fielded the ball at the State seven-yard line and made a couple of would-be Tiger tacklers miss just before he sprinted to daylight. The return covered 93 yards and gave the Maroons their first lead of the day at 20-14.

State took complete control later in the third quarter when McWilliams and company had just won a war of attrition in the trenches. The drive ended with McWilliams scoring his third touchdown of the day. The fourth quarter opened with State ahead 26-14.

Auburn inched closer with just minutes to play and pulled within five points at 26-21. The Maroon defense got the stops they needed, and the State offense moved the chains just enough to exhaust the remaining time on the clock.

Chatter about another SEC title began making the rounds in the media as State prepared to take on Alabama. If the Maroons could take down the Tide, then the path to a conference championship and a Sugar Bowl bid were possible.

The biggest issue facing the Maroons wasn't Alabama. It was the fact that McWilliams was banged up.

The State star played sparingly and struggled to exert his normal influence on the game. McWilliams rushed for just five yards on eight carries.

McKeen elected to try to throw the ball more to spread the workload around, but the plan failed.

Over 23,000 fans packed Denny Stadium, setting a program attendance record. Those who wore Crimson went home happy as Alabama shut down and shut out the Maroons 19-0.

McWilliams' health and availability dominated the headlines leading up to the Battle for the Golden Egg.

Once again, McWilliams was limited in both snaps and good health when the game kicked off.

Ole Miss captain Bob McCain put the Rebels ahead 6-0 early in the second quarter. The point after attempt was blocked.

Colston engineered an 80-yard scoring drive to tie the game at 6-6. Owen Moore reeled in a Colston pass from the Rebel 4-yard line to force the tie. The extra point kick was no good, as it had the score level at the halftime whistle.

In the third quarter, Rebel quarterback Johnny Bruce of West Point put together a drive that got inside the State five. With the Maroon pass rush forcing Bruce to scramble, he elected to call his own number and dive ahead on a quarterback sneak for the score. The conversion proved true, giving Ole Miss a 13-6 lead heading to the fourth quarter.

With just five minutes left to play, State forced a safety to pull within five. Set to receive the free kick, the Maroons knew full well that if they could put one in the end zone, they would escape Oxford with the Golden Egg for the fifth straight time.

The kick was shanked out of bounds at the Ole Miss 32-yard line. State fans roared their approval as the Rebels were up against it late. Perhaps some maroon magic was in store.

McWilliams entered the game with the Egg on the line. Despite his limitations, he gutted it out and got the team into a first-and-goal situation inside the Rebel five-yard line.

McWilliams took the snap with the clock winding down and rolled right with a run-pass option called play. As the Ole Miss defense closed in, McWilliams had to pass. Jerry Tiblier intercepted his attempt toward the end zone for the winning score. Game over.

For the first time in his Mississippi State tenure, McKeen tasted defeat at the hands of the Rebels.

McWilliams was named SEC Player of the Year after leading the league in scoring. The Associated Press included McWilliams on their second-team All-American list.

McWilliams became the first Mississippi State player to receive votes when the Heisman ballots were counted. He finished 10th despite being a freshman.

Football was back in Mississippi, and McKeen had a player to build a team around, or so he thought.

State didn't receive a bowl bid or finish with a Top-20 ranking.

McKeen had also seen the Golden Egg leave Starkville for the first time in his tenure. That development ruffled some feathers within the fan base, especially with some benefactors with influence around Jackson.

Chapter 20

Unrest in the House of Maroon

Bob Sanders loved Mississippi State. There is no question about this. He was involved with many projects to help make his alma mater great academically and athletically.

After an outstanding prep career in Tuscaloosa, Alabama, and ended in Meridian, Mississippi, Sanders enrolled for classes at Sewanee as a multi-sport athlete.

The stay on the mountain lasted just one semester. Sanders landed at Mercer and then completed his education and playing career at Mississippi State. Sanders played quarterback on the 1917 Aggie team, just two years after Dudy Noble's senior season.

As one of the wealthiest men in Mississippi and perhaps the most business-savvy Mississippi State alum, Sanders had power. He had money and influence. Sanders also had connections throughout the South and friends who could make things happen.

An enterprising industrialist, Sanders ran his textile manufacturing business like a sewing machine. He was a smooth operator who set up factories around the state and employed thousands.

Hazlehurst was home to Sanders in those days. He set up a sprawling homestead at Kaywood Plantation on 4,000 acres. Sanders even raised a massive flock of pheasants on his land for hunting trips with his family and friends.

Sanders was also a man people knew not to mess with. This wasn't just because he had power but because he was strong-willed and well-educated. In a battle of wills, he was determined to win.

One example of Sanders' fury allegedly occurred on March 8, 1944. At issue was a workman's compensation bill before the state legislature that 66-year-old Julian Morrison supported. The matter had grown contentious between Morrison and Sanders.

If passed, the bill would have cost Sanders big money as one of the state's largest employers, so he fought hard against it. Seeking to discuss the matter with Morrison, a former administrator at Belhaven, Sanders took the matter up in person.

The conversation didn't go to Sanders' liking, and the two men came to blows, with Morrison getting the business end of the beating.

Three weeks later, future Mississippi Governor Ross Barnett filed a lawsuit against Sanders on Morrison's behalf, seeking $40,000 in damages.

The suit alleged that Sanders attacked Morrison, leaving him with a broken jaw and a concussion. The matter was big news around the state of Mississippi.

Just as the case was set for trial with Hinds County Judge Hugh Gillespie presiding, a settlement was reached. The case was settled on October 4th, with Sanders agreeing to pay Morrison $5,000 in damages.

Years later, the workman's compensation bill that Sanders opposed became state law.

Sanders was used to writing checks, but they were typically for much more noble pursuits.

While he was a gritty businessman, Sanders was also very generous with his money and not just with Mississippi State. In 1945, Sanders donated $100,000 to Millsaps.

Sanders was a fat cat who could gain an audience with anyone. He was well respected for his contributions to the state.

"Bob Sanders is doing more for the industrialization of Mississippi than any other industrialist," then-Governor Thomas Bailey told the *Enterprise Journal*. "He is leading in the sphere of processing Mississippi raw materials, and this is the only way that Mississippi industry can really expand."

As a leader in the Jackson Touchdown Club, Sanders helped grow the organization's membership and prestige to greater heights.

Sanders even personally delivered legendary speakers like Red Grange and Jim Thorpe to address the membership.

When Hinds Junior College returned to Mississippi as Junior College Bowl Champions in 1946, Sanders hosted them at a celebratory banquet at Le Fleur's restaurant in Jackson.

Mississippi State needed to build a student union. Sanders was asked to help raise $1 million for the construction costs. He planted the first seeds with $100,000 of his own money.

At the time, the only revenue sources for college athletic programs were ticket sales and private donations. As a result of that arrangement, Sanders carried a big stick regarding Mississippi State sports.

McKeen and Sanders had a solid relationship, but the foundation of that alliance was soon tested.

Even though McKeen had brought State football into the national spotlight, Sanders felt State could accomplish more. He pushed both McKeen and Noble for loftier results.

If he was the prime benefactor bankrolling the great Maroon machine, he felt he should have a more significant say in how things were done. As a former quarterback, Sanders felt McKeen's offensive approach was antiquated and that the attack should be modernized.

McKeen added a few wrinkles and ran some sets from the Wing-T, but he returned to what he knew best. After all, he was the coach. He was also the mentor who had done more with less than any football coach ever to call the Starkville campus home.

As spring practice was set to begin for the 1945 season, there was a noticeable absence. Shorty McWilliams had knee surgery to repair an injury he suffered late in the 1944 season.

While McWilliams was expected to be at full strength when the season opened, he would wear different school colors. McWilliams received an appointment to West Point and was set to report on July 2nd.

It was a massive blow to the Mississippi State offense. McKeen had a history of coach speak and poor-mouthing in the pre-season, but this year was different. The Maroon headman did his best to encourage all invested in State football to stay the course.

"There's not a Shorty to be found in our 50-man squad," McKeen told the *Clarion-Ledger*. "But we'll be a bit more substantial this fall because of our reserve strength, something we didn't have last year."

McKeen wanted that to be true, but no team gets better by losing its best player, especially when that player led the SEC in scoring a season before.

WWII was ending, and some servicemen were getting their releases. College coaches around the country were given clearance to recruit them. Many men went to war as boys and came home as hardened men. They made good football players.

McKeen hoped to get some of his players back, but he wasn't an avid pursuer of war veterans. There were some exceptions, though.

As Harper Davis was set to finish his service with the Navy at Corpus Christi, Texas, McKeen called him. In many respects, all McKeen had to do was tell Davis to come on.

As a high school football star from Clarksdale, Davis saw Blondy Black play a game over in Starkville. Black dominated, and Davis told himself that if he ever had the opportunity to play at Mississippi State, he would take it so he could be like Black.

McKeen began to make that dream become a reality. Davis needed to get his release from the service. Before that could happen, Mississippi State had to play a football game.

The Maroons won a turnover-filled slop fest over Southwestern Louisiana to open the 1945 campaign, 31-0. State piled up over 300 yards rushing, but it was far from a masterpiece of offensive brilliance.

Just a few days later, Davis received his discharge papers. McKeen was so desperate to have an offensive playmaker that he sent a car from Starkville to Texas to fetch Davis.

On the ride back to Mississippi, Davis studied the Maroon playbook and readied himself for the next game. Davis arrived on campus in time to work through the final walk-through with the team and boarded the bus to Birmingham to play Auburn.

Davis broke loose for a 61-yard sweep play, resulting in a touchdown in the game's second quarter. Davis ran wild again in the third quarter, scoring from 43 yards out. A final touchdown was scored after Auburn failed to convert on a fourth down deep in their own territory. Don Robinson scored for State on the next play to cap the scoring at 20-0.

The game's story was Davis, who ran for 166 yards and two touchdowns on 22 carries. The fact that Davis was leaned on so heavily after having only one practice under his belt is a testament to his talent and an indictment of the quality of the returning roster.

While Davis may not have been a Heisman candidate like McWilliams, he had the makings of a star. Clearly, the Maroons would go as far as Davis would carry them.

In week two, the Titans from the University of Detroit melted in the southern sun. The teams met in Memphis at Crump Stadium.

The visitors got ahead 6-0 but were outscored the rest of the game in a blowout led by Davis, 41-6.

John Sabo of the *Detroit Free Press* wrote, "There was no Southern hospitality for University of Detroit's football team down on the banks of the Mississippi Saturday afternoon."

In that same paper issue, a recap detailing Army's 28-7 victory over Michigan was at the top of the page. The Cadets ran up 380 yards rushing. Among the stars of the game was Shorty McWilliams.

State welcomed another military team in week three when they played Eastern Flying Training Command. The Eagles took a 6-0 lead, but the visitors' celebration was short-lived.

Davis and Graham Bramlett led the comeback, and State ran through the airmen en route to a 16-6 win.

Enjoying their third week in the Top-20, the #15 ranked Maroons headed to New Orleans to put their four-game winning streak on the line against the struggling Green Wave that was just 2-2-1.

State's Don Robinson provided the icebreaker with a 22-yard run. The extra point was wide of the uprights.

Before the first quarter ended, Tulane took a 7-6 lead. State almost regained the lead on their first possession of the second quarter, but the Green Wave turned them away with a goal line stand.

Davis pushed State back into the lead with a short run just before the first half ended. With the extra point, the Maroons moved ahead 13-7.

State looked ready to put the game away in the third as they marched inside the Tulane 10-yard line. A Robinson fumble was lost at the seven, turning the ball over to the Green Wave.

From there, the Tulane Stadium crowd had plenty to cheer about as their team marched 93 yards to tie the game. The good conversion gave the Greenies a 14-13 lead.

Late in the fourth quarter, State mounted a drive that got as deep as the Tulane four, but the Maroons were denied on fourth down, and the upset was official.

"My boys are capable of playing a much finer brand of ball than they did last Saturday," McKeen told the *Clarion-Ledger*. "I hope they'll play their greatest game against LSU."

Many, including donors like Sanders and his associates, saw the bloom coming off the McKeen rose.

Fortunately, State rallied to beat LSU 27-20 and then rolled over Northwestern Louisiana 54-0. The Maroons were 6-1 heading into the Battle for the Golden Egg.

Ole Miss was 3-4 on the season as they boarded the bus to Starkville. Things weren't good in Oxford, as Coach Harry Mehre was mired in his third straight losing season. The Rebels needed something to feel good about and found it at Scott Field.

In a surprising upset, Ole Miss defeated State, 7-6, in a game in which the Rebels outrushed the Maroons by nearly 200 yards. Harper Davis scored for State. The extra point was no good, which proved to be the difference. The Maroons had three promising drives that yielded zero points in the loss.

In the campaign's final week, #3 Alabama ran roughshod over

State, 55-13, ending State's season with a 6-3 mark. It was a winning year but a year without the Golden Egg, a bowl bid, or a final national ranking.

The back-channel chatter regarding McKeen's employment status wasn't positive among donors. Sanders and others pushed Noble to consider making a change, but the State AD couldn't be persuaded. Noble stuck behind McKeen, suggesting that a winning record under the circumstances was a significant accomplishment.

The unexpected loss of Shorty McWilliams would have put most teams in a tailspin, but McKeen found a way to post a winning season without him.

Even though support for McKeen was dwindling among some of the most prominent and wealthy alums, the rank-and-file State fans remained in McKeen's corner.

Their support would soon be rewarded, and a surprise fueled a turnaround of McKeen's fortunes.

As the summer of 1946 began, rumors were ripening about McWilliams returning to Mississippi State to resume his education and playing career. Media reports around the country suggested that with the war over, the star halfback may resign from the Army to return to the Magnolia State.

"I cannot confirm anything at this time, but when Shorty resigns from the Point, he will come here," McKeen told the Associated Press. "I will be delighted to have him.

"I do know that Shorty wants to resign because he doesn't want to stay in the Army. If he graduates from West Point, he must stay in the Army for at least four years.

"I know, too, that his family wants him to return to Mississippi."

While McWilliams' family told inquiring media members that the decision was ultimately Shorty's, there was truth in McKeen's comments. Those in Meridian who missed him while he was away were ready for him to come home.

Before settling the matter, McWilliams penned three letters of resignation to the Army. His first two were rejected as the Army wanted to keep the Heisman trophy candidate on their football roster.

Ultimately, the War Department accepted McWilliams' resignation, albeit begrudgingly. The military brass alleged malfeasance.

West Point superintendent Major General Maxwell Taylor alleged that McWilliams had "received a lucrative financial offer designed to induce him to leave West Point to play football elsewhere."

McKeen barked back in response, saying that the Army was denying McWilliams the chance to resign because he was a star football player. Thousands of other enlisted men were allowed the opportunity to resign from the military once the war ended, but they weren't Heisman candidates.

There is a substantial amount of circumstantial evidence that supports the belief that the Army simply wanted to hold McWilliams hostage so they could continue to thrive on the football field. They weren't concerned about Shorty. They were consumed with their self-interests.

With McWilliams joining Harper Davis in the State backfield, business was about to pick up. Adding to the offensive threats for McKeen were the returns of Eagle Mautlich and Spook Murphy. The Maroons had a four-pronged attack that rivaled most in all of college football.

State easily rolled over Chattanooga 41-7, setting up a massive showdown with LSU.

Approximately 44,000 people crammed into Tiger Stadium, making the match-up with the Maroons the most well-attended college football game in Louisiana at that time.

Legendary quarterback Y.A. Tittle led the Tigers. LSU had a 7-0 lead at the half as the Maroons kept turning the football over. A critical fumble from McWilliams thwarted a potential State scoring drive.

In the fourth quarter, McWilliams fumbled again deep in State territory. The Tigers cashed in but missed the extra point to make the score 13-0.

McWilliams left the game due to an injury. The Maroons avoided the shutout thanks to a Mautlich touchdown. The point after was no good, and LSU won 13-6.

In week three, Mississippi State traveled to East Lansing, Michigan, to battle Michigan State. As part of a gentlemen's agreement, northern teams with integrated rosters agreed to bench their black players when they played against southern teams.

Just before kickoff, Michigan State head coach Charlie Bachman informed McKeen that he had no choice but to play Horace Smith, a black player, due to injuries on the Spartan roster.

McKeen met with his team and explained the situation to them. He agreed to abide by his players' will and allowed them to decide whether to play or return home.

Mautlich said, "Let him play." The rest of the team agreed, and the game went as scheduled. Despite some of the misplaced Southern fears back home, no one died. Two teams filled with college kids played a game.

The 1946 Mississippi State football team became the first college sports team from the Magnolia State to play a game against an integrated opponent.

As fate would have it, Mautlich scored the game's only touchdown with a two-yard plunge in the first quarter. State edged out the Spartans 6-0.

Three weeks later, Michigan State visited Lexington, Kentucky, to play the Wildcats led by Coach Paul "Bear" Bryant. Smith, the Spartans' lone black player, didn't play in the game due to the gentlemen's agreement between the North and the South.

State's win over Michigan State was the first game in a seven-game win streak. During that stretch, the Maroons dispatched of San Francisco, Tulane, Murray State, Auburn, and Northwestern Louisiana.

The final win came in a convincing victory over Ole Miss. Led by first-year coach Harold "Red" Drew, the Rebels had no answer for State's ground game.

McWilliams threw for one touchdown and ran another one. The

final points of the day game came on a pick-six from Mautlich, who reportedly broke through tackles from half of the Ole Miss offense on his way to the endzone. State won 20-0, and Drew never coached another game for the Rebels. After just one season, he was gone.

The Golden Egg was back in Maroon and White hands, quieting the last dissenters. State was still alive for a bowl bid but needed to beat Alabama.

There weren't many highlights for the Maroons in that 24-7 loss to the Tide, save a fourth-quarter Mautlich touchdown.

The season ended with an 8-2 record, but State was out of the bowl picture again and saw another season without a Top-20 finish.

Many State supporters were happy to see a step in the right direction and a win in the Egg Bowl. There was still a core group who had lost confidence in McKeen and wondered if he could get State back over the hump.

Blessed with the gift of hindsight, we know Mississippi State was the best football program in Mississippi then. The Maroons had won an SEC football championship and had been to a pair of bowl games, winning one.

Ole Miss had never won the league, no matter what it was called, and had taken just one bowl trip. The school that would eventually be known as Southern Miss had neither a conference title nor a bowl bid at any point in their history.

Still, Sanders and some of the wealthiest alums wanted more. They felt that State should compete on the same level as programs like Alabama and Tennessee. They pushed Noble and McKeen to do more to make the Maroons a national-level program.

The 1947 season failed to meet those aspirations, but McKeen and the Maroons posted another winning season at 7-3. Seven weeks into the season, State held a 6-1 record, with the lone loss coming to out-of-conference foe Michigan State.

Undefeated in SEC play, the Maroons had the chance to get back to the top of the heap and finally earn a Sugar Bowl bid.

A tough 21-6 loss at LSU extinguished those hopes. State knocked off Southern Miss 14-7 before losing to Ole Miss 33-14 in Starkville.

The Rebels celebrated their first SEC championship on Scott Field under first-year head coach Johnny Vaught. He was a former military team coach who was highly aggressive in recruiting war veterans. At times, playing the Rebels was like pitting boys against men.

There was no NCAA transfer portal back then, but Vaught used his resources and relationships to generate an influx of talent. In just one season, Vaught had turned Ole Miss from SEC also-rans to champions.

The turnaround in Oxford only fueled the voices of discontent in Starkville. Sanders urged Noble to make a change but was rebuffed once again. Sanders went to work networking with other donors to apply pressure on the Mississippi State College administration.

Some allies were found in the Mississippi Delta among the state's most distinguished and prosperous farmers. McKeen was scheduled to appear there, but at the last minute, he sent an assistant coach in his place. The abrupt change of plans didn't go well with the attendees.

Many began pointing to Vaught's work at Ole Miss and felt that a change at State might yield similar results. Despite several discussions with Noble, the group saw their concerns fall on deaf ears. Noble backed his coach.

It is important to note that heading into the 1948 football season, Mississippi State had posted eight straight winning campaigns under McKeen's direction. He was winning, but Sanders and many like him didn't believe the Maroon mentor was winning enough.

The 1948 season was the worst under McKeen as the program experienced a down year at 4-4-1. The year ended with a humiliating loss to Ole Miss in Oxford, 34-7.

McKeen's critics pointed to a few issues that they believed were crucial. They felt McKeen was too stubborn to change offensively with the times. They believed McKeen was stuck in his ways and not open to innovation.

They also thought that Ole Miss and Vaught were leaving State behind due to their decision to sign as many veterans as possible, while McKeen was reluctant to do so.

McKeen had also grown reclusive and walled up. He rarely made trips to meet with alums, so those folks were offended and felt he didn't respect them.

Sanders, and many aligned with him, threatened to pull or reduce their financial support of the athletic department if McKeen was retained another season.

Led by the mob to fire McKeen, the Mississippi State students signed petitions calling for his ouster. They also announced that they would boycott on-campus football games if McKeen remained.

The petition didn't stop with just requesting McKeen's dismissal, but Noble's, too.

"Mr. Noble has served the school well over a long period of years," one of the petitioners told the *Clarion-Ledger* without using his name. "It is felt his retirement will facilitate a thorough and much-needed reorganization of the athletic department under a new director."

In the end, Allyn McKeen was a man without a country. Despite never having a losing season, he had lost the support of the school's donorship, many fans, and the student body.

Noble was left with no choice but to move on from McKeen. There were three years left on McKeen's five-year contract, but a settlement was reached. While it was a firing at the urging of malcontented voices, Noble afforded McKeen the grace of calling it a resignation.

The news hit the media on December 1st. While McKeen tendered his resignation on November 30th, his departure became official on January 1, 1949.

In his written resignation letter, McKeen penned that his leaving "was in the best interests of the college and the team."

Noble told the Associated Press, "Everything was entirely amicable between McKeen and the college. He has served State well during his ten years here."

During his nine seasons at State, McKeen was 65-19-3. He stuck with State even though other programs courted him to leave, most notably in 1943 when few were playing college football in the South.

McKeen was tossed out like trash without ever recording a losing season. He deserved much better. Firing McKeen is among, if not the worst, decisions anyone at Mississippi State has ever made, but the blame doesn't belong to Dudy Noble.

When the mob has money, the mob rules. Noble was at their mercy, though he backed his coach until he was backed into a corner. Little did Dudy know then that the mob would soon be coming for him, too, and they would have to be dealt with.

Chapter 21

Honoring the Legend

In the late 1940s, college baseball had become a much grander event. Noble's demands of running the athletic department scarcely left him time to manage the Mississippi State baseball program.

The decline of the proud Diamond Maroons was a source of disappointment for State fans.

Noble had taken Mississippi State baseball to new heights, and the Maroons were considered the diamond kings of the South throughout the 1920s.

As the Southeastern Conference was founded, more extensive schedules with bigger opponents occurred annually. New rivalries were formed, and there was plenty of carryover from year to year. As a result, scouting became a more important facet of running a baseball operation in the South.

State was still an excellent baseball program in the 1930s, finishing in the top three in the SEC standings each year between 1933 and 1937. However, the Maroons closed out the decade with three straight losing seasons.

In 1939, Noble's squad lost a league-high 10 games, finishing 11th. The only thing that prevented the team from the SEC cellar was that Tulane played only three conference games and lost them all.

In 1940 and 1941 State finished seventh in the league. Finally, in 1942, State returned to the winning side of things, but barely. The 1942 squad posted an 8-6-1 record.

The centerpiece of that turnaround was pitcher David "Boo" Ferriss. As a senior out of Shaw High School in the Mississippi Delta, Ferriss' exploits were well known.

Ferriss began playing varsity baseball in the seventh grade. As an eighth grader, he earned a starting spot at second base. There were no state playoffs back then, but Ferriss made Shaw a championship contender in Delta baseball, winning a championship as a junior in 1937.

Alabama wanted him, Mississippi State wanted him, Ole Miss and Tulane wanted him, among others. Almost all Major League Baseball teams, including the New York Yankees, wanted Ferriss.

After graduating from high school in 1939, Ferriss had two decisions: Would he turn pro or go to college? If he opted for school, where would he enroll?

Ferriss had some time to consider his way as he had no deadline to sign a pro contract. Ultimately, his family convinced him to go to college to further his education and gain more playing experience.

Ferriss's final two college choices were Alabama and Mississippi State. After a trip to Tuscaloosa, it appeared the Crimson Tide would win out, but Noble had a plan.

On his way home to Shaw, Ferriss stopped in Starkville to sit down with Noble and his top assistant, Doc Patty. A historic moment happened during that meeting; Noble did something completely unprecedented, he offered Ferriss a full scholarship to play baseball, making Boo the first Mississippi player ever to receive that honor.

Not only was Ferriss a dominant pitcher, but he was also a bit of an oddity as a baseball player. When he pitched, Ferriss threw right-handed. As a first baseman, the lanky star fielded with his right hand and threw with his left. While he didn't pitch with both hands, he learned to be ambidextrous as a youngster after suffering a broken right wrist that required a cast.

After sharing the good news of the full scholarship with his family, who was still battling through the end of The Great Depression, Ferriss accepted the offer to join the Mississippi State roster.

Ferriss played freshman ball in 1940 and joined the varsity in 1941. In his major college debut on March 28, Ferriss fanned 10, including striking out the side in the ninth in a 6-3 win over Minnesota. Thanks to an error, all three runs were scored in the eighth inning.

Ferriss had three hits in his second start, limiting LSU to just five in a 14-0 shutout.

A 4-2 win over Tulane advanced Ferriss' record to 3-0. A week later, Boo shut down LSU for the second time on the season, taking a shutout into the ninth. State closed it out with a 4-1 victory to make Ferriss undefeated in four starts.

Just three days later, Ferriss was back on the bump, leading the Maroons to a 29-2 rout of Kentucky. Now 5-0, many wondered if Ferriss would remain a college player for more than just a single season in Starkville.

The winning streak ended against Ole Miss, as Ferriss struck out 10 in a losing effort. The Rebels found some success as the State defense committed eight errors in the game, leading the way to a 6-0 win.

Alabama won over Ferriss in his next start with a 6-3 decision. The decisive inning came in the eighth when the Tide scored three runs without hitting a ball out of the infield.

State led the SEC for a spell, but Alabama swept all four games from the Maroons and took control of the league standings. A pair of those losses came at Ferriss' expense.

The losing skid ended when Ferriss shut down Ole Miss in a 4-2 victory. State won just eight games that season, and Ferriss was the winning pitcher in six of those victories.

The attack on Pearl Harbor happened as the year ended, and Ferriss had to consider his plans. The initial intention was to play four years at Mississippi State and then turn pro, but with so much unsettled in the world, Ferriss decided to turn pro after his junior season in 1942.

Looking to pick up where he left off the previous year, Ferriss worked hard to improve his game in his final season in a Mississippi State uniform.

Noble sent Ferriss to the mound in the season opener, and the brilliant junior came through with a 1-0 win over LSU in Baton Rouge. The only run scored was on a sacrifice fly.

State dropped the second game of the series 3-2. Ferriss's friend and summer league teammate from Minter City, Homer Spraggins, started the game. In the first inning of the contest, Spraggins was slightly injured when LSU senior star outfielder Alex Box, a native of Quitman, Mississippi, smashed a line drive off the Maroon pitcher's right arm.

Less than a year later, Box was killed while planting land mines in Tunisia as a member of the U.S. Army. To this day, LSU's home baseball stadium bears his name in tribute to his ultimate sacrifice.

State swept a midweek SEC series from Tulane, with Ferriss fanning 14 and allowing just four hits in a 4-0 shutout in game one. *The Mississippi State College M Book of Athletics* incorrectly reports the score as 4-3.

LSU got revenge over the Maroons in game one of the two-game series in Starkville. Ferris was locked into a masterful pitching duel with Tiger hurler Jim Hall.

The State defense booted the ball around in the ninth, loading the bases. Gerald Hightower came through with a bases-clearing triple to give LSU a 4-1 win.

The Maroons roared back in game two, whipping the Tigers 26-3.

Ferriss had another tough outing against Ole Miss in the first game of the two scheduled for Oxford. The Rebels jumped out to a 7-0 lead and hung on to win 7-6 after State scored three runs in the ninth.

Spraggins evened things up in the second game, tossing a 7-0 shutout. He retired the Rebels in order in all but one inning.

The season got away from State when they had to face Alabama again. The Tide took three of the four games to eliminate the Maroons from league title contention. All State had left to play for was bragging rights with Ole Miss.

In his final game in a Mississippi State uniform, Ferriss defeated the hated Rebels in a 3-1 win that saw him scatter seven hits.

The regular season finale ended in a 5-5 tie after 12 innings due to darkness. With that game in the books, State claimed a 2-1-1 record against the Rebels for the year.

State ended the schedule with an 8-6-1 record to post the program's first winning season in five years.

Unfortunately, the 1943 season was a return to futility, but that 3-9 season had much to do with the loss of Ferriss and other upperclassmen, along with several players who enlisted in the armed forces.

State didn't field a baseball team in 1944 or 1945. Many supporters of Maroon sports felt that Noble should step down as baseball coach and focus his full energies on running the athletic department.

While Noble was officially the baseball coach after the war ended, Doc Patty handled the team's day-to-day operations and facilitated the training and practice sessions.

The 1946 season was a complete disaster. State lacked talent, which showed in every aspect of baseball. They couldn't throw strikes, field, or hit. Outside of those three things, they were pretty good.

The Maroons turned in a 2-10 season. The only saving grace for State was that three of the four games against Ole Miss were rained out. It was clear something had to change.

Many of the same donors keeping the pot stirred with McKeen also took some shots at Noble. McKeen was winning. Noble wasn't.

The biggest problem that those pushing for change had been that Noble was beloved by Mississippi State and most of the fanbase. Noble loved them all right back in his way.

Noble also loved that baseball program. Because of his love and respect for what he helped build as a player and a coach, he began quietly taking steps toward retiring from coaching. While there was no official declaration, as the fall semester began, it was widely known that 1947 would be the final year of Noble's coaching career. Many thought he might resign as Athletic Director, but Noble had no plans to do that.

On October 10, 1946, Noble and other State dignitaries spoke in Columbus, Mississippi. After concluding his remarks, Noble was informed that the Lowndes County Chapter of the Mississippi State Alumni Association had introduced a resolution to name State's baseball field after him.

The crowd roared as Noble offered a wry smile and shook hands with all who extended theirs to offer congratulations.

A vote of the rest of the alumni chapters around the state quickly approved the measure. On December 26, 1946, the news of the state college board's decision to grant their permission for the naming ceremony was released.

Like his friend and former teammate, Don Scott, Dudy Noble was about to see an athletic field named after him at his Alma Mater.

On May 14, 1947, Mississippi State dubbed their home diamond Dudy Noble Field. Over 3,000 fans and friends attended the ceremony to pay tribute to the most decorated student-athlete in school history and a director of athletics who had steered the State ship through some troubling waters over the years.

Boo Ferriss was unable to attend the ceremony as he and the Boston Red Sox were already in season themselves. The day before the field dedication, Ferriss was the starting pitching in Boston's 19-6 win over the Chicago White Sox.

Ferriss still found time to send a telegram to offer his well wishes to his former coach.

"Miss. State is fortunate to have you as its athletic head," Ferriss's message read. "I was lucky to spend three years with you. Sorry I cannot be there to witness the ceremonies in your honor today, but I send my very best wishes."

In Dudy Noble's final season as the head baseball coach at Mississippi State, the Maroons went 8-8. Ironically, that was the same record as his first season in 1920.

Of course, in the final game of his long career as the State baseball coach, Noble led the Maroons to one last blowout of Ole Miss, 11-1. It was a fitting end to his time as a Rebel-rouser.

Once the dust settled, Noble turned the reigns of State baseball over to Patty full-time. Patty led the Maroons to back-to-back Southeastern Conference championships in his first two seasons as the head man.

The College World Series was founded in 1947. Regional committees selected the participants. Some districts had tournaments, while others selected teams based on regular season performances.

In 1948, Auburn and Mississippi State played in the SEC Championship series. Organizers elected to send Alabama and Georgia Tech, the SEC division runners-up, to the NCAA District III tournament in Gastonia, North Carolina.

The following year, Mississippi State was selected to play in the NCAA tournament for the first time. The Maroons defeated the Richmond Spiders 6-2 in their first District III game.

In game two, State lost to eventual tournament winner Wake Forest in 13 innings by the score of 4-3. Kentucky eliminated the Maroons a day later.

Under Patty's leadership, State's baseball team quickly regained its strength. This success prevented significant competition from threatening Noble's position, but the public was still unsatisfied. While the resurgence of baseball may have appeased them, they remained dissatisfied with McKeen and State's football team. An ominous storm was brewing in and around Starkville, Mississippi.

Chapter 22

Be Careful What You Wish For

As Mississippi State began its first search for a new football coach in over a decade, there appeared to be a shift in power within the Maroon family.

Dudy Noble hired Allyn McKeen based on his own sense of coaching and character. Familiarity brought some hometown contempt related to McKeen, but it was impossible to ignore that Noble had hit a home run during that coaching search.

His previous boss, Duke Humphrey, left Starkville to become president of the University of Wyoming in 1945.

The man hired to succeed Humphrey was Fred Tom Mitchell. A native of Clarksdale, Mississippi, Mitchell was well acquainted with Noble as the two overlapped as students at Mississippi A&M.

After graduating from A&M, Mitchell worked tirelessly as an Arkansas public school system educator. He earned his master's degree from Peabody, now Vanderbilt, and his doctorate from Cornell.

Mitchell had a vision for Mississippi State and sought to grow the campus and the student enrollment.

He was also a man known to be a Master of Diplomacy. Mitchell supported Noble, but due to the tension between the administration and the fanbase, the new president sought to enable at least the alums an opportunity to speak their minds about the direction of the football program.

With Noble's agreement, a search committee was formed to replace McKeen, allowing alums a voice. A week after McKeen's resignation, the alumni group representing all 24 districts offered their unanimous support of the decision to move on from McKeen. It was an odd move, considering it was billed as a resignation.

It was also an unnecessary vote. McKeen was already gone, but the pomp and circumstance of the balloting perhaps provided some sense of unity. It was a dog and pony show at its core as a considerable power struggle was about to occur with that newly formed bloc of alumni leaders squarely in the middle.

Following the announcement that Mississippi State had a head coaching vacancy, the *Clarion-Ledger* reported a list of potential candidates to succeed McKeen.

Like all early lists, the names of potential replacements in the newspaper were a hodge podge of obvious candidates and coaches who wanted their names attached to the search.

Tulane assistant coach John Read was among the most dogged pursuers of the position. Read told the *Clarion-Ledger* he was going after the job lock, stock, and barrel.

"I've already made formal applications with the authorities," Read said.

The report mentioned Southern Miss mentor Reed Green, former McKeen assistant Bowden Wyatt, and Farmer Johnson of Vanderbilt as names of interest.

Of course, none of those men got the job. On New Year's Eve, it was announced that former VMI headman Athur Wilson "Slick" Morton was headed to Starkville after two seasons with the Keydets.

A former state champion quarterback in Louisiana, Morton spent his college career with LSU before going into coaching. His first stop was St. Stanislaus in Bay St. Louis, Mississippi.

At that prep school stop, Morton coached future Heisman Trophy winner Doc Blanchard who played alongside Shorty McWilliams at Army.

After high school coaching, Morton accepted the head coaching position at Southeastern Louisiana, where he went 5-5 in his lone season in Hammond.

The call home to LSU came the following year, where Morton coached the backfield for the Tigers. After four years as a Tiger assistant, Morton accepted his post at VMI where he posted an unimpressive 9-8-1 record.

It boggles the mind to consider that the winningest coach in Mississippi State football history was run off to hire a coach with three years of head coaching experience and just one game over .500 in his career.

But the meddling alums wanted a new brand of offense, and Morton ran the Wing-T, which was all the rage in a new generation of college football. Morton's hire came at the urging of the same group that pushed McKeen to be fired.

1949, Mississippi State went winless in Morton's "innovative" offense. The Maroons scored just 38 points all season. The year ended with an embarrassing 26-0 loss to Ole Miss in Starkville.

The 1950 season ended with a 4-5 record and another Egg Bowl loss. One of the only highlights of the year was a 7-0 win over #4 Tennessee in Starkville.

Morton's final season, 1951, was another 4-5 year. Again, there was an upset of a ranked opponent. This time, it was #13 Georgia, who struggled to a 5-5 record.

Ole Miss destroyed State 49-7. "Showboat" Boykin scored all seven touchdowns for the Rebels.

The alumni-appointed hire of Slick Morton went about as one would expect: terrible.

Morton gave up coaching and went to work with the Stribling Brothers' Machinery Company after his three years at State. His career record as a head coach was 22-31-2.

Once again, Noble allowed his outgoing coach to make it appear it was on his terms. Noble even called the announcement a surprise, but Morton made it seem like it was a long time coming.

"Last August, I made up my mind that the 1951 season would be my last year in the coaching profession, win, lose or draw," Morton said in a prepared statement.

If Morton knew he was leaving the summer before the season started, why would it have surprised Noble? In the end, it was nothing more than face-saving bravado.

Call it what you want, but Morton wasn't returning to Mississippi State except as a visitor in 1952.

With Morton's time at State a colossal failure, those working behind the scenes to pull the strings got a pretty hefty dose of humble pie, but it didn't suit their palate.

Rather than stay out of the football business and mind their own, they doubled down. If Morton, their hand-picked coach, couldn't win, the problem must be Dudy Noble. There was simply no way they could have been wrong. It had to be someone else's fault.

If the plot to topple McKeen wasn't traumatic enough for Mississippi State, Sanders and some connected with him turned their vitriol towards Noble.

A grassroots campaign emerged to push for Noble to be removed as the director of State athletics.

Some of the most ardent supporters of Maroon athletics felt that athletics at Mississippi State had become stale under Noble's direction and that the school needed new blood and new ideas.

The cry for change in leadership was floated to President Mitchell, who rebuffed the group's suggestions. Soon, Mitchell was in the crosshairs of the agents for chaos.

What began as idle chatter soon became action as several alumni association chapters drafted formal demands to force Noble into retirement. The Hinds County Alumni group took the first steps. Not only were they targeting Noble, but Mitchell as well. The mob wanted to clean house.

(Mississippi State) "has and continues to rapidly diminish with respect to its academic standing and reputation for progress.

"The administrative head (Mitchell) has not been able to coordinate the several departments within the institution so that they can work in harmony."

The statement also shared the group's concerns about Noble and their feelings about his leadership.

"The athletic director through his conduct has seriously deterred and marred the confidence in respect of prospective students and the student body as well as the general citizenry in the alumni of Mississippi State College."

The dissenters in Jackson were not alone. Several chapters of alumni groups around the state supported the ouster of Mitchell and Noble, including a group from Kosciusko.

"We deplore the ineffective and inefficient handling of athletics by the director, we therefore join with the group of associations throughout Mississippi in an earnest request that Noble be replaced by a man who will meet the qualities for honor, respect, and confidence that this place deserves," their statement read.

The Covington County alumni chapter supported the dismissal of Noble but was opposed to the firing of Mitchell.

There were some pockets of support for both Noble and Mitchell within some other groups, including the one in Lowndes County.

"The association believes," according to a statement from chapter president Mike Kerby, "that the college is being injured by such attempts and that the responsibility for changes should come from the appointed college board of trustees."

When the resolution was considered in Oktibbeha County, the Starkville Alumni Association voted 16-0 to table the measure. President Wilburn Sudduth recommended that a committee be empaneled to investigate the claims of others regarding Mitchell and Noble. Those asked to serve on the committee refused to do so. The chapter took no action.

The Mississippi State alumni executive committee met at the Heidelberg Hotel in Jackson to address the concerns of chapters across the state. The state president of the association was Buck Palmer of Clarksdale.

L.A. Latimer, who represented Sharkey, Issaquena, and Warren counties, read the resolution and asked for a vote on the motion to terminate Mitchell and Noble.

The group eventually went into private session, only to emerge after taking no action. The room was split, and Palmer kicked the can down the road a bit and said the matter would be taken back up in the spring meeting.

Some of the political enemies of Mitchell and Noble were working to engineer some clandestine plots to overthrow the administration. Rumors of misconduct made the rounds. Those whispers found the ears of many in the state senate, who instructed the state college board to investigate the charges.

One of the charges was especially troublesome. A group of men accused Noble and some of the Mississippi State football staffers of acting inappropriately towards a young woman on the return trip from Knoxville to Starkville aboard the Southern Railway train, The Tennesseean, in 1951.

The accusers levied allegations that Noble was drunk in public and acting in a less than chivalrous fashion during the trip. According to an affidavit, the men involved with the claims of boorish behavior by Noble and the State traveling party were T.S. Aderholt Jr., Claud D. Williams, W.A. Hughes, and W.B. Puckett.

Details in cases like these always tend to vary. Still, the Maroon version of the evening suggested that Slick Morton and the rest of the staff played Gin Rummy and discussed State's 14-0 loss to #1 Tennessee.

Noble and Mississippi State Sports Information Director Bob Hartley joined the group and sat at a table behind the coaches. Across from the contingent sat a young woman, a civilian, and two service members.

The statement says that no comments were made to the other group or about the group and that no liquor was consumed by Hartley, Noble, or the rest of the State staff. Noble and his media relations agent were said to have ordered sandwiches and soft drinks.

Puckett, a resident of Clarksdale, Mississippi, allegedly approached Morton and the rest of the coaches to voice his displeasure with the play of the Maroon offense and the kicking game.

In addition to his complaints about the loss to the Volunteers, Puckett reportedly voiced concerns about the staff's recruiting efforts in the Mississippi Delta.

Eventually, Puckett and State assistant Jesse Fatherree became engulfed in a heated discussion, and Puckett was asked to leave the area.

Noble was said to have intervened and told Fatherree to return to his seat and end the confrontation. Once Noble spoke, Puckett turned his attention toward the State athletic director.

Puckett allegedly accused Noble of mishandling tickets, failing to recruit talented football players from the Delta, and not giving him a fair chance to play baseball at State during his college days in Starkville.

The State staffers said that Puckett was intoxicated and was later found asleep on the Club Car table shortly after the alleged incident.

The affidavit was signed by Fatherree, Hartley, Morton, and Coach Clarence Strange. Henry F. Meyer notarized the document.

In addition to his work as a notary public, Meyer owned and operated the *Starkville Daily News* and taught journalism at State. He was later inducted into the Mississippi Press Hall of Fame, and the former student media center at Mississippi State was named in his honor.

The state college board acted quickly and thoroughly probed the allegations against Mitchell and Noble. Both were entirely exonerated by the February 1, 1952, scathing report that called the charges against both men completely erroneous.

Mitchell was given a full vote of confidence by the board of trustees.

"It is shocking that men and women of fine character and scholastic standing and many of whom have given most of their lives to the teaching profession should be charged with corruption, immorality and inebriate condition," the report read.

The urging of state senator William McGraw of Bentonia, a lifelong friend of Mitchell, prompted the investigation.

The final findings suggested no evidence of wrongdoing and that the entire fiasco stemmed from some alums with an ax to grind over State's poor showing on the football field.

In a move of support for Noble and a message to his detractors, the state college board gave the athletic director a brand-new four-year contract.

"We are surprised that those who made these charges did not bring factual evidence before this board to substantiate same," the report continued.

"There was not a whisper of evidence presented before the board that tended in the least to discredit the reputation of the faculty of Mississippi State College, and there was no evidence in any way of dissatisfaction or that Mississippi State does not enjoy a good scholastic standing."

In short, the witch hunt ended, and there would soon be consequences for the accusers who did their best to manipulate the situation to undermine both Mitchell and Noble.

One of Mitchell's first acts of order after receiving the vote of confidence from the state college board was to restructure the alumni association completely.

Noble would later say that in the years that followed, he never had a better relationship with the college's alumni after those changes brought by Mitchell.

With his job secure and the wolves at bay for a bit, Noble called on former McKeen assistant Murray Warmath to turn the football program around.

Warmath left Starkville after four seasons to enlist for military service. Once his service was complete, Warmath landed at his Alma Mater, Tennessee, for four years.

After leaving Knoxville, Warmath worked with legendary coach Vince Lombardi with Army. Noble was able to lure Warmath away from West Point and back to Starkville to replace Morton.

Adding former Jones County Junior College quarterback Jackie Parker aided the turnaround.

The influx of new talent and ideas netted a winning season under the direction of Warmath. The Maroons finished 5-4 with big wins at

Auburn and LSU.

Parker was named the Southeastern Conference Player of the Year at season's end.

Parker nearly brought the Golden Egg back to Starkville as well. Ole Miss had a tremendous season that year and didn't lose a regular season game, so a nail-biter with the Rebels was no small feat.

Down 13-0 at the half, Parker and hard-charging running back Joe Fortunato took over in the second half and nearly pulled off the upset of the #6 ranked Ole Miss squad.

Parker engineered a final drive with just minutes to play that looked bound for the end zone. Instead, Ole Miss defensive back Pete Mangum intercepted Parker deep in Rebel territory to seal the deal in favor of Ole Miss, 20-14.

The 1953 season, much like the '52 year, was fair to middling. State got off to a big start that year, winning their first three games against Memphis State, #17 Tennessee, and North Texas State.

After that trio of wins, the Maroons rose to #11 in the polls, and visions of Sugar Bowls danced in their heads. A tie against Auburn did little to dampen the spirits or hurt State in the polls.

Good fortune ran out in Lexington as the Wildcats recorded the first blemish on the Maroon schedule with a 32-13 victory.

State lost just one more game that year, which came to nonconference foe Texas Tech. The tale of the season was a trio of ties against Auburn, Alabama, and Ole Miss as the Maroons finished the year 5-2-3.

Parker was named SEC Player of the Year for the second straight season even though State failed to make a bowl game or win a conference title. He was simply that good.

At the end of that second year in Starkville, Warmath resigned to take the head coaching job at Minnesota, where he won the national title in 1960.

"It is with deep regret that I leave Mississippi State and the Southeastern Conference," Warmath said in a statement released by the school. "My association here with President Hilbun and athletic director Dudy Noble has always been most happy and satisfactory. They have always complied with my every request.

"I regret leaving the football squad. It is composed of the finest group of boys I have ever coached. I wish them all the luck in the world. The job at Minnesota is a tremendous challenge to me and offers me an opportunity that I feel that I cannot resist."

The search for Warmath's replacement drew tons of interested parties. Noble had to make an important decision and would have to do it without President Mitchell, who resigned in April 1952 due to illness.

How much the stress of being accused of impropriety contributed to Mitchell's health issues? It was a shameful and embarrassing time in the history of Mississippi State. Sadly, Mitchell was unable to overcome his illness and passed away on December 5, 1953.

The man who replaced Mitchell was long-time faculty member Benjamin Franklin Hilbun.

When asked about the quest to replace Warmath, Hilbun told the *Clarion-Ledger*, "I wish we could name one today. The new coach will definitely hold spring football. We usually start here around the latter part of February to take advantage of the better weather, but nothing has been done at this time. As soon as we come to any decision, the news will be released immediately."

The newspaper also listed another crop of obvious candidates who failed to get the job. Most weren't even interviewed.

Noble turned to another former State football assistant, Darrell Royal. During the 1952 season, Royal coached the Maroon backfield before leaving Starkville for a position with the Edmonton Eskimos of the Canadian Football League.

Like Warmath before him, Royal posted a pair of winning seasons and saw a player, halfback Art Davis, earn SEC Player of the Year honors.

After two 6-4 seasons, Royal left for the University of Washington but ultimately landed at Texas, where he won three national championships (1963, 1969, and 1970).

Because of Warmath and Royal's future successes, Mississippi State football began being viewed as a stepping stone job. It also demonstrated that Noble had a keen eye for coaching talent.

McKeen had taken State football to heights never seen before. Warmath and Royal were winners and went on to win big elsewhere. Morton, the lone clunker in the bunch, was forced on Noble by meddling alums.

In 1956, Noble made the final football hire of his life when he elected to promote from within and named Wade Walker the head coach. Walker coached the line under Royal and knew the playbook and personnel well.

The lone season of joyous remembrance of the Walker era came in 1957. State went 6-2-1 and finished third in the Southeastern Conference standings behind Ole Miss (9-1-1) and Auburn (10-0). The Tigers, led by Coach "Shug" Jordan, were one of only two teams to beat the Maroons that year, and they went on to finish #1 in the final Associated Press football poll.

Football never regained the previous glory of the McKeen years during the final years of Noble's tenure as State's athletic director. What could have happened if Noble and the presidents he served under had the freedom to run the show without outside interference?

Mississippi State has won just one Southeastern Conference football championship in its history, and that was under McKeen.

After the McKeen era ended, six State coaches failed to win a single Egg Bowl. From 1947 to 1963, Ole Miss dominated the series without one defeat at the hands of the Maroon and White. Some may be willing to surmise that the program was cursed for forcing McKeen out.

Bob Sanders, who helped orchestrate the end of the McKeen era, passed away in September of 1954 at 55. Sanders fell ill on a business trip to Kosciusko and died several days later at his home in Hazlehurst.

Sanders' untimely death brought an end to a tempest that brought some real damage to the school and athletics programs that he loved so dearly and followed so closely. Though that may not have been his intention, it remains his legacy.

His actions were often misunderstood, and his motives were misguided, but Sanders loved Mississippi State. In fact, he may have loved her too much, which gave way to obsession. He wanted State to be prosperous in all areas of academics and athletics. Sanders was a generous man, but when it came time to share his affection for his college Alma Mater, he squeezed too tight.

There is a Shakespearean quality in the story's climax with Noble, Mitchell, and Sanders. Strong-willed men eventually try each other on for size, no matter the consequences.

After the final conflict ended, only Noble, our protagonist, soldiered on. A Mississippi State man to his core, Noble had lived through WWI, The Bilbo Purge, The Great Depression, WWII, what amounted to a not-so-Civil War among his people within the State family, and he had come out on the other side to tell the tale.

Chapter 23

Atta Babe!

While baseball and football had enjoyed some incredible moments in the three decades since Dudy Noble was a player, basketball was another story. Yes, there were some winning seasons, but State hadn't won a single conference title since before Noble graduated in 1917.

Noble was part of a great run in Mississippi A&M hoops history when the Aggies won four SIAA titles in five seasons (1912-1916). In the nearly five decades that followed, no one in Starkville was hoisting basketball trophies or cutting down nets.

As noted earlier, Frank Carideo took over the basketball program in 1935 in addition to his football coaching duties. In his four seasons at the helm of State basketball, Carideo posted a 43-39 record.

Carideo had a Hall of Fame resume as a football player, leading Notre Dame to back-to-back undefeated seasons as a quarterback. Legendary coach Knute Rockne once called Carideo the best quarterback who ever lived.

Despite the All-American accolades and praise from one of the gridiron's finest coaches, Carideo struggled to become a head coach in any sport.

Before his time as a Mississippi State assistant football coach, Carideo ran the Missouri program and won just two games in three seasons with an overall record of 2-23-2.

After his final season in Starkville, Carideo took an assistant coaching job with the Iowa football program. It proved to be his final college coaching stop of any kind.

The man Noble hired to replace Carideo was Thomas Stanfield "Dick" Hitt, a former Mississippi College sports star. Hitt spent his childhood in the Marion County, Mississippi, community known as Bunker Hill.

He went on to football glory at Mississippi College as a halfback. In his three seasons in Clinton, Mississippi College went 21-4-2.

Once his playing days were over, Hitt started coaching, taking his first step as a head basketball coach at Biloxi High School. A natural progression followed. Hitt graduated to the junior college ranks and took over at Copiah-Lincoln Junior College. A return to his college Alma Mater followed before Dudy Noble came calling.

Known as a gentleman and a strict disciplinarian, Hitt had the Maroons on the upswing until WWII paused the program. His first four years in Starkville were winning campaigns, but the team failed to find any solid footing once the program resumed activity following the 1944 abbreviation. Three years of losing followed.

Times were tough, but like many schools, State had problems putting competitive teams on the floor or field immediately after the war ended. The paltry results don't rest fully at Hitt's feet.

As Noble began searching for a coach to replace Hitt, he reached out to Paul Gregory, his former player. While known best for his exploits on the baseball diamond, Gregory was a three-sport star during his college career, lettering in baseball, basketball, and football.

Gregory began his professional career with the Atlanta Crackers in 1931. A year later, he was in the Big Leagues with the Chicago White Sox. Gregory's pro claim to fame is that he once retired Babe Ruth in five at-bats in a single game.

Following the 1932 season, Gregory returned to the Minor League Baseball, where he toiled earnestly to return to the Major League Baseball level.

When World War II broke out, Gregory enlisted in the service and spent time in the United States Navy from 1943 to 1945. Once his tour of duty ended, Gregory took one more shot at pro ball.

Two more seasons in the Pacific Coast League followed before Gregory hung up his playing spikes for good.

Enter Dudy Noble. Gregory, a native of Tomnolen, Mississippi, was more than eager to listen to Noble about the opportunity to return home and take a job in sports.

The catch was that Noble wanted Gregory to coach basketball rather than baseball. Gregory reportedly told Noble he was concerned that he didn't know enough about coaching on the hardwood to win many games.

As recounted by Gregory's son, Beau Gregory, Noble said, "Well, when I get ready to win, I'll hire somebody else."

The elder Gregory's concerns were well founded, and on-court results left much to be desired. Throughout eight seasons, Gregory's charges turned in a combined record of 58-100. The teams hovered around .500 and never finished better than seventh in the SEC standings.

There was a bigger plan in place that had little to do with basketball. Gregory was, in many respects, the coach in waiting for baseball. Noble simply parked him down the hall with the basketball team until the time came.

Doc Patty won back-to-back SEC titles in 1948 and 1949. For the next seven seasons, Patty's club only challenged for league supremacy one other time, in 1953. It was the lone season outside those two title years where the Maroons even posted double-digit wins.

State dropped the SEC championship series to Georgia in two games but still managed to get invited to the NCAA District III tournament in Durham, North Carolina. The team was eliminated in three games.

Athletics were growing at State, and the responsibilities were becoming more demanding. In addition to managing the baseball program, Patty was the business manager for the athletics department. Like he had been on the baseball diamond, Patty was Noble's right-hand man in the administration. Things would have to change as more staff were required to meet the needs of a growing college.

In 1955, Noble was ready to win in basketball. Gregory was reassigned to the school to help run the physical education program. A year later, he succeeded Patty as the head baseball coach.

The man replacing Gregory as head basketball coach was a surprise hire. No one knows precisely what Noble saw in James "Babe" McCarthy, but it was clear he was intrigued. Maybe it was a penny-pinching move, but it paid off handsomely.

McCarthy was an SEC basketball official and worked as a high school basketball coach, making stops at Baldwyn and Tupelo. McCarthy's 1948 squad at Baldwyn won the state championship.

Much like the hiring of Allyn McKeen, Noble went with his instincts and hired a virtual unknown.

McCarthy's first season at State finished at 12-12. The team's star, Jim Ashmore, was one of the country's best players, making him a target for opposing defenses.

State needed a complimentary player to force defenses to play honestly and not cheat on Ashmore. Help was on the way. A talented freshman had come to Starkville from across the Tennessee line.

Bailey Howell was one of about 400 residents in tiny Middleton, Tennessee. That hamlet's population would grow considerably whenever Howell took the court.

Earning All-State honors as a junior and All-American honors as a senior, Howell was one of the top prospects in the country. A who's who in college basketball coaching made their way to Hardeman County to see Howell play in person. One such coach was Babe McCarthy.

"Coach McCarthy recruited me," Howell said in an exclusive interview. "I kind of wanted to go to an SEC school. At that time, I was a big Tennessee fan.

"Memphis State had a great program at that time as well. It came down to Memphis State or Mississippi State.

"Coach McCarthy had such a great personality. Every time you saw him, you felt he was thrilled to see you. He was way ahead of his time as a recruiter. He visited me in my little hometown of Middleton more than all the other coaches combined.

"He came to Middelton and brought his wife and two little boys. They all met my parents. With his personality and his gift of gab, he really sold them."

McCarthy didn't stop until he convinced Howell to join the rising program at State. McCarthy played every card he had to increase his chances of landing a blue-chip recruit.

"A guy from Corinth, Mississippi, played second base for the St. Louis Cardinals (Don Blasingame). Babe had coached him in the military. He sent Don to my hometown to vouch for Babe, as a coach."

The competition for Howell's signing day signature was intense. National power, Kentucky, even beat a path to the Howell family door.

"Coach Harry Lancaster was an assistant at Kentucky," Howell said. "He came to see me play, and he met my parents. He told them they were offering me a scholarship and that when he got back to Lexington, he would send us a letter to make it all official. That's the way they recruited."

Kentucky didn't make the list of finalists. Perhaps the fact that Adolph Rupp didn't make an in-person visit was a part of their exclusion. McCarthy also decided to sign Don Mott, a high school friend and teammate of Howell's.

Freshmen weren't allowed to play on the varsity team then, so Howell sharpened his skills on the first-year squad against other freshman teams and some junior college programs.

His second season in a maroon and white uniform proved to be very good for Mississippi State. The Maroons got off to a hot start.

Seven games into the 1956-57 season, Howell and the Maroons were 6-1. The lone loss had come at home to Memphis State, the team that had come in second in his recruitment.

McCarthy and the team hit the road for a Christmas Tournament in Evansville, Indiana. State took on Denver in the first round and defeated them by the score of 69-65. Howell had 22 points and converted 10 of 11 free throws.

The Denver Pioneers had a pair of black players named Bill Peay and Rocephus Sligh on their roster. Once word got back to Mississippi that State had played an integrated team, all hell broke loose.

While State had earned the right to play Evansville in the tournament final, the squad was called back to Starkville.

"There weren't many Christmas tournaments back then," Howell explained. "Evansville had one every year, and we got invited. I was a sophomore then.

"We had played the University of Denver, which had two black players. Evansville had one black player. Once it was found out that we were playing against integrated teams, some of the politicians out of Jackson got involved. I don't know who they were. They called Babe and told us to come home.

"We had eaten our pre-game meal and were getting ready to play the championship. We went and walked a few blocks around Evansville and then walked back to the room.

"The manager knocked on the door and told us to get our stuff and get on the bus. It wasn't time to go to the game yet, but he said not to say anything to anybody and just get our stuff and get on the bus. We did.

"Before we left, some newspaper people found out about it. They were at the bus trying to get some comments, but we drove right out of there.

"Coach McCarthy said that it was his second year as coach. If he defied the order and we played the game anyway, they would have fired him. I don't know who the power was behind it, but I guess they called President Hilbun, he called Dudy, and Dudy called Babe.

"All I know is that we got on the bus and left. I was disappointed, of course. We didn't have any trouble playing against black guys. They were just like anybody else. They were just basketball players to us."

Don Ping, the athletic director of Evansville, read a statement to the crowd that Mississippi State had been called home and that Denver would play in their place in the tournament championship game.

President Hilbun played both sides when assigning blame for the early exit. Hilbun told the Associated Press that the directive came from Noble and not from him or the state legislature.

"We just want to play like we do at home," Hilbun told the Associated Press in a contradictory statement.

Days later, Noble told the *Clarion-Ledger*, "It is my understanding that we didn't know beforehand that there would be negroes in the tournament. It's always been our policy that our teams would not compete against negroes. That's traditional with our institution."

Ironically, Ole Miss director of athletics Tad Smith issued a similar statement as his Rebel squad was called home from playing Iona in a consolation game in a Christmas tourney called the All-American City Tournament in Owensboro, Kentucky, a day later. Tournament officials were told that Ole Miss wouldn't take the court unless Iona withheld their one black player, Stanley Hill, from the competition.

"When we accepted an invitation to the tournament, it was with the understanding that there would be no negroes in it," Smith told the *Clarion-Ledger*.

Like his Mississippi State counterpart, Ole Miss chancellor, Dr. John Davis Williams, sent some mixed messages, initially saying he had no knowledge of the incident and Smith must have made the decision.

Williams said, "It's the school's policy to maintain segregation so far as team play is concerned inside and outside the state."

Several fingers were pointed directly at Mississippi Governor James Plemon Coleman. Still, the state's highest elected official denied comment and passed the buck. Plemon suggested it would be wrong of him to comment because "under the constitution of Mississippi, control of such institutions is vested solely in the board of trustees."

The truth is that race problems weren't a Mississippi State problem or even an Ole Miss problem. They were a Mississippi problem that plagued the state for decades.

Hilbun would later imply what everyone else knew but couldn't prove. He said that state government didn't control the state's colleges and universities regarding decision-making, but they did control their funding.

As documented earlier in this book, Mississippi State played against an integrated football team in 1946 when it traveled to East Lasing to play Michigan State, so what changed?

In the fall of 1955, Jones Junior College was invited to play for the national championship against Compton in the Little Rose Bowl. Compton was an integrated squad with eight black players.

Before the game, *Jackson Daily News* editor Frederick Sullens wrote a front-page editorial blasting the Bobcats for even considering playing a team with black players.

Sullens labeled the acceptance of the bowl invitation as a "flagrant violation to the Southern way of life," and a "spineless surrender to the principles all true white Mississippians hold near and dear, and all who are in any measure responsible deserve the sharpest rebuke it is possible to administer."

Sullens wasn't alone. Several media members around the state called for the state government to pull funding from Jones and suggested that the Bobcats deserved to be soundly defeated for turning their backs on the ideals of Mississippi.

Natchez Times columnist Jeanerette Harlow penned, "They say that history often repeats itself, and this seems to be true the case in Mississippi's Jones County. For the second time within a century, the county of Jones has failed to live up to the standards and traditions of the South.

"When Mississippi seceded from the Union during the War Between the States, Jones County refused to abide by the decision of the sovereign mother state to secede and set itself up as the Free State of Jones, remaining a part of the Union."

Harlow also alleges that bowl officials and those connected with both Compton and Jones junior colleges asked media members not to publish that Compton was an integrated team.

"As far as we are concerned," Harlow offered. "Jones County is still the Free State of Jones and not a part of our own Mississippi."

Several state officials withdrew pledges to assist financially with funding the trip to California. Lieutenant Governor Carroll Garlin even canceled his plans to attend the game. While Garlin never disclosed the actual reasoning regarding his about-face, it is reasonable to assume he simply didn't want to raise the ire of public sentiment that was clearly against Jones playing a team with black players.

To suggest that Mississippi was the only state with this stance would be to miss the mark. Georgia Governor Marvin Griffin blasted Georgia Tech for playing Pittsburgh in the Sugar Bowl because the Panthers had a black player.

Griffin even threatened to close the state parks if there was co-mingling between the races.

The prohibition on playing integrated teams wasn't limited to college programs either.

In September of 1955, Fort Smith High School in Arkansas canceled their game with Fayetteville High School because Fayetteville had four black players.

Old habits and ideals die hard, but in the Magnolia State some lawmakers were prepared to put some bass in their voices and bite into their bark.

Dr. E.R. Jobe, the executive secretary of the board of trustees that oversaw Mississippi's Institutes of Higher Education, may have been the only state official to take any accountability for State and Ole Miss being called home from their Christmas tournaments that featured integrated teams when he said, "the two schools were following state policy."

Jobe said that Delta State had opted out of athletic events against integrated teams and that extra precautions had been taken to prevent such matchups.

The *Clarion-Ledger* polled several state lawmakers, and segregation sentiments were essentially unanimous.

"The officials of the two colleges took the only honorable course they could in good conscience follow," – State Senator and President Pro Tem of the State Senate, Earl Evans, of Canton.

"They did just exactly what they should have done by withdrawing their teams," said Speaker of the State House Walter Sillers of Rosedale "I commend the authorities of both schools for taking the position they have taken."

"I approve of the withdrawal," Representative Russell Fox of Port Gibson echoed. "We can compromise on method and manner, but never on principle."

Itawamba state representative R.C. McCarver introduced a bill that would have levied a $2,500 fine on any school playing integrated teams and imprisoned, for one year, any school official who violated the law (copy of original bill on page 220). In addition to those penalties, McCarver wanted all state funds cut off from the offending institutions.

While the bill failed to pass, it had support. Many in the state legislature were more than willing to vote to cut funds from schools that dared challenge the authority of state government even if they couldn't throw school officials in jail.

It is unfair to judge the people of yesterday by today's standards. Still, documenting the environment in which those school administrators had to function is also worth noting.

The message from the legislature was clear, even if it wasn't a written decree—any school that played integrated schools faced the possible forfeiture of future funding.

Mississippi State wouldn't play another integrated basketball team until March 15, 1963, when McCarthy and his team defied the state legislature and snuck out of the state to play Loyola in an NCAA tournament game. Before that significant game was played, McCarthy had plenty of time and reasons to build up a healthy resentment against the powers that be.

Despite the controversy over backing out of that Evansville tournament in 1956, the '56-'57 team had a great year.

State knocked off #3 Kentucky 89-81. The victory was just the third win over the Wildcats in school history and the first since 1926. That's right. It had been over 30 years since State beat Kentucky.

ATTA BABE!

HOUSE BILL NO. 47

AN ACT MAKING IT A FELONY TO HOLD, OR CAUSE TO BE CONDUCTED, ATHLETIC CONTESTS OPEN TO THE PUBLIC WHEREIN NEGROES OR PERSONS OF MONGOLOID DESCENT PARTICIPATE WITH WHITE PERSONS AND PROVIDING THE PENALTY THEREFOR.

BE IT ENACTED BY THE LEGISLATURE OF THE STATE OF MISSISSIPPI:

SECTION 1. It shall be unlawful for any person, firm, corporation, school, college or university to hold, produce, direct, sponsor, supervise, or otherwise cause to be conducted any athletic contest, game, program or event open to the public, wherein Negroes or persons of Mongoloid descent are permitted to play or participate therein with persons of the white race.

SECTION 2. Any person, firm or corporation violating the provisions of this act shall be guilty of a felony and, upon conviction, shall be punished by imprisonment for one (1) year or be fined two thousand five hundred dollars ($2,500.00), or both.

SECTION 3. The state treasurer, state department of education, state educational finance commission, county board of education or board of trustees of a municipal separate school district, shall not pay, distribute, allot or disburse any money to any school, college or university that violates this act either within or outside the State of Mississippi, and all appropriations by the legislature to any school, college or university shall be subject to this act.

SECTION 4. This act shall take effect and be in force from and after its passage.

HB-47
ms

DIED IN HOUSE COMMITTEE

The Maroons finished third in the SEC that year and duplicated the feat the following season. Both years saw the program ranked #15 in the final AP Poll.

Howell's senior year came in 1959. He was 1-1 against Kentucky in his career, and Rupp had a fascinating proposal for the rubber game. Rather than play the game as scheduled in Starkville, Rupp offered State administrators a sack full of money to play the game on a "neutral" floor in Louisville, Kentucky.

Knowing that money was nearly always an issue for State, McCarthy went to Noble to convey Rupp's offer.

After hearing the opportunity in detail, Noble turned to McCarthy and said, "You bring them down here, and you beat the hell out of them."

That year State had a squad that could accomplish such a task. The Maroons went 24-1. Those two dozen wins included a 66-58 victory over #1 Kentucky.

For the first time in school history, Mississippi State earned an SEC championship in men's basketball. State qualified for the NCAA tournament by winning the league, but the state legislature wouldn't permit the team to participate.

Kentucky, a team State had defeated and finished ahead of in the standings, went as the SEC representative.

California won the tournament and the national championship with a 25-4 record. Mississippi State was the best team in college basketball but was denied the opportunity to prove it by their own state government.

In a strong statement of faith in McCarthy's team, the Associated Press voted Mississippi State as the number three team in the country despite not playing in the NCAA tournament. Short-sighted state lawmakers likely cost State a national championship.

McCarthy would go on to win three more SEC titles. In two of those three years, his team was banned from playing in the NCAA tournament. In 1963, he got tired of being pushed around. With the backing of President Dean Colvard, McCarthy defied state government and the co-authors of Jim Crow laws by taking a plane to play a basketball game he was forbidden to coach.

Those young men took the court not knowing if they would be arrested when they returned to Starkville. They could have been kicked out of school and branded as race traitors, but they weren't. They were welcomed home as heroes.

McCarthy was hailed as a champion for change. Through his acts of rebellion, he opened the door for all state-funded institutions to play in NCAA tournaments, including against integrated teams.

The seeds of that change were first planted when McCarthy had to put his team on a bus in Evansville, Indiana, and leave town without playing in a tournament championship game they deserved to participate in.

Bailey Howell was on that bus but never got to play in an NCAA tournament game. When State took the tourney floor in 1963, Howell was in attendance.

After his college career ended at State, he was the second pick in the 1959 NBA draft by the Detroit Pistons. Howell finished second in the Rookie of the Year voting to a familiar name—Wilt Chamberlin.

Howell played for four NBA teams in a dozen pro seasons. He won a pair of NBA titles with the Boston Celtics. Howell was a member of six NBA All-Star teams.

Once his pro career ended, Howell was named to the Basketball Hall of Fame and the College Basketball Hall of Fame. His jersey #52 hangs from the rafters of Humphrey Coliseum. Howell is the only men's basketball player in Mississippi State history to have had that honor bestowed upon him.

Chapter 24

The End of the Road

By the end of the 1950s, there was change afoot. Dudy Noble and the Mississippi State Alumni Association were working together more closely, presenting a more unified front. That's not to suggest Noble didn't have critics. He did, but they weren't as well-funded or influential as those who had vied for his position in the wake of the Slick Morton era of Maroon and White football.

After Morton "resigned," State experienced six winning seasons in seven years. In 1957, the Maroons were ranked #14 in the Associated Press postseason poll. That end-of-year ranking was the first since the termination of Allyn McKeen.

Mississippi State baseball was winning under Coach Paul Gregory. While the diamond dwellers weren't yet competing for championships, they were turning in winning seasons with Gregory at the helm.

As noted in the last chapter, Babe McCarthy was winning and winning big. The Maroons won 20 games in 1958 and the Southeastern Conference title in 1959.

The bottom line is the Maroon sports programs were healthy toward the end of Noble's tenure as State athletic director, at least relative to previous school standards.

Mississippi politics was still infected with the virus of segregation. Countless articles and stories have been written about State's 1959 team being denied the opportunity to accept an invitation to the NCAA tournament.

Some on the university level have been unfairly maligned for decisions above their pay grade. While I never had the chance to talk with President Hilbun and Dudy Noble about their politics, the newspaper accounts of their day suggest that they were pawns in a political chess game.

In the days before State withdrew from the 1959 NCAA tourney, Hilbun said he had a "tough decision" to make.

Many Mississippi State student body members did their best to help Hilbun as he considered the next move for the basketball program. Looking to make their voices heard, the students turned to the ballot box.

Approximately 25% of the students cast votes for or against the team playing in the NCAA tournament, regardless of the racial composition of opposing rosters.

Some 1,135 ballots were tallied, with 973 students voting for playing in the tournament and only 162 voting against it. Those with a B.S. degree in revisionist history will tell you that Mississippi was racist to its Magnolia State core, but those results suggest a much different story.

Ultimately, State didn't accept the invitation despite the students' will.

"Policy is not set by the student body," Hilbun told the *Jackson Daily News*. "It's set by the state college board and the legislature.

"Well, the students of today are the adults of tomorrow, and that 973 to 162 vote is a sign of things to come."

Mississippi State's coaches, fans, and players were mistreated, but that brand of medicine isn't without precedent. There is another element to this story that has been rarely told until now.

In 1957, the historically black college, Jackson State College, had an outstanding basketball team. The Tigers roared through the regular season with a 22-2 record, winning the Midwest Athletic Conference championship. The title included a berth in the NCAA Division Tournament for smaller colleges.

What may surprise many is that Jackson State got to play—at least for a while.

The Tigers trounced Philander Smith, another historically black school, 93-65. Jackson State was considered one of the favorites in the tournament as they awaited the winner of Monmouth and South Dakota. The Coyotes of South Dakota advanced and were set to host the

Tigers in Vermillion, South Dakota.

Just days before the game was set to take place, Mississippi politics reared its ugly head again. Incredibly, Jackson State was forced to withdraw from the tournament. The reason given was that Mississippi schools weren't permitted to play against teams of other races. Since South Dakota was an all-white team, Jackson State wasn't allowed to play against them, as any comingling of the races was prohibited by Mississippi's policy of segregation.

"It is the policy of the board that state institutions of higher learning shall not participate in national athletic tournaments under the present conditions," Jackson State president Dr. Jacob Reddix shared in a school statement. "Under the present circumstances, our basketball team will not compete further in the NCAA."

When questioned about the decision, Dr. E.R. Jobe, the executive secretary of the college board, claimed that he was unaware of the incident.

Sound familiar?

Jobe told the Associated Press that it was "generally understood that was the accepted policy," when asked about Jackson State being barred from further competition due to playing against integrated teams.

"I am disappointed," Jackson State captain Billy McDonald told the Associated Press. "I've worked four years to play in a national tournament."

There was no law on the books that the state college board, the state legislature, or the Governor's office could stand on. Instead, there was an unwritten policy that all the decision-makers referenced when questioned.

One could easily surmise that Dr. Reddix wanted his team to continue playing. The same could likely be said of Dr. Hilbun at Mississippi State and Dr. Williams of Ole Miss, but those who controlled the purse strings dashed their real or perceived wishes.

Hilbun had some other fish to fry beyond athletics. State College had grown under Hilbun's leadership and not just with enrollment. The school had matured, adding more fields of study, graduate programs, and the advancements of several schools like forestry and agriculture.

Simply put, the old girl had outgrown her old name, and Hilbun aimed to change it.

A handful of state representatives who helped champion the bill through the state legislature were Vernon Bullock (Walthall), who authored the measure; Rip Collins (Union), Leon Hannaford (Tate), and Fay Willis (Monroe).

The lower house passed the measure with a near-unanimous vote. The state senate followed suit in short order, and Sonny Montgomery did his part to ensure the matter was handled in the senate.

While state officials rubber-stamped the change in terminology, Ole Miss and Southern Miss opposed the decision.

State's transition from college to university fit national trends as most other land grant schools had been promoted to university status.

There was chatter about Hilbun leaving State for a potential run at the Governor's office. Some advisors suggested that votes from the Ole Miss and Southern Miss sides may be hard to come by.

In the end, Hilbun elected not to run. As of the writing of this book, there has never been a Mississippi State-educated governor in Mississippi. Make of that what you will, but it is noteworthy.

Hilbun, a lifelong Mississippi State man like Dudy Noble, had strong opinions. As did Noble. The two had some heated disagreements. Considering some of the conversations Noble had in the presence of all forms of company, it isn't surprising.

Noble was a staunch advocate for rules. He felt that if the Southeastern Conference was going to have rules, they must be followed and enforced.

At one meeting between league officials and the SEC athletic directors, Noble became increasingly frustrated as the group began to focus on minor matters.

"You guys are talking about a bunch of rat pellets when there are elephant turds laying all around the room," Noble said. "When y'all are ready to get serious, then let me know."

With the stench of that surly comment hanging in the air, Noble got up and walked out of the meeting.

Noble detested Ole Miss as both a player and a coach. He intensely hated Ole Miss teams in a way that is hard to describe. One time, Noble stated that if he were to die and accidentally end up in Hell instead of Heaven, he should be given credit for time served for the two years he toiled in Oxford. Once Noble became an athletic director, he realized that for Mississippi State and Ole Miss to be treated fairly within the rugged SEC, the two schools would have to work together.

Noble and Ole Miss director of athletics, Tad Smith, became allies towards that cause. While Noble wanted to beat the Rebels without mercy in competition, State and Ole Miss needed each other. Noble had the good sense to recognize that.

The common enemy between the two schools was LSU. As shared with me by multiple sources, Noble saw the Tigers as the most rogue program in a band of branded outlaws.

It wasn't until 1953 that the NCAA sanctioned member institutions for coloring outside the lines. Almost half of all the schools in the SEC were sanctioned in the '50s, beginning with Kentucky in 1953, due to illegal inducements in basketball recruiting.

Auburn (1956, 1958), Florida (1957), and Ole Miss (1959) were all penalized for football violations. The penalties of yesteryear pale in comparison to those of today. Schools sometimes lost their right to vote in NCAA matters or were publicly reprimanded. It was a penalty structure of "Stop, or I'll say stop again."

LSU won the national title in football in 1958, which only added to Noble and Smith's distaste.

With some rifts behind the scenes between Noble and Hilbun, Smith would soon need a new brother in arms.

The relationship between Hilbun and Noble had grown contentious. On opposite pages, you had the most powerful man on campus in Hilbun and the most popular man on campus in Noble.

One legendary battle for power involved a parking lot. As the University grew and more and more students had automobiles on campus, parking became a real challenge.

Hilbun opened the lot outside the athletic department to provide more parking places on a first-come, first-served basis.

This became a real issue for Noble. As he traveled the State on athletics business or drove downtown to have lunch, he would return to find no room to park his car near his office.

Noble addressed the issue directly with Hilbun, but the two couldn't find common ground. It was a battle of egos, and both men were determined to win.

The State athletic director hatched a plan. Hilbun had to be away from campus for a few days, so Noble instructed some campus workers to erect a fence around athletic parking, complete with a locked gate.

Once Hilbun returned to campus, he had the fence taken down. This became a tipping point between the two. There were other grudge matches of pettiness, but this one was the straw that broke the camel's back.

Mississippi had a compulsory retirement law that said any state employee aged 65 or older with 15 years of service could be forced to retire. There was a little wiggle room, as there always seems to be, but Hilbun chose to act and attempted to force Noble into retirement.

Hilbun was facing the same fate. He, too, was approaching retirement age and had more than enough years in the state system to retire. Hilbun was determined to be the last to go.

As the fall semester opened, Hilbun was very vocal about his plans for change. While no official action had been taken, things were moving behind the scenes and within President Hilbun's mind.

While Noble may have planned to retire, his time frame and Hilbun's didn't align. As Noble drove through Jackson, a radio report crackled through the static announcing State would promote Wade Walker to the athletic director, ending the Dudy Noble era.

Noble's next stop was to the offices of the *Clarion-Ledger* to tell his side of the story. Noble reportedly called Hilbun a coward for not having the courage to tell him face-to-face that he was out and that he wasn't surprised to see Hilbun take the easy way out.

The report shared that Noble's final day at Mississippi State would be December 31, 1958, but the state college board had the final say.

When the board met later that month, they extended Noble's contract through the spring semester, ending on July 1, 1959. It was official: The Dudy Noble era had an expiration date.

The board also rebuked Hilbun and told him Noble would stay on through the end of the academic calendar, whether he liked it or not.

In January 1959, the state college board approved Walker's promotion and formally announced Noble's retirement.

Once word spread around the state of Mississippi through the various media reports, there was great sadness within the fanbase. While Noble had his critics over the years, the changing of the guard didn't sit well with many.

William Stone and other supporters put together a Dudy Noble gift fund. This allowed Mississippi State fans to contribute and give Noble a retirement gift as a token of their appreciation for his many years of service.

When the funds were collected, a three-carat yellow diamond ring was fashioned and presented to Noble. It was a prized possession that stayed with him. The engraving inside the band of that ring thanked Noble for his decades of service to Mississippi State.

Noble made good use of his final months in Starkville. He secured a new four-year contract for Babe McCarthy, ensuring the basketball program remained on an upward trajectory.

When Noble's forced retirement news reached the former players, a once-dormant M-Club was revitalized. Mississippi State sports alums wanted to have a voice in things.

Hilbun got his wish in many respects and would have a new director of athletics. He was also dealing with the aftermath of the Old

Main dormitory burning down earlier in the year.

Over 1,000 students called the Old Main home, and one, Henry Allen Williamson of Columbus, Mississippi, lost his life in the fire.

Six others were injured: Glen Allen, Sidney Bounds, Doyle Collins, John Duke, Kenneth Middleton, and Parker Sullivan.

Sullivan was hospitalized and was nearly the second fatality. According to the *Clarion-Ledger*, students hailed Joe Denton of Cleveland, Mississippi, as a hero after he helped rescue Sullivan from his burning room.

The displaced students had to have housing. Many were crammed into other residence halls, while others settled for temporary housing in makeshift camps.

A fire fund was established to help students who lost everything in the fire. Those dollars provided some help to those impacted, giving them a slight head start on recovery. Thousands of dollars in relief aid were contributed and distributed.

The bricks from the Old Main, affectionately known as "Polecat Alley," were salvaged and used to build the Chapel of Memories on the Mississippi State campus.

"Old Main dormitory has been a landmark at Mississippi State and in Mississippi since 1880," Hilbun told the *Clarion-Ledger*. "I can think of no better way to preserve its memory than with a small chapel."

The landscape at Mississippi State was changing, both literally and figuratively. Things would never be the same. They may be better, but not the same.

As State looked to complete construction on newer residence halls, Noble and his wife Elizabeth discussed building their retirement home in Learned, Mississippi.

Instead, Noble moved back into the old homestead where he grew up. Before he and Elizabeth gave way to peaceful days in rockers on the front porch, the Southeastern Conference elected to honor Dudy at a banquet at The Club atop Red Mountain in Birmingham.

A huge plaque was presented to Noble on behalf of the conference for their appreciation of his long and distinguished career as a student-athlete, coach, and administrator.

Several dignitaries spoke and shared stories of both gratitude and humor about their dealings with Noble over the years.

Every school in the SEC was represented, and representatives from the Gator Bowl, Orange Bowl, and Sugar Bowl also attended.

"We regret that an outstanding figure like Dudy is retiring," SEC commissioner Bernie Moore said. "He has meant a great deal to intercollegiate sports."

Legendary *Birmingham News* sportswriter Zipp Newman's career lasted throughout Noble's time as a player, coach, and athletic director.

"State has played like this man we honor tonight, unafraid and daring," Newman said.

Newman also recounted when a local Birmingham hospital had a charity drive to raise operating capital. Noble brought Mississippi State's freshman football teams over and played. Noble agreed to cover all the team's expenses so that the money raised by the event went to the hospital and the children it cared for.

Ole Miss athletic director Tad Smith shared that many people considered him and Noble like brothers because of their tireless work together to help the Mississippi schools.

"You have done loads for us at Ole Miss," Smith said. "Anytime you want, you will have a 50-yard line ticket with me in the press box."

"I don't have words to express thanks," Noble told the assembly. "We owe so much to you all."

Not one to show emotion, Noble was touched by the ceremony and the many coaches and administrators who had made the trip to Birmingham to honor him and his career.

"It's so hard to say anything when you have so much to say," Noble told reporters after the event.

After a distinguished journey marked by grandeur and significance, Dudy returned to his hometown of Learned, where his remarkable story had begun. This homecoming marked the end of his tenure in Starkville and his iconic status in Mississippi State athletics.

Chapter 25

A Lasting Legacy

Life on the farm was a lot quieter for Dudy and Elizabeth Noble. Learned, Mississippi was a smaller dot on the map than when Noble left home to begin his college career at Mississippi A&M in 1910.

The 1960 census registered the rural Hinds County community with just 96 year-round residents.

For Noble, there were no longer any budget meetings, coaching searches, or southern bureaucrats to deal with, and no warring factions from the State alumni groups who were out for his job.

There was just Dudy and Elizabeth.

Gone were the football game weekends where Mississippi State's first athletic couple hosted family reunions after each home game. Those parties brought most of Noble's siblings and their children to town.

Those special weekends allowed the cousins to get to know each other better. Just as night fell, the children were ushered off to bed, and the adults would sit and visit. An adult beverage was shared, but not in the presence of the children.

Even though Elizabeth never had children, Dudy could be heard bellowing "Maw" in his booming voice when he beckoned his better half.

The Noble nieces and nephews began to call Elizabeth "Dranma" as a term of endearment. To hear them tell it, she was their bonus grandma.

Dranma had some nesting to do when she landed in Learned full-time. As a young girl, one of the things she wanted most in life was a four-poster bed. Of course, Dudy ensured she had one shortly after they were married.

That four-poster bed made its way down to the farm along with everything the couple had amassed and collected during Dudy's time as a coach and athletic director at State.

One of the things that Elizabeth left Starkville with that she never planned for was bitter resentment. She was disgusted over how her husband was treated at the end of his tenure. Dudy wasn't ready to retire, but he was pushed out. She felt he should have been able to go out on his terms on his own time.

No matter the circumstances, Elizabeth had her hero with her full time, except for the time he spent hunting.

Many coaches and staffers from around the SEC visited the Noble place to participate in outdoor activities. While Dudy was a man of accomplishment, he was also a country boy who enjoyed wetting a line in a stream occasionally. He also loved to hunt deer, rabbits, and birds.

As famously noted over the years, Noble had a good-for-nothing bird dog that couldn't hunt acorns under an oak tree. Dudy called him "Mr. Ole Miss" because he lacked fetching prowess.

Noble believed that naming dogs was necessary, almost prophetic, when he gave a pair of bird dogs to his brother, James Phillips Noble. Being a man of the cloth, Phillips gave the canines biblical names Jacob and Esau.

As fate would have it, those bird dogs failed to live up to their Presbyterian province. Jacob proved to be the better hunter in this case, while Esau was just another pot licker.

The younger Noble is credited with a significant role in integrating the Anniston, Alabama school system. He penned a book entitled *Beyond the Burning Bus: The Civil Rights Revolution in a Southern Town*. It was the first of four published works written by Dr. Noble.

The Noble children were all accomplished adults who lived life independently. Perhaps inspired by their eldest brother, Dudy, or the civic example set by their father, the rest of the group went on to big things. The Nobles felt that more was expected of them, and they did their best to live up to it.

All of Will Noble's children earned honors, including the girls.

They grew up in a time when girls didn't go to college, but the Noble daughters went and graduated.

In April 1961, Noble was selected as a charter member of the Mississippi Sports Hall of Fame. Goat Hale, Bruiser Kinard, Noble, and Stanley Robinson were the first four inductees. They are all mentioned extensively in this book as Noble's contemporaries.

The induction was the second honor for Noble, who was also selected in 1954 to the Helms Baseball Hall of Fame, making him the first coach from the Southeastern Conference to receive such distinction.

The news in 1961 wasn't all good. In the fall of 1961, Noble underwent an operation that many wondered if he would recover from. He did and even made a couple of return trips to campus, including one to be honored at halftime of the home football game against Alabama. The 1948 and 1949 SEC baseball champion teams were celebrated, and Noble was a part of the ceremony. That Homecoming trip to Starkville would be the final one of Noble's life.

Even in his final days, the ordinarily gruff Noble had a sense of humor. As his siblings visited, Dudy saw his nieces and nephews playing outside his bedroom window. At times, they would attempt to get a peek at their uncle, and Noble would offer them a playful growl to hear them squeal as they ran away out of sight.

Those who knew him personally often said his bark was worse than his bite, but those who had to compete against Noble or beat him in an argument would beg to differ.

In late January of 1963, Noble was hospitalized for what doctors diagnosed as a stomach hemorrhage. The staff of Mercy Hospital in Vicksburg conducted Dudy's final care. His last days were spent in room 325 with his devoted wife, Elizabeth, praying at his bedside without ceasing.

A cry went out for O Positive blood as doctors worked to save him from his critical condition. Those efforts proved to be unsuccessful.

On February 2, 1963, Clark Randolph "Dudy" Noble took his final breath. It was a Saturday afternoon. He was just 69.

And with that, Mississippi State's most decorated student-athlete and longtime leader was gone.

As a student-athlete, Noble won a school record 14 varsity letters. Only an injury prevented a full 16. While it is a shared record, it is a benchmark that no future student-athlete will ever touch.

On the baseball diamond as a coach, Noble led the Aggies to three SIAA titles. He was the first coach in program history to reach that number of championships.

Noble made some of the best hiring decisions in the school's history as an administrator. He was an icon hiring icons. Those around him didn't realize it at the time.

One of those hires was the legendary voice of Jack Cristil, who told the Mississippi State story with artistry and panache.

Cristil is famously quoted as saying that Noble gave him some simple instructions when he hired him in August of 1953, "You tell that radio audience what the score is and who's got the ball and how much time is left, and you cut out the bull."

"The best advice I ever got," Cristil said.

When Noble arrived in Starkville, the athletic facilities weren't much more than a dirt farm with a shed to house the equipment.

After his retirement, Scott Field had a capacity of 35,000. The basketball gym that would later bear the name of Babe McCarthy was one of the finest in the SEC, with enough room to host 5,000 fans.

The baseball field that bore his name was one of the best, if not the best, in the country. In modern times, there is no question about where that great stadium ranks, but even in the decades before, Mississippi State had a field of dreams.

Several friends and peers from around the league shared their comments and stories of "Coach Dudy" in the days after his passing. One of the most poignant came from Coach Paul Gregory.

State was in the process of making plans for a new baseball stadium. When asked if the new park would still be called Dudy Noble

Field, Gregory didn't hesitate to answer.

"That's a heritage that can't be shifted around," Gregory told the *Clarion-Ledger*.

Former Mississippi College star and Mississippi State assistant coach Goat Hale praised Noble without reservation.

"Nobody thinks more of him than I do," Hale told the *Ledger*. "Mississippi has lost a great athletic director and coach. I've looked up to him ever since I was one of his football players at Mississippi College back in 1916. In my book, he was the greatest."

Clarion-Ledger columnist Carl Walters shared, "Noble's greatest work at State, however, was probably as athletic director. In this capacity, he pushed and fought for State in both good times and bad.

"He was a strong-minded individual who fought for what he believed in and always fought for the good of Mississippi State. Because he was so strong-minded, he made some enemies, but even his enemies were quick to tell you he was 'All for State.'"

Noble's funeral was held at the Alumni Hall on the Mississippi State campus. An overflow crowd showed up to pay their respects.

There were no hymns sung. There was no grandstanding about his accomplishments as an athlete, coach, or administrator.

Four ministers eulogized Noble, including his younger brother, Dr. Phillips Noble. A few scriptures were read, and many tears were shed.

Dudy was laid to rest at the Memorial Garden Park Cemetery in Starkville, close enough to the Mississippi State campus where he could hear the cheers from the crowds at the athletic venues he helped cultivate and renovate.

Following Noble's death, Elizabeth devoted her time and effort to the church, rising to state president of the Mississippi Church Women's Association.

Dudy's "Maw" never dated or remarried. She remained devoted to him for the rest of her life. There are even some stories of former players stopping by to check in on her. She would entertain them on her front porch so as not to welcome any appearance of impropriety.

Elizabeth transformed her dining room into a shrine of Dudy Noble. His awards and memorabilia filled the room. As one visitor to her residence shared, she would allow folks to look at Dudy's things but not touch them. She stood dutifully by to ensure nothing walked off or got damaged. They were the last remnants she had of her beloved husband. They were vital to her.

In time, Elizabeth always wanted a piece of Dudy with her. She had a ring forged with the yellow diamond from Noble's retirement gift from the alumni and friends of Mississippi State.

Sadly, one day, walking down a gravel drive, she realized the stone was gone. Neighbors and friends were fetched to help search for it, but the stone was never found. Elizabeth never forgave herself for it. She looked for it regularly but never found it.

Those who knew her the best and loved her the most will tell you that she worshiped Dudy long after his passing. While his death did do them part, in her heart, the covenant between the two of them was a lifetime commitment on her part.

It took some time, but she even forgave Mississippi State for forcing him out because that's what Dudy would have wanted.

Elizabeth began going to baseball and football games again. The university provided tickets for her and her guests whenever she needed them. Some say that she made those trips not just to support the teams but to represent Dudy. As one family member shared, she felt closer to Dudy by attending those games that had been such a significant part of their lives and marriage.

Dudy Noble was Mississippi State in the eyes of many. He was a towering figure in Southern college sports. Elizabeth's attendance, in many ways, kept his name on the lips and ears of those involved with State athletics.

Elizabeth sold the old Noble farm and moved to Edwards for a bit before settling in Batesville, Mississippi. The final years of her 17 years without Dudy were spent spoiling her nieces and nephews and their families. She loved them deeply.

Elizabeth passed away in April of 1980. Dr. Phillips Noble was once again one of the presiding clergymen. She was laid to rest next to Dudy. The inscription on their shared headstone reads "Together Forever." One can only imagine the reunion on the other side.

In the days leading up to her passing, Elizabeth spoke of Dudy often as if she was fully aware of her pending earthly exit. The time for them to be together for eternity was drawing nigh. She appears to have embraced it.

Since Noble passed away, Mississippi State has moved his namesake stadium once and renovated it multiple times. Brand new ballparks were constructed in 1967, 1987, and 2018. All continue to bear the name of Dudy Noble Field.

Dudy picked up some company when legendary Mississippi State baseball coach Ron Polk retired. The stadium surrounding Dudy Noble Field is now called Polk-DeMent Stadium.

The DeMent name was added following a generous one-million-dollar gift from Bonnie DeMent of Indianola in honor of her late husband, Gordon DeMent. A portion of that incredible donation went toward constructing a new band hall and the rest toward baseball.

Dudy Noble Field is synonymous with big-time college baseball. The greatest fans in the country consider the venue their home away from home. It's where new friends meet, and old friends reunite, all supporting the Diamond Dawgs.

In the early days of Mississippi A&M, player-coach William Jennings tossed out some makeshift bases near the old railroad tracks to help facilitate a game.

Now, some of the greatest players in the country get to perform regularly in front of record crowds in the grandest cathedral in college baseball. That holy house surrounding the most sacred patch of grass in the southland still bears the name of Dudy Noble.

Legendary writer Ernest Hemingway once wrote, "Every man has two deaths, when he is buried in the ground and the last time someone says his name. In some ways, men can be immortal."

Those are salient and profound words. With the sentiment of Hemingway in mind, Dudy Noble will live forever. His name will always be spoken. He shall be immortal.

Pictures and Letters

A bright-eyed and bushy-tailed Dudy Noble growing accustomed to college life.

Dudy Noble likely thinking about a way to beat Ole Miss.

Dudy's father, William Alexander Noble, was a distinguished man.

An older Dudy Noble admiring the spoils of a hunt.

Dudy rarely kept a clean desk as he led the State athletic department.

His hat and tie indicate that Dudy was a right-hander on the field and off.

Dudy handling State business

Alabama Polytechnic Institute
Auburn, Alabama

AUBURN ATHLETIC DEPARTMENT
BOX 432   —   PHONE 2488

January 27, 1959

Mr. C. R. Noble
Athletic Department
Mississippi State University
State College, Mississippi

Dear Dudy:

As I told you in Baton Rouge, it saddens us all to see you step down as Athletic Director at Mississippi State. We have always felt that you have been a friend to Auburn both on and off the athletic field and that your contribution to this conference, and to all of us who have had the opportunity of knowing you, has been great.

Maybe after you get down on the farm there will still be time for us to have that much talked about rabbit hunt. I am sure we will never get off probation and we will always have plenty of time around New Year's for just such a thing.

Best of luck and I hope you can find it possible to come to the meetings and to Auburn when ever the occasion arises.

Sincerely yours,

G. W. Beard
Director of Athletics

Dudy through the years

Dudy's adoring wife, Elizabeth.

Dudy's baseball club team photo.

Coach Dudy back at A&M

State College, Mississippi
January 20, 1952

To Whom It May Concern:

The undersigned, do hearby swear, that the accusations toward C. R. Noble, director of athletics, by T. S. Aderholdt, Jr., Claud D. Williams, W. A. Hughes and W. B. Puckett following the Mississippi State-Tennessee football game concerning the trip back from Knoxville on the Southern Railway train, the Tennessean, on September 29, 1951, are absolutely false and without foundation.

Our version of what happened is as follows: Coaches A. W. Morton, Jesse Fatherree, C. M. Strange and Mr. Norman Davis of Baton Rouge, La., were sitting in the Club Car playing gin rummy and discussing the game that was played that afternoon.

Coach Noble and Bob Hartley, sports publicity director, came in later and sat at a table directly behind the above mentioned. Across the aisle from the group playing cards was a young lady with a civilian and two servicemen. No remarks were made by Coach Noble or any of the Mississippi State athletic staff directed to this party or concerning this party.

Neither Coach Noble nor any members of the Mississippi State athletic staff had any liquor in their possession at anytime.

After being seated at the table Coach Noble and Bob Hartley ordered sandwiches and soft drinks.

A person, who later identified himself as Mr. Puckett of Clarksdale, came up to the table where the coaches were sitting playing cards. Mr. Puckett began critizing the quarterbacking and kicking in the game played that afternoon against Tennessee. He was very critical of the coaching staff and accused the coaches of not making an extended effort to get Delta athletes.

Coach Fatherree then asked Mr. Puckett to leave the coaches alone and Puckett would not leave. This brought on a heated discussion between Fatherree and Puckett and involved no one else.

At this time Coach Noble told Coach Fatherree to sit down and it was at this point that Puckett began accusing Mr. Noble of mishandling tickets, failing to take athletes from the Delta, and said that when he was in school Coach Noble did not give him an opportunity to demonstrate his baseball ability.

The only misconduct we observed on the train was by Puckett, who was most definitely under the influence of alcoholic beverages and Mr. Norman Davis of Baton Rouge, La., can verify that Puckett was asleep on the Club Car table when Mr. Davis retired to his berth.

[Signatures: Jesse L. Fatherree, C. M. Strange, A. W. Morton, Bob Hartley]

STATE OF MISSISSIPPI
OKTIBBEHA COUNTY

Personally appeared before me, a Notary Public, in and for said county and state Jesse Fatherree, C. M. Strange, A. W. Morton and Bob Hartley, signers of the above statement, who swear and depose that all statements made therein are true and correct.
Signed in my presence this the 20th day of January, 1952.

HENRY F. MEYER
NOTARY PUBLIC

My Commission Expires April 25, 1954

Spike Nelson staff
Back row Left to right: Carideo, Wendler
Front row left to right: Noble, Nelson, Calhoun

Ralph Sasse staff
Back row left to right: Fatheree, Noble, Armstrong, Wendler
Front row left to right: Aiken, Stokes, Sasse, Carideo

President Ben Hilbun addresses the homecoming crowd
with Dudy standing off his left shoulder.

Dudy's headshot from the
1918 Ole Miss yearbook

MISSISSIPPI STATE UNIVERSITY
STATE COLLEGE, MISSISSIPPI

OFFICE OF THE PRESIDENT

February 7, 1963

Mrs. C. R. Noble
Learned
Mississippi

Dear Mrs. Noble:

    I am pleased to transmit to you a resolution which was passed by the Administrative Council on February 4, 1963, expressive of the sentiments of that group toward Mr. Noble.

Sincerely yours,

D. W. Colvard
President

DWC:ps

Enclosure

MISSISSIPPI STATE UNIVERSITY
STATE COLLEGE, MISSISSIPPI

DEPARTMENT OF ATHLETICS

February 20, 1962

Coach Dudy Noble
Learned, Mississippi

Dear Coach:

    Just as always, I put off things that I should have done many days ago, but at last I have gotten around to saying thanks for making possible all the many wonderful things that have happened to me in the last few months. I doubt that any coach in America has ever had the satisfaction that I have had in my seven years here at Mississippi State, all seven of which were made possible through the faith that you showed in me by giving me my first chance. I am sorry that I have not given you the credit due as often as I should, but on every occasion that I have the opportunity I have told people how much I appreciate what you did for me. I have been to Jackson on a number of occasions in the past few months, but I have always been busy as a bee while there. I plan to come to see you and Mrs. Noble in the near future, but I want you to know that in my happiest hours I thought about you a lot of times.

    If I can ever be of service to you in any way, please feel free to call on me and know that anything that I might do could not be enough to repay you for what you have done for me.

    With every good wish and with kindest personal regards, I remain

                                  Sincerely yours,

                                  "Babe"

P.S. George Boyd said that he would like to come to see you, but would need bus fare in order to get down there and thought maybe you might send it to him. I would send him, but I am afraid you don't want him down there in the first place.

The Birmingham News
EVENING AND SUNDAY

ZIPP NEWMAN
SPORTS EDITOR EMERITUS

2959 MONTEVALLO RD.
MOUNTAIN BROOK, ALABAMA

Feb. 20, 1963

Mrs. C.R. Noble,

Learned, Miss.

Dear Elizabeth:

    I have never known a man, who did more for his alma mater than Dudy. You know I loved him like a brother. And some of the most wonderful memories I have- were the visits in your home- with Granny and Dudy- and going to the little church with you.

    I am sorry I never got to visit with the Nobles in Learned . I retired -semi- in 1959- writing books and doing three cols a week.

    It has been a pleasant life, but I must admit losing friends like Dudy has encimbered the heart with longings .

    Forget the small people-they soon pass away-forgotten and pitied.

    I sent you four clippings, if you need more, let me know.

    Be of good cheer,

UNIVERSITY OF MISSISSIPPI
UNIVERSITY, MISS.

DEPARTMENT OF INTERCOLLEGIATE ATHLETICS

April 4, 1959

Mr. C. R. Noble
Director of Athletics
Mississippi State College
State College, Mississippi

Dear "Dudy":

Someone sent me the last Miss. State Alumni magazine which was dedicated to you. I thought it was very nice and know that you deserve a lot more than this but only time will make them realize the many problems that you have had.

I am going to miss you as I have told you several times and the little things that irritate people so much are already beginning. I am like you, hoping that they will not be too numerous or to put it this way, make mountains out of mole hills.

Give my best regards to Ma and tell her that this is one piece of literature from Miss. State that I will keep and cherish at my home.

Sincerely yours,

Tad

C. M. "Tad" Smith
Athletic Director

CMS/jt

HELMS HALL COLLEGE BASEBALL HALL OF FAME... COACHES

*GEORGE A. HUFF... Coached at University of Illinois for 24 years. .. 1896-1919. Served as Illinois' Director of Athletics from 1901 through 1924. A leader in Big Ten athletics throughout his collegiate career. Arranged and sent an Illinois diamond squad on a tour of Japan in 1928. Won 10 Big Ten Baseball crowns, and nabbed the runner-up position on 11 occasions.

*JOHN H. KOBS... Michigan State's sterling coach for 29 seasons -- 1925-1954. Current President of the American Assn. of College Baseball Coaches, and has been an officer of the association since 1945. Through the season of 1953, Kobs' Spartans have won 386 diamond encounters, losing 252.

*WILLIAM V. MC CARTHY... Baseball Coach at New York University for 33 years. One of the founders of the Metropolitan (New York) Conference. McCarthy's teams at N.Y.U -- 1922-1953 -- won 386 engagements, and lost 194. He guided the Violets to 7 Metropolitan crowns -- six of them in succession.

*JAMES F. "POP" MC KALE... Tutored University of Arizona Baseball teams for 35 years, during the period 1911-1948. His all-time record was 318 triumphs and 124 setbacks. McKale served as President of the American Assn. of Baseball Coaches in 1950. He was an important factor in the establishment and growth of the Border Conference, of which Arizona is a member. He gained 14 consecutive Border loop crowns for his beloved Arizona Wildcats.

C. R. "DUDY" NOBLE... Clarke Randolph Noble has played a prominent role in the development of athletics at Mississippi State College -- as Baseball Coach, and as Athletic Director. "Dudy" joined the Mississippi State coaching staff in 1919. He took over duties as diamond mentor in 1920, and handled the post for 29 seasons, through 1948. His teams were always among the strongest in the Dixie circuit.

*WARREN E. STELLER... Presently in his 30th year as Baseball Coach at Bowling Green State University (Ohio) -- 1925-1954. Previously he coached 3 years at Wesleyan (Connecticut). Steller's top team was that in 1943, which won 18 and lost 2, and which was chosen mythical college champion of Ohio.

*HENRY C. SWASEY... Coach of Baseball at University of New Hampshire for 33 seasons -- 1922-1954. He spent three years, prior to his New Hampshire tenure, at Adelphia Academy (Brooklyn, N.Y.) One of Swasey's top teams was that in 1936, which won 13 and lost 1.

*OTTO H. VOGEL... Teacher of Baseball, and an exceptional one, at University of Iowa for 27 seasons -- 1925-1954 -- with the exception of World War II years, when he served as a Naval officer. Vogel's Hawkeyes teams tied for the Big Ten championship on 4 occasions, and won it once, in 1939. For the period 1925-1953, Vogel's Iowans won 357 diamond clashes, and lost 234.

*PAUL B. "BILLY" WILLIAMS... Pilot of 31 Ball State (Indiana) Teachers College Baseball teams -- 1921-1954. It was "Billy" Williams who gave Ball State its first Indiana Conference championship (in Baseball) in any sport... in 1939.

West Virginia University
DEPARTMENT OF INTERCOLLEGIATE ATHLETICS
ROBERT H. (RED) BROWN · DIRECTOR OF ATHLETICS
P. O. BOX 877 · MORGANTOWN · TELEPHONE 2411

January 29, 1959

C. R. Noble
Athletic Director
Mississippi State College
Starkville, Mississippi

Dear Dude:

I for one didn't like it. You have done a tremendous job at Mississippi State under difficult circumstances, and for many years inferior athletic facilities, particularly in reference to your natural rivals.

You taught me a lot of football years ago—more than you realized and I want to express my appreciation to you for doing so. Since I left Mississippi State in 1935 I've only been with you for doing so. Since I came to West Virginia in 1952, I've had nine all American linemen, many now playing in pro ball. Yess, I've learned more football around you than I ever did with Zuppke.

I want to apologize for recommending "Slick" Morton. I'm still a little gun shy about blowing that one, but I guess he just went crazy.

Art Lewis, who is doing a terrific job here said he worked them so hard they were dead on Saturdays and that experience has benefited us because we're not dead physically Saturday afternoons. We make mistakes alright, but not that mistake.

Sorry I haven't been able to come down and visit during Christmas, or summer vacations, but just been scared of winter driving and the hot summer.

Kindest regards to you and MJ

Russell J. Crane

Memphis State University
MEMPHIS, TENNESSEE
ATHLETIC DEPARTMENT

February 9, 1959

Mr. C. R. Noble
Director of Athletics
Mississippi State College
State College, Mississippi

Dear Dudy:

Received your note with the check today and wanted to let you know how much I have enjoyed working with you through the past several years. In this business there are a few bright spots and pleasant memories and my association with you has certainly been one of the few. I have wanted to write for sometime to tell you this since I wanted you to know that I shall always treasure my association with you and remember your kindness and good judgment through the years.

I did want you to know that there is no one in the whole field of athletics that I have worked with that I have more respect for or a higher personal regard. I shall remember your many kindnesses and hope that you will give me the opportunity someday of repaying in a small part the many fine things that you have done to help me out. May our paths continue to cross frequently as I shall always look forward to renewing our personal friendship.

With kindest personal regards, I am

Very truly yours,

C. C. Humphreys
Athletic Director
Assistant to the President

CCH:hb

TULANE UNIVERSITY

NEW ORLEANS 18

Division of Athletics

April 15, 1959

Mr. C. R. Noble
Director of Athletics
Mississippi State College
State College, Mississippi

Dear Dudy:

Recently a March issue of the Mississippi State Alumnus magazine came to my desk. Your cover picture was great. It almost made me feel that you were sitting in the room with me. I know your long service at State justifies your getting more time in the future to hunt those rabbits and quail. However, our conference will not be the same without you in it. Athletic Director's meetings in the future will be drab and uninteresting without you to spice it up from time to time.

Just thought you'd like to know Dick Baumbach will miss you a lot and hope that you will look him up whenever you come to New Orleans. All of your Tulane friends here join me in sending you best wishes for many more years of a happy and healthful life.

Sincerely yours,

Dick

ROB:ld
R. O. Baumbach
Director of Athletics

THE UNIVERSITY OF WYOMING
OFFICE OF THE PRESIDENT
OLD MAIN
LARAMIE, WYOMING

January 31, 1957

Mr. C. R. Noble
Mississippi State College
State College, Mississippi

Dear "Dudy":

I appreciate your sending me a copy of the memorandum from Bernie Moore on the new NCAA rules. I agree with you that a pat on the back is due the six "knotheads" who went to Chicago to see Major Griffith and then came back and "paddled our own canoe." Right does eventually prevail.

We have not yet decided on a new football coach. We have decided, however, that it is not going to be anybody from Tennessee. We are going to look in other pastures this time. We have been a great developing ground for coaches, because we give them all the backing in the world and give them every chance to win. So they use us as a stepping stone. Perhaps it will always be so.

I have about recovered from my illness, although I still tire easily. This is no time to admit it, however, as the Legislature is in session and we have to hire a coach in the middle of it—and still try to keep up with the daily routine of running a university.

I hope we can get together sometime in the next few months. Perhaps I will have a chance to get down in that direction—at least near enough so that we can make connections.

I hope you and Mrs. Noble are enjoying the best of health. Good wishes to you both as always.

Sincerely yours,

G. D. Humphrey
President

GDH:TW

LOUISIANA STATE UNIVERSITY
Baton Rouge, Louisiana

DEPARTMENT OF ATHLETICS

February 6, 1959

Mr. C.R. Noble
Director of Athletics
Mississippi State College
State College, Mississippi

Dear Coach Dudy:

Many thanks for the check, and for the nice words you had to say regarding our Conference meeting here. It certainly was wonderful having you down, and I sincerely hope that you will not be a stranger in these parts ever. In our book you're one of the finest people we've ever known, Dudy, and have done a tremendous job for Mississippi State. You have the respect of everyone who knows you, and your contributions to intercollegiate athletics at your school, in your state, and throughout the Conference has been one of the outstanding features of athletic administration that we know.

Come see us, Dudy, and don't hesitate to call on me if I can ever be of any assistance in any way.

Sincerely,

James J. Corbett
Director of Athletics

2613 Lackawana Street
Adelphi, Maryland
1-20-59

Dear Coach Dudy:

I just received a newspaper clipping from home reporting the recent action of the Board of Trustees. I deeply regret that the "powers that be" have terminated the services of one who has served the State, the school, athletics and athletes so well for so long. This of course is their prerogative but it does seem to me that it could have been handled in a more straightforward manner. I have never been able to understand why people with authority should lack the courage to stand up and be counted. Knowing you I can just hear you answer "No guts", and who can dispute you?

I have no knowledge whatever of the circumstances leading to the Board's action and when one is ignorant perhaps he has no grounds for argument. However, sentiment alone is a powerful argument and I do have that. The world would be a helluva place without it. In your case mine is based on the knowledge of the great many boys you have encouraged to get an education and saw to it one way or another that they got it. I am also aware that a lot of these boys were never athletes enough to justify your help on this basis alone. No doubt you have been criticized for this by those without sentiment and those who evaluate success only by wins and losses. I feel sure that the great majority of those you helped have not and will not forget and you must not lose sight of this. Of course, one cannot help but dwell on the old saying "nothing is so fleeting as human gratitude". It's just something a man has to accept and live with whether he likes it or not.

It has now been almost 28 years since I last played for you. All this time I have looked back with regret at my inability to produce as I wanted to for you. However, my failures in no way dim the happy memories of being on your teams and of having you as a personal friend. I shall always consider you one and hope the feeling is mutual. This is not much solace after what has happened but I wanted you to know anyway.

With very best regards, I am,

Most sincerely,

Bill M. Diggin

MISSISSIPPI STATE COLLEGE
STATE COLLEGE, MISSISSIPPI

DEPARTMENT OF ATHLETICS

Nov. 30, 1948

Mr. C. R. Noble
Director of Athletics
Mississippi State College
State College, Miss.

Dear Mr. Noble,

Believing that it is for the best interest of the College, and for myself, I do hereby tender my resignation, effective January 1, 1949.

This resignation is in consideration of an agreement this day entered into between Dr. Fred T. Mitchell and C. R. Noble, acting for Mississippi State College, and me.

Very truly yours,
Allyn McKeen

JOHN STENNIS
MISSISSIPPI

United States Senate
WASHINGTON, D.C.

February 8, 1963

Dear Mrs. Noble,

As one among the many, many thousands of friends and former Mississippi State students who loved and esteemed you and your late husband, I hasten to extend to you my deepest and heartfelt sympathy in your earthly loss. And at the same time, I want to express my deepest gratitude for the friendship of the two of you over the years.

Both as a student and in later years I went to Dudy many times for advice and counsel, and I was always rewarded by his sound and solid suggestions and counsel. And I know that my experiences in this way were shared by thousands.

Let me also commend and congratulate you, as well as sincerely thank you, for the life you have lived by his side as you both supported and inspired him. With you, I shall ever treasure his memory. My prayer is that God will sustain you, as I know He will, and enable you to see the wisdom of His ways. And I know you will make the years ahead for you useful years and that they will be full of rich satisfaction.

Fondly and with appreciation, I am

Your friend,

John Stennis

Mrs. C. R. Noble
State College, Mississippi

JS/ll
Air Mail

RESOLUTION

WHEREAS, Clarke Randolph Noble entered this institution more than fifty years ago, and as a student, coach, and director of athletics had great influence in and upon it; and

WHEREAS, he inspired his athletes and staff members as he taught and directed them; and

WHEREAS, he was a broadly educated and genuinely cultured gentleman; and

WHEREAS, he was deeply sensitive, penetrating in his understanding of men, scrupulously honest, and eminently generous in his dealings with them; and

WHEREAS, those who knew him best loved him most; and

WHEREAS, on February 2, 1963, the Great Scorer released him from further competition;

NOW THEREFORE BE IT RESOLVED, that the Administrative Council of Mississippi State University take note of the passing of this peerless colleague and that it communicate to Mrs. Noble its tenderest sentiments, along with its hopes that she will find joy in the realization of the full and influential life that her helpmeet lived among his many friends;

BE IT FURTHER RESOLVED, that a copy of this resolution be spread upon the official minutes of the Administrative Council of Mississippi State University.

D. W. Colvard
President

This Resolution was unanimously passed by the Administrative Council, Mississippi State University, at its meeting on February 4, 1963.

Epilogue

Embarking on this book has been a transformative journey that has deepened my understanding of Mississippi State University's history. Through my words, I hope you can share this profound connection and uncover the untold stories that have shaped our beloved University.

When I first began considering this project, I contacted Mississippi State icon writer Sid Salter and asked him what he thought about me writing a biography of Dudy Noble. His response? "Whoa!"

I called legendary Mississippi sportswriter Rick Cleveland to ask if he felt it was a worthy project. Rick said, "I think so. I wish I would have thought of it."

From the depths of my soul, I knew this book wasn't just a personal endeavor but a necessity for the Mississippi State community. It's a story, long overdue, that should have been told decades ago, and I'm humbled to have been the one to pen it finally.

As the final chapters took shape, I was in a whirlwind of emotions. Anticipation for you to experience the incredible stories I had unearthed was mixed with a sense of loss as I bid farewell to the journey of discovery I had embarked upon. In the days to come, I promise to continue sharing stories like this one, hoping to keep the spirit of this journey alive.

A part of me was also sad to say goodbye to Dudy. On the pages of this book, the characters are alive to me. After finishing writing about Billy Chadwick, I was so moved that I felt I needed to go to his grave and say, "I'm sorry."

After I had written the final chapter, I went to the graves of Dudy and Elizabeth Noble to pay my respects. I left a few flowers. I stood there and told them goodbye, and to Dudy, I said I had done my best to share the truth and majesty of his life growing up and his time at

Mississippi State.

He was with us through the best and worst of times. Little did I know when I sat down to organize the outline that I would soon be writing about a pair of World Wars, The Great Depression, and some of the most challenging times in Mississippi State athletics.

All of that mattered. All of it made us who we are. All of it had an impact on the direction of State sports.

I love Mississippi State and always have. I suspect I always will. I sincerely hope you love State a little more after reading about the life and times of Dudy Noble.

He earned everything from start to finish. He fought for the State of old and the State of the future. We owe a profound debt of gratitude to Dudy. My aim wasn't just to shed light on who and what he was but also to meticulously honor his legacy and inspire deep admiration for his achievements.

Some of these stories are over 100 years old, and the only ones alive to share them are retelling stories passed down by an earlier generation.

There's only so much you can learn from online searches. The real stuff is buried and hidden from view. Now, it is available for all who love State and have wondered about the man with the intriguing name—the legend named Dudy Noble.

Hail State!

Acknowledgments

I fully understand the importance of this segment of the book. In previous books, I have made some glaring omissions. I have done my best to be diligent about this, but I know there will be someone who deserves inclusion that will likely slip my mind.

I sincerely apologize for any omissions. Your contribution isn't just beneficial; it is the very foundation of this book. My appreciation for your help isn't just endless; it's immeasurable.

Like all the others, this book was written with my wife, Dana, to deal with my long hours and obsession with the subject matter. One night, during my research for this work, a friend told me, "You may be the world's definitive expert on Dudy Noble." I couldn't help but chuckle and reply, "Then, that makes Dana number two on that list."

When I met Dana, I had nothing to offer but my unwavering love and support. I didn't even have much hair or job prospects at the time. There was just me; soon, there was just us, a bond I cherish more than anything.

I couldn't have been married to some "fru fru" girl. It had to be her. Only she could put up with me. She knew I was a dreamer and has helped me realize most of those dreams.

I've often joked with her that we did the world a disservice by not having more children. Everyone dotes on their kids, but I have the receipts to document how amazing my children are.

People always talk to me about legacy; my children are the most incredible legacy I can leave. They are the best of me.

Oni, Audrey, Mia, and Ian have enriched my life. Watching them grow into adults is one of the greatest gifts God has ever given me.

Oni and his wife, Betsy, have proven to be wonderful parents to our grandgirls, Vivi and Lily. That boy of mine can be a handful; he found a peach of a bride in the hills of northern Arkansas.

I am what I am because of the people who loved me long before anyone knew my name. I owe a debt of gratitude to Louis, Beth Crout, and Dolores Robertson for showing me the way. Most of my greatest attributes came from my father, Freddie. I wear that like a badge of honor. May he rest in peace.

Many thanks to my siblings: David & Kim Kennedy, Pat and Stephanie Robertson, Mark & Nikki Smith, Gordon and Tara Foil, and William and Regan Lunceford. I love you, your children, and your grandchildren very much.

Special thanks to the educators who not only challenged me to be a better writer but also played a significant role in shaping my writing journey: Mary Jean McKay (RIP), Karen (Purvis) Callendar, Maryanne (Boutwell) Simpson, and Judy Gordon. Your guidance and teachings have been instrumental in my growth as a writer.

I'm a huge proponent of the Mississippi independent bookstores, even those that don't carry my books. Support them before ordering from Amazon. I have few friends in the literary community who are better than Carolyn Abadie at Book Mart and Café in Starkville, John Evans at Lemuria in Jackson, and Shelby Gorman at Turnrow in Greenwood.

None of this would be possible without Paul Brown and my favorite Ole Miss girl, Vicki Gardner. Paul believed in me enough to allow me to begin writing books. I can never repay what I owe him, but I try. We have an excellent working relationship. He has been a part of six of my books. I hope we get to write twenty more before we're done.

Chris Boudreaux and Dennis Heckler work behind the scenes but play an essential part in bringing these books to life. I am grateful for their contributions.

I cannot begin to express my gratitude to the family of Dudy Noble, the legendary baseball coach. We have spent a lot of time visiting, talking, and texting. From the beginning of this process, I wasn't sure how they would feel about me writing this book, a tribute to their beloved patriarch. I had to have their blessing before I wrote the first page. They gave it.

I consider Frances Banks Amis and Mitzi Banks Still among my friends now. They are Dudy's nieces and have been amazing to me.

Thanks to Phil Noble, the rest of the Nobles, Ted, and the Harpole family for sharing your stories with me. The same goes for Mississippi State Hall of Famer Charlie Weatherly and my friend William Hilbun.

This book wouldn't have been complete without the assistance of state Representative Sam Creekmore, Delvan Irwin, Brandon Langlois, Travis Rae, and Sid Salter.

Thanks as always to David Murray and Mike Nemeth for always being my sounding boards and steering wheels at times. My respect for you both continues to overflow.

God bless the family of Chris Cornell!

Finally, thanks to all of you for buying this book and all the others. I'm just an old boy from South Mississippi. You sure know how to make a fellow feel proud.

While I have plans to write several more books, you never know when it's your last one. If this proves to be it, then know I put my heart in every word.

I love my life, family, and friends, and I count you within that number. Go forth and spread love and happiness into all parts of the world.

Hail State!